Chandralekha: Woman [obscured by barcode] searched critical perspec[tive on the uniquely] radical artist of contemporary India. Moving beyond the biographical genre, the book deals comprehensively with her interventions as a choreographer, graphic designer, writer, cultural activist. It investigates the manner in which Yoga and martial arts provide the foundations for her bold rearticulation of Bharatanatyam. It also explores her close affinities to the women's and ecological movements which have inspired her profound understanding of the body.

'Tradition' and 'modernity' meet in the life and work of this activist/performer, whose position as an artist offers one of the most subtle critiques of official and fundamentalist cultural appropriations. The book celebrates the non-conformist questioning spirit of its subject while placing it in the cultural history of post-Independence India as represented in critical issues like the 'invention of tradition', censorship, 'festival culture' and the struggle against fundamentalism. It will be of vital interest not only to dancers and artists, but to feminists, activists and cultural historians.

Trained as a dramaturg at the Yale School of Drama, Rustom Bharucha has been actively involved in the production and critical formulation of the performing arts in India. Author of *Rehearsals of Revolution, Theatre and the World, The Theatre of Kanhailal* and *The Question of Faith*, he divides his time between writing and directing, teaching and travel. This book has emerged out of his close association with the *Request Concert* intercultural theatre project in 1987.

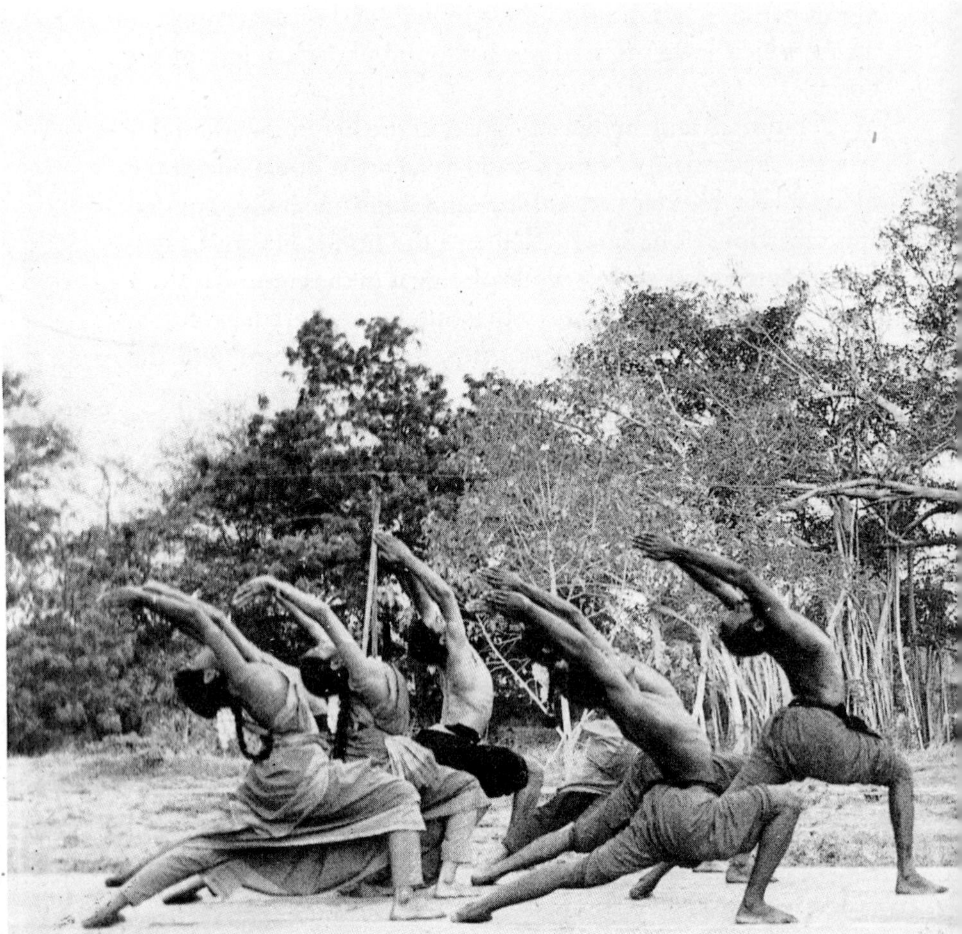

1

CHANDRALEKHA

WOMAN DANCE RESISTANCE

Rustom Bharucha

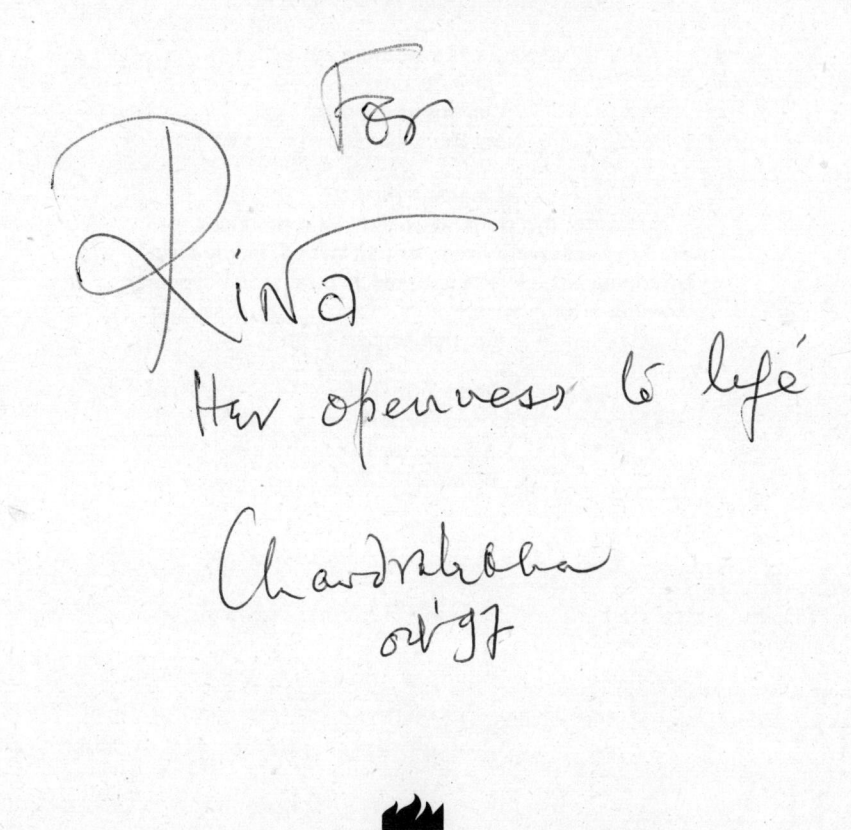

For Rina
Her openness to life

Chandralekha
oct '97

HarperCollins *Publishers* India

HarperCollins Publishers India Pvt Ltd
7/16 Ansari Road, New Delhi 110 002

First Published in Hardback 1995 by
HarperCollins Publishers India
First in Paperback 1997

© Rustom Bharucha 1995

Rustom Bharucha asserts the moral right
to be identified as the author of this work

ISBN 81-7223-254-3

Book & jacket design by Dashrath Patel

Typeset in 11 pt Garamond by
Megatechnics
19A Ansari Road
New Delhi 110 002

All rights reserved.
No part of this publication may be reproduced,
stored in a retrieval system, or transmitted, in any form,
or by any means, electronic or mechanical, photocopying,
recording or otherwise, without the prior permission of
the publishers.

Printed in India by
Gopsons Papers Ltd
A-28 Sector IX
Noida 201 301

If they see
breasts and long hair coming
they call it woman,

if beards and whiskers
they call it man:

but, look, the self that hovers
in between
is neither man
nor woman

O Ramanatha

      DEVARA DASIMAYYA
      (trans. A.K. Ramanujan)

Acknowledgements

The structure of this book was framed in September 1991 at the Bellagio Centre in Italy where, as a writer-in-residence, I found an ideal space in which to connect the multiple strands of the narrative. Shortly after, I was invited most graciously by Murari Ballal to draft the earliest chapters of the book at his home in Ambalapady, Karnataka. Through the intervening years (and earlier, as this book was researched between 1989-91), I have been supported by many of Chandra's friends and associates in India and other parts of the world. I hope to be forgiven for not naming these numerous friends who have nurtured the innerworld of this book.

To name just a few contributions, I would like to acknowledge the insights I have received from Chandra's dancers and performing artists, both past and present, those who remain with her and those who have moved on to other pursuits. Among the numerous feminists and women who have contributed to Chandra's work as active supporters, observers, critics, I would like to acknowledge in particular the sensitive observations of Kamala Ganesh, Vibhuti Patel, Neela Bhagwat, Vidya Shankar and Indira Jaising. Some meetings with unknown women at seminars and backstage after a performance have been very fleeting but intense. The emotions underlying these exchanges have lingered with me.

The core of my acknowledgements, however, is centered around three people without whom this book would not have been possible — Sadanand Menon, Dashrath Patel, and Chandra herself. Without their collaboration and close tuning to each other's sensibilities, there would have been no work to be addressed in the first place. To Sadanand, who knows Chandra more deeply than anyone I know, I am indebted for his unfailing generosity and presence of mind in addition to his empathetic reading and editing of my manuscript. To Dashrath, I am grateful for his keen eye and warmth of feeling which have contributed so perceptibly to the design of the book.

And finally, to Chandra... what can I say? Neither her fan nor *shishya* but intimate critic, I have been opened through her creativity to knowledge that would have been denied to me — the *mandalas* inscribed in our bodies; the interrelationships between Yoga, martial arts, and dance; the rigour in sensuality; the links between breath and planetary forces; and so many deviant, playful, and fluid sources of energy that have brought me closer to an understanding of femininity within myself. Without problematising this connection, I trust that it underlies the narrative which follows, testifying to some of the sources of renewal and resistance that I have imbibed from Chandra. In a very small way, this book is a tribute to what I have received.

Contents

Introduction   1

1   8

Memories of the Body
Return to Childhood
Life with Baba
Harindranath's Legacy
The 'Trinity': Baba, Guru Ellappa, and Dashrath
The 'Contradiction' of Life and Dance
Art and Survival

2   37

Early Career
Bharatanatyam: An 'Invention' of tradition?
For and Against Devadasis
Balasaraswati's Parampara
Chandra's *Devadasi*
Conceptualising *Devadasi*
Tillana

3   69

Living in the Sixties
Kamala
An Illumination through Flowers
Sources of Experience
Navagraha
Homage to the sun
Exploring the Media: a. Posters
                            b. Cinema

4   103

The Politics of Friendship
Dashrath's Dilemma
The Space of 'Skills'
Workshop

Learning through Posters
Street Theatre
The Raid
After the Raid

5   125

The East-West Dance Encounter
Problematising the Encounter
Primal Energy
Mandala

6   147

Angika
'Cosmic Energy'
Martial Sequences
The Animal World
The 'Grammar' of Bharatanatyam
The Socialisation of Dance
The 'Male Gaze' of the *Varnam*
Naravahana
Tillana
The Impact of *Angika*

7   177

After *Angika*
The 'Critical' Reception
Power Play
Namaskar

8   195

Background on *Lilavati*
Principles of Selection
'*Amala-kamala-rashe....*'
'*Panchamsho-alikulat...*'
'*Yatam-hamsakulasya....*'
'*Chakrakrauncha-akulita salile...*'
'*Haras-taras-tarunya...*'
Touring *Lilavati*

9   217

Homage to Breath
Asanas/Adavus
Returning to *Navagraha Kritis*
The Opening of *Prana*
Planetary *Yantras*
From *Namaskar* to 'Shanti'
Beyond the Disaster of Opening Night

10   241

Relationships with Dancers
The Body Freed and in Pain
Dancers on Chandralekha
The Male Dancer
'Foreign' Connections
The Walk Workshop
Against Aridity
Outside Professionalism

11   270

In Search of Freedom
'Freeing Myself from the Wall': *Request Concert*
One More News
Fire, Counter-Fire
Posters for the Women's Movement
Stree
Sahaja

12   307

Sri: a. Pre-History
     b. The Feminine Principle
     c. Towards Empowerment
Beginning with *Sakambhari*
Against Motherhood
Dreaming of the Future

Postscript   337
Notes   342
Photographs   353
Index   355

2

Introduction

The subject of this book is a woman called Chandralekha. Known primarily (and perhaps, misleadingly) as a dancer, she has been associated with more creative disciplines and activities than almost any other artist living in India today. She has danced; choreographed; designed exhibitions, posters, logos, graphics; conducted workshops with development and feminist groups; written poems, tracts, essays, and a novella; travelled widely and committed herself to the 'art of living' in a highly original and creative way.

If this sounds somewhat too rapturous, I should also add that she has struggled 'to be free/be herself' by fighting numerous battles with the cultural establishment and the State. Within the last twelve years she has resisted censorship and fought a false charge of 'sedition'. She continues to fight, firmly convinced that 'freedom' can never be taken for granted. Through this ongoing struggle, Chandra (as I address her in this book, and as she is normally addressed by her dancers and associates) has emerged as a woman whose life is as vital as her art. Not only has she broken new ground in the 'language' of dance, she has resisted the norms of 'Indian womanhood' by rejecting the institutions of family, marriage, and motherhood. Resplendently, yet consciously, she remains her own woman.

Inevitably, the very exceptionality of Chandra makes it difficult for any writer to categorise her. Her subjectivity is intense, and perhaps egotistic at times, but never isolationist. On the contrary, she has always attempted to connect her work to all kinds of movements committed towards realising a more humane and ecologically balanced world. To categorise her as an 'iconoclast' is to negate the depth and range of her involvements with varied groups of people particularly in the 'alternative' and 'marginal' sectors of society.

While some of Chandra's critics may disagree with the 'style' of her 'radical will', few would deny that she has the courage of her conviction. Quite simply, she practises what she preaches. Her theory has been tested through work. Moreover, in an age when most artists (and dancers in particular) seem obliged to kowtow to the establishment, if not play to the whims of ministers in increasingly humiliating ways, it is refreshing to know that we have an artist like Chandra who can say in plain terms: 'I exist in spite of you'.

At one level, this could be regarded as a disingenuous statement because Chandra is now becoming increasingly famous as a choreographer. 'The days of brickbats are over', as she says reflectively, 'people are now beginning to dive at my feet'. It should be remembered, however, that this change in attitude towards Chandra (officially recognised by her 1990-91 award for 'Creative Dance' from the Sangeet Natak Akademi) is of very recent origin. Since she staged her first production *Devadasi* in 1960, the road has been rough.

Indeed, we tend to forget that Chandra has opted out of dance for long stretches of time in her volatile career. Between 1962-84, she staged just one production, *Navagraha* (1972), participating in all kinds of activities relating to politics, education, feminism, design, far removed from the norms assumed by the dance establishment. Much of what we see today in Chandra's most widely acclaimed work — *Angika, Lilavati, Prana, Sri* and *Yantra* — has evolved after years of meditation, fantasy, and experiments in other forms and media.

It is, perhaps, only inevitable that the narrative of this book should be intercut with the lives of many artists, thinkers, and companions who have played a significant role in the shaping of Chandra's creativity. Harindranath Chattopadhyay, Guru Ellappa Pillai, Balasaraswati, Rukmini Devi, Dashrath Patel, Sadanand Menon are just a few of the figures in the landscape of this book, who have either influenced Chandra deeply or with whom she has lived and interacted at creative levels. If I had attempted to write a biography of Chandra, I would have had to dwell on many more relationships which are fleetingly addressed in this book. My focus, I must emphasise, is not biography, but the study of a particular artistic sensibility and the sources that have contributed to its growth in concrete ways.

This fact needs to be emphasised because there is a certain mystique around Chandra largely fed by the media, which has tended to sensationalise her as a 'silver-haired danseuse', a 'revolutionary mystic', and even a 'living Shakti'. Most of these reports have focused on her personality rather than her work, with a subtext that suggests a rather torrid and flamboyant life-style. In demystifying this totally false image, I have been compelled to highlight the critical nature of my inquiry dwelling on those aspects of Chandra's biography that are pertinent to her work.

My own association with Chandra began almost seven years ago when I invited her along with my German colleague, Manuel Lutgenhorst, to participate in an adaptation of a one-woman, wordless play called *Request Concert* by Franz Xaver Kroetz. From this first involvement, I have deepened the relationship over the years through conversations, discussions, rehearsals, and performances. Predictably, the closest moments have been spent backstage when I have accompanied Chandra and her troupe on tour to Germany, Italy, Canada, and in India to a range of places in Jaipur, Baroda, Auroville, and smaller towns like Manchikere and the village of Heggodu in Karnataka. It is on these travels that I was able to observe the dynamics of the group at very close quarters.

My most important task on these tours was to 'protect' the performance space from any kind of undue interference particularly moments before the show would start. It is during this time that Chandra's group improvises a ritual of solidarity backstage — not a *puja*, but just a holding of hands in a circle followed by movements, deep breathing, and meditation. It is telling that I have not participated in this act myself, maintaining a certain distance from the 'inner core' of the group.

This very choice, however, is what has enabled me to write this book from the perspective of a 'critical insider' rather than a 'total insider' or a 'critic'. What I have attempted is to find the necessary balance between 'distance' and 'belongingness', expressing my very real affinities to Chandra's ideas on creativity, femininity, and resistance, with a more critical perspective of her life and work within the larger cultural history of post-Independence India.

Woman, Dance, Resistance: these are the central motifs of the book which are thoroughly implicated in each other's discourses. One cannot schematise them into water-tight compartments. On the contrary, one is constantly flowing into the other. Thus, instead of structuring the book on rigid lines, I have opted for a narrative based on what I would like to describe as a web of inner connections.

Occasionally, I have had to intervene more academically as in the section on *Devadasi*, where it was expedient to provide a short but critical account of the history of Bharatanatyam. I should add, however, that I have consciously minimised the use of technical language to describe Chandra's choreography, focusing on principles of movement rather than the minutiae of dance terminology. In the final chapters of this book describing Chandra's relationship to feminism and the women's movement, I have found it necessary to broaden the critical inquiry by addressing the different 'languages' that Chandra has explored beyond dance — in theatre, posters, exhibitions, visual texts, and polemical interventions in women's conferences.

The range of this book is undeniably wide focusing as much on the sensibility and consciousness of a particular artist as on a spectrum of social and political forces that have shaped the cultural history of India since Independence. Writing about Chandra has necessitated a confrontation of some of the burning questions of our times concerning art and survival, the invention of 'tradition', the fundamentalist appropriation of 'Indian culture' in the name of 'religion', as well as larger contradictions relating to 'festival culture', censorship, and the increasingly difficult quest to sustain 'alternatives' within the cultural politics of our times.

Chandra's work embraces these contradictions in which she is, at one level, implicated and yet resistant through her deep and continuing struggle for self-realisation as a woman. If I have been inspired to write this book, it is not simply because Chandra is a 'great artist', but more specifically, because her art, in my view, is vital to our times. It is not hagiography that concerns me but a living history in which we can learn to discriminate the possibilities of our cultural praxis with greater rigour and sensitivity.

1

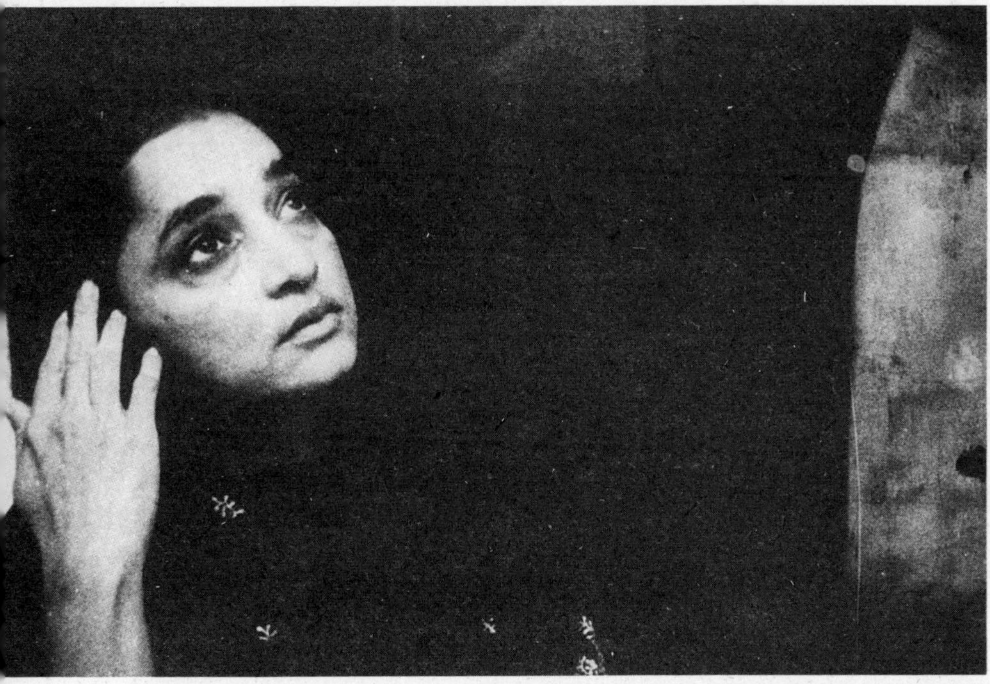

> I wish to invent
> a heredity
> for me
> I would like
> to think
> wistfully
> of my grandfather
> being a
> still-born baby
> who died
> as
> soon
> as
> he was born.

Memories of the Body

To begin on a note of fantasy, an 'invented' heredity rather than a biography, Chandra's rejection of genealogy and the institution of family is playfully evident in this excerpt from her '*68 Poems*. Never is the family a source of nostalgia for her as it so often is for many Indian dancers, who invariably ascribe their artistry to the blessings received from a particular heritage. Nor is the family an object of fear for Chandra, some kind of dark secret that she represses silently. If I had to choose a single word to describe her attitude to the family, I would say that it is a non-issue. She is neither derisive nor bitter about it. Indeed, she has lived independently since she was seventeen.

At home you will find some mementoes of the past relating primarily to her work—books, posters, handicrafts, terra cotta figures, a selection of brass vessels (collected, I should add, as much for the beauty of form as for the utilitarian purpose of cooking). But nowhere can one find the familiar memorabilia associated with Indian families: garlanded portraits of ancestors, wedding photographs, pictures of babies. These, I think, would be odious to

Chandra.

With this scrupulously defined rejection of the family, where then does one begin? Most memories of childhood are frequently forgotten; if remembered, they also tend to be invented. Chandra's earliest memory (which could be a viable point to begin an exploration of her creativity) is not a fiction like her 'still-born' grandfather. 'It is not what I have invented', as she emphasises, 'but something that happened'. These to her mind, are the only memories to be trusted: the memories of the body.

What was it? A child (herself) picking up some shell-like objects, gathering them in a kerchief, and placing them in the corner of a living room, a room with a lot of sofas and armchairs. Then, the family goes in for dinner. As they are about to leave, they see the shells scattered on the floor. And out of these shells, living creatures are crawling. 'Those shells had life in them', Chandra remembers. In all probability, they were minuscule clams, her first concrete images of contact with nature.

As a child, she was almost always outdoors, roaming the numerous compounds attached to the houses in which she was privileged to live. Invariably, she sought out areas with rough and dense undergrowth, and would sometimes fall asleep under trees. 'Then father's peon would come with a lantern — yes, it was a lantern, not a torch — and carry me into the house', Chandra recalls, adding that her mother 'would get into a real state because it happened so often'.

A need to be outdoors, sleeping under trees, being awakened, carried indoors: these are some of the recurring motifs in Chandra's memories of childhood. What needs to be stressed here is not so much the location of these memories and their rootedness in biographical details, but their sense of life that seems to emerge from 'another time'. At least this is how Chandra herself tends to value memories as an artist.

Remembering the touch of a shell at another period in her life, she continues to marvel at the experience and is genuinely puzzled. 'The touch was so familiar. The colour in the inside of the shell — mauve — something I had seen before, physical, sensual. This kind of experience cuts across time'.

So also the combination of red, black, and white, her favourite colours for which she is known so well — they are intensely familiar to Chandra, evoking inexplicable sensations. 'These colours remind you of blood. They take you somewhere in time that you have known in your body'. Then, reflecting on the difficulty of representing memory, she adds, 'That word "known" does not have a linguistic meaning'. It is more like a perception that has been 'memorised' by the body, surfacing at moments in life with a clarity that is startling, yet elusive.

It is this 'memory of the body' which has haunted Chandra throughout her life that has enabled her to remember the minutiae of dance even after long breaks and stretches of silence. In more recent times, she has been inspired by the 'ancient memory' of mythic figures like Sakambhari and the *matrikas*, which she has attempted to embody through performance. The actual construction of these images and the feminist responses to them will be discussed later in the book. For the moment, let us simply acknowledge the potency of these images in Chandra's 'memory' as an artist.

Return to Childhood

To return to Chandra's childhood and ceaseless need to be outdoors, to 'run wild, naked, and free', there are some memories that blend with thoughts of her family, others which exist in defiance of the family as an institution. Perhaps, one of Chandra's most tender memories relates to her father. She remembers his voice early in the morning, just before dawn, 'Like to come for a walk?' Instantly, Chandra is up, raring to go out in the open in the dark night, and sit somewhere near a railway track. It is this sense of the 'open' in which she traces her earliest images of freedom.

Her sense of freedom was, to a large extent, stimulated through travel. At different points in time, her family had lived in Saurashtra, Pune, and at one time, in Aden. Gujarat is, originally, Chandra's home-state, but she is not rooted there geographically. Since the age of seventeen, she has spent most of her time in Madras and for the last fourteen years at least, has lived by the sea on Elliots Beach. Her peripatetic existence as a child has clearly influenced her more recent perception of herself and most of her friends as 'urban nomads', a cultural phenomenon which will be described later.

Some facts of Chandra's childhood are worth noting. Her father was a free-thinking doctor in whose company she found stimulation and comfort. 'My real contact', as she once confided in a rare outburst of emotion, 'was with my father and none else'. What she respected most about him was his 'life of the mind'. In his library (which is almost always synonymous with Chandra's memory of her father), she read a wide range of books, 'devouring' them without necessarily understanding everything she read. It was an ambitious reading list by any standard, including the *Ramayana*, *Mahabharata*, the *Bhagavad Gita* and commentaries on these texts. At the same time she read *Manusmriti* which provoked her first suspicions of patriarchal values apart from influencing her early decision to remain unmarried. Among foreign classics she read Thoreau, Ruskin, Ingersoll, the complete plays of Bernard Shaw (Anne from *Man and Superman* being one of her favourite characters), and a lot of Dostoevsky ('to soak in the atmosphere').

Frequently, Chandra discussed these books and issues of freedom with her father, countering his pragmatism with dreams of a more individual, less 'responsible' existence. In her father, who often joked about the excess of omniscience in the *Bhagavad Gita*, Chandra also found an ally for her instinctive rejection of orthodox religious values.

If her father was a 'total iconoclast', in her words, her mother was 'highly religious'. She performed many rituals at home in which Chandra showed some interest particularly when it came to performing actions like lighting the lamp with oil, drawing *kolams*, stringing flowers. However her spirit was more clearly drawn to reading books in her father's library and roaming about in the compound where Chandra found an 'entire education' in nature.

At the age of thirteen, she had her first major confrontation with her father. While she wanted to study the fine arts, her father wanted her to graduate from college, believing that she was too young to make decisions which required 'development of the mind'. 'I told him I didn't believe in the development of the mind', says Chandra. 'I wanted to experience things'.

Perhaps if Chandra had stayed on at home after high school, these tensions could have resulted in bitterness, even hostility towards the family. Already in her college years, which were spent in Bombay, she was relatively free of parental pressures. Consequently, it is possible for her to look back on this period in her life with a matter-of-fact honesty and grace: 'They (the family) were very nice people. No, there was no repression, no orthodoxy. It was quite a liberal surrounding, but they were conventional. I realised that at an early age. They did not have this need, this compulsion I had, to run away. Where to, I didn't know'.

The conventionality of 'family life' has often been the source of Chandra's most witty criticism both in conversation and occasionally in poems. Thus, in her '68 Poems — a collection of irreverent verse written in the summer of '68 — we have some fairly vicious vignettes of a 'man from Cuddalore' sequestered in his 'world of toys', which he meticulously winds while 'waiting for an issue, preferably male' from his 'brand-new wife'.

More outrageously, there is a disquisition on farts in which Chandra focuses on an aunt, a 'connoisseur of farts' who can chant the 'sacred OM' through a series of small farts. Apart from versifying on the range of her aunt's farts, Chandra uses this biological propensity to explode the institution of marriage:

> I have heard it said of my aunt
> with a wee little fart
> she blew up
> her marriage pandal

> in fact
> it flew up
> in the air
> parents, guests, groom, and all.

Along with this total irreverence, there is also, in a very different poem, a more candid admission of hatred for 'old ladies', especially 'very old ladies.' They are 'cunning', 'selfish', 'inconsiderate', 'jealous of everything good, strong, and healthy.' Most unpardonably, they 'make you feel guilty for no reason.'

These snippets from her poems provide some playful clues to Chandra's early distrust of the larger institutions of family, marriage, and the self-righteous morality of 'old ladies.' Even before she had left home, Chandra was convinced that she did not want to get married: 'I would think ... this man and woman who are so different, how can they live under the same roof? Is it possible to live like that without hating each other?' Though this statement can be read as a literal comment on 'bad marriages' in general, it also indicates Chandra's early awareness of her own differentiation through self. She knew that she was not like the people around her. At the same time, she didn't know what she would do with her life. Today Chandra is capable of reflecting on the ambivalences of her adolescence:

> People are so stupid. They keep asking children: What do you want to do? I had no answer at that time. Even where I stand today, I realise that there can be no answer. One's learning is part of a long process. For anyone who is a seeker, I would say that you must know what you don't want to do. That 'No' is very important. Most young people succumb to pressure in moments of indecision. That's when 'they' can trap you.

Defying the imposition of societal norms on her own growth, Chandra gradually moved away from home and created a life for herself. The beginnings of her freedom had already emerged through her decision to study law in Bombay where she experienced hostel life and the first glimmers of her own search for identity. The study of law itself was not motivated by any conscious need to fight for feminist rights. Chandra was merely 'curious' about it and thought that it would be more useful to study than the arts (which 'you can always do better by yourself').

When it came to the finals, however, she decided to opt out of college. At a certain level, it was a gesture of protest against the system, but as Chandra emphasises, it was made at a 'simple, intuitive level. I was not emphatic about the decision. I was confused for a long time.' It was during this period of confusion that Chandra came to Madras, debating whether or not to sit for her exams, in the company of her newly-found mentor and friend, Harindranath Chattopadhyay, whom she lovingly calls 'Baba' to this day.

Life with Baba

What was it that attracted a 51-year old man, a celebrity who was lionised in the world of arts, to a college girl still in her teens? The question is open to much speculation and has been the source of misunderstanding, gossip, if not sheer bewilderment. Such an open relationship would make headlines today in our increasingly lurid press coverage of artists' lives. In 1949, just two years after Independence, in the proverbially conservative city of Madras, this kind of relationship was altogether unprecedented. Nonetheless, if it was sustained, nourished and gradually accepted, it was not only because of the sheer weight of Baba's personality. The relationship itself was honest and creative testifying to what Harindranath himself has described as the 'art of living.'

In a response that has been frequently quoted, Harindranath claimed that the first time he saw Chandra, 'this thin lovely girl with the long black hair', he knew that she was 'someone special. I could see the spark in her.'[1] Brushing aside the sexual innuendoes read into the relationship as 'so much damn nonsense', he asserted that, 'Sex as such hardly exists. Each time you create something beautiful you have in fact something akin to a sexual experience.'[2] Known for his numerous relationships with women, Harindranath was, nonetheless, equally vehement about his 'affairs' with Nature. Recalling his early morning walks to which he was particularly devoted, he captures a most amazing sense of life:

> On such walks I have several 'affairs' which are strictly private ... Enough if I say that they have to do with secret tunnels murmuring down boulders, wild flowers which flash a purity as of God, birds twittering in a thicket, grey fields taking on a sense of awakening ... and a hundred other sights — nay — even sounds and smells ... involving deep love and mating.[3]

If I had to characterise the very special friendship that existed between Harindranath and Chandra, glimpses of which I have sensed in his writings and her vivid reminiscences, I would say that it was an intrinsically playful relationship. Its intimacy was coloured and textured through a sense of fun. When they met, the 'child-soul' in Harindranath, which he called 'Mana,' had already manifest itself in his writings and perspectives of himself. In his 'toy-shop of a world', Chandra was as much a playmate as a source of inspiration.

Certainly, what she recalls most of all about the relationship was its abundance of laughter. 'I remember laughing and laughing in his company.' To this day Chandra is known for her laugh, which is strangely girlish and infectious. I remind her of it. With a touch of sadness she acknowledges: 'It is nothing compared to my days with Baba. From morning to evening I remember laughing.' Baba would play the fool, which was a role that he cultivated very seriously and with a considerable degree of skill. Chandra remembers his ceaseless word-play, rhyming, punning, and improvised songs and verse, many of which she recorded as the unofficial 'scribe' of Baba, thereby sharpening her own skills as a writer.

This 'play' with language coexisted with a more serious exploration of different poetic idioms. As one of the most famous poets of post-independence India known as much for his patriotic and satirical verse as for his political songs composed for the Indian Peoples' Theatre Association (IPTA) and the Peoples' Squad, Harindranath had wide contacts with the major poets and literary figures of India. In Madras, Chandra remembers meeting poets from all over India. 'People came and stayed. There were also activists of the Telengana movement. We didn't know what the future would hold for them.' There was a constant exposure to other languages and cultural idioms, so much so that when Chandra herself had learnt barely 200 words in her newly-acquired Tamil, she immediately started composing rhymes and verses, some of which came in handy later on as part of her contribution to live-demonstrations and *morchas* against price-rise and corruption.

This proximity to diverse languages and cultures was one of the major characteristics of Harindranath's all-India personality and image. It was nurtured to a large extent through his own childhood in Hyderabad, where (as a Bengali) he was more closely acquainted with 'Christians, Anglo-Indians, Hyderabad Hindus, and Muslims.'[4] As he recalls in his autobiography, which deserves to be more widely known and read, 'Mother spoke to father in Bengali, to us in Hindustani and to the servants in Telugu.'[5] Only later did Harindranath develop his instinctive affinity for his mother-tongue, Bengali.

This multilingualism is an important trait in Chandra's life and relationships with other artists as well. Her mother-tongue is Gujarati, but most of her exchanges with her dancers are in a combination of English and Tamil. To her *nattuvanar*, Udupi Lakshminarayan, she speaks almost exclusively in Hindi. This openness in Chandra's attitude to languages and cultures in general clearly reflects the anti-parochial affinities of her mentor, Harindranath. Both of them are in a sense distanced from their 'mother-tongue' and 'place of birth' — details which have become increasingly valorised in determining the 'rootedness' of Indian artists.

What makes artists like Harindranath and Chandra so special in the Indian context, to my mind, is their 'rootedness' in self which enables them to be 'at home' in a widely disparate range of circumstances. The very concept of 'home' for them is a fluid reality capable of incorporating diverse relationships and experiences that transcend the strictures of 'regionalism.' Chandra's sense of 'home' became more clear (yet elusive) to me one night as she was watching the waves on the sea from her house. Totally at peace with herself, she confided: 'You know what I like about being here. You could be anywhere.'

I think this provides a very interesting clue to her temperament as an artist which, to a large extent, accepts and even rejoices in the possibility of anonymity. Along with this very real need for solitude is an obligation to interact with diverse communities. Earlier in her life, this interaction bordered on gregariousness as Chandra participated in Baba's numerous interventions in political, social, and cultural forums. He was the prototype of the 'urban nomad', to use Chandra's phrase. Stirred by a certain restlessness emerging from metropolitan conditions of life and the need to actualise post-Independence ideals, the 'urban nomad' was driven by a combination of inner necessities and external drives, a ceaseless search for inner solitude coexisting with an absorption in a range of worldly desires and pursuits.

This 'worldliness' brings me to one of the important qualities that Chandra has derived from Harindranath: a vibrant secular spirit grounded in the multiple resources of our cultural history. I will be dealing with aspects of the 'secular' in Chandra's work at various points in this study. For the moment I would like to contextualise its underpinnings within the specific details of Harindranath's biography.

Harindranath's Legacy

It is a little known, yet telling fact that Harindranath's father, Aghorenath Chattopadhyay, was one of India's leading scientists and alchemists in the early half of this century.

A 'walking Encyclopaedia' who had gathered his knowledge from books written in Hebrew, French, German, Greek, Sanskrit, Bengali, Urdu, he instilled in his children a scientific sense of inquiry about the laws of the universe. The formation of stones, the composition of flowers, the flight of birds, the direction of wind, the orbits and speed of stars ... these were some of the ordinary things of life that he reflected on. Tellingly, this scientific temperament was affirmed in constant counterpoint to his wife's more religious explanations of natural laws. As Harindranath reveals in his autobiography:

> When thunder rumbled my mother would say poetically, 'There goes the golden chariot of God. Its wheels are rumbling. Wonderful!... and the next moment, scientific father would very politely and tactfully seat us beside him and explain that two clouds had in a hurry met each other with a terrific bump and that friction was created and there was, as a result, the lightning that we saw and the thunder ... At an early age, we got to know, therefore, that light travelled faster than sound.[6]

Though their family backgrounds were entirely different, it is significant how Chandra faced the same kind of counterpoint of 'reason' and 'faith' in dealing with her own parents. Over the years, she has evolved a seemingly irreligious attitude to life in general and is particularly critical of religiosity in dance.

In Harindranath, we find a more double-edged attitude to issues of 'religion' and 'faith.' On the one hand, he is remembered as one of the most outspoken and irreverent critics of religious orthodoxy. Writing at a very different point in Indian history when the separation of 'state' and 'religion' was the *sine qua non* of a secular 'Indian' identity, he could assert his position with an inimitable directness as in *The Curd-Seller Quatrains*:

> O I am sure that God above
> Would cease to feel a fool

> If every temple would become
> A hospital or school!

Or still more mischievously:

> I would not call the temple priest
> A parrot in a cage
> Since that might hurt the parrot's pride
> And put it in a rage.[7]

However, it is necessary to point out that for all the immediacy of Harindranath's attack on religious bigotry and cant, which Chandra has imbibed and extended in her own critiques of religiosity in art, there is no dismissal of 'faith' as such in his vision of life. In fact, there is an acknowledgment in Harindranath of the profound value of his mother's faith, which 'instilled' in his heart 'a belief in a Great Being called God.'[8] This God had many names in his house — Bhagwan, Khuda, Devadu — but 'He remained one and unchanging in our home.'

More than to ritual or prayer, however, Harindranath was drawn from his youth to a deep awareness of the interconnectedness of elements in the cosmos. In a memorable passage from his autobiography, steeped in a childlike wonder of Nature that he never lost, Harindranath speculated on God as an Artist:

> I always imagined that there was a huge Being called God seated behind the sky paring His nails; I imagined Him to have long, tapering fingers, too! Fingers of an artist. For he would paint the sunset and the dawn and the petals of flowers and the beaks of birds. He could change the tints of clouds at will. So He must be an artist, and, at an early age, I heard it said that long tapering fingers indicated the temperament of an artist. God was an artist who was always in hiding; I never understood why, though.[9]

This could be dismissed as a fanciful passage, but it reveals a certain poetic 'temperament' to which seers like Sri Aurobindo responded with considerable warmth. Indeed,

Aurobindo had written a seven-page review of Harindranath's first published work, *The Feast of Youth*, in his journal *Arya*, hailing the young poet 'as a supreme singer of the fusion of God with Nature and human existence.' It is equally necessary to point out, however, that when Harindranath spent some time as a poet-in-residence at the Aurobindo Ashram, he ultimately resisted and rejected the regimentation and austerity of the environment. If we have to speak of Harindranath's 'religion' therefore, it would be best to qualify it as a 'poet's religion', which had been apotheosised by yet another of Harindranath's admirers, Rabindranath Tagore himself, who in a much-quoted comment once remarked, 'After me the mantle falls on Harindranath.'

This is not the place to discuss why Harindranath did not ultimately come anywhere near realising this ideal. If I can venture a hypothesis for the purpose of this study, I would say that he was a prodigy who never really grew up. It is one thing for the 'little poet of ten' to make Gopal Krishna Gokhale cry with the reading of his poem commemorating the death of Khudiram Bose:

> When I am lifeless and upon the pyre,...
> Mine ashes will arise and sing in joy;
> It will proceed like music from the fire:
> Weep not, my country! for this patriot boy![10]

Similarly, when we hear the patriotic rhetoric of *Freedom Come* (written a few days before Independence), we can also accept Harindranath's poetic diction as part of a larger nationalist rhetoric:

> But we will rise and re-unite the mother,
> Yes, we shall move together towards our goal;
> Inseparable, brother one with brother,
> One India, one nation, and one soul.

The problem arises when this kind of Poet Laureate verse became a norm, which is unfortunately what tended to happen with much of Harindranath's later writing. What remains vibrant today are his comments and verses in a more satirical vein precisely because he was able to shift between different idioms in response to the forum he was addressing.

Imagine the electricity created in the seemingly august forum of the Lok Sabha, where Harindranath was once an Independent member, who would occasionally intervene in the sessions with verses like:

> The increment in railway fares
> Is very very fair,
> It does not touch the ministers
> Who always go by air.
>
> Our Five Year Plan is very like
> A piece of chewing gum
> We'll draw it out and draw it out
> For fifty years to come.[12]

This is where the *performer* in Harindranath, I imagine, came to the fore, combining the deadly wit of a satirist with the political acuity of an independent activist, a contemporary Vidhushaka who had earned the privilege to speak out.

Apart from the doggerel verse in which he excelled, Harindranath could formulate his critique in the most concise prose. For example:

> There are two sorts of democracy in the world:
> 1) of the people, for the people, by the people.
> 2) minus the first two and change the spelling of the last: just buy the people.[13]

Still more memorable are his political songs for which he is still remembered by some of our most radical writers like Mahasweta Devi who took pains to point out to various newspapers that obituaries of Harindranath (who passed away in 1990, at the age of 92) failed to mention his spirited contribution to IPTA and the Peoples' Squad through his rousing songs. An entire study should be made of these songs not only for their political content and rhetoric, but for the inimitable style of Harindranath's singing that could switch from classical to folk to sheer buffoonery, and then suddenly and totally unexpectedly switch back to a classical style. It is a most outstanding display of a histrionic temperament, at once frontal in its attack, and yet so full of play, irony and self-mockery. No one, including close friends and artists like Chandra, have been able to capture this unique gift of Harindranath's — to be alone and with thousands of people at the same time, at once jocular and critical, sophisticated and blunt. Most paradoxically, he was most true to himself when he was least serious about himself. This, to my mind, is his extraordinary quality (or quirk) that has yet to be studied in the larger context of political idioms in our cultural history.

I have dwelt briefly on Harindranath's qualities as a writer to provide some context of the artistic temperament to which Chandra was exposed at the very start of her life as a dancer. As yet, she had no career. What she did have was a most playful and creative relationship with a man who was both a friend and mentor, 'Mana' (child-spirit) and 'Baba'. It is in this context that one should situate Harindranath's seemingly authoritarian statement that he 'took charge of her mind.'[14] While one should not underestimate the power and influence of his charisma, it is equally necessary to point out that he was neither a guru nor a father in a conventional sense. As Chandra clarifies: 'Baba helped me to *see*. He watched what I was responding to. If he didn't agree, he would still go with me.' There was an honesty and freshness in their relationship that was only to be expected in its unorthodox, creative sense of 'play.'

In Harindranath's company, Chandra was also exposed to some of the most significant artists and cultural activists. Together they attended seminars, lectures, plays, poetry-readings, and most of all, dance performances. Bharatanatyam was Chandra's new love, a discipline to which she surrendered after abandoning her study of law. Now she knew what she wanted to do: dance. Earlier she had participated in some amateur performances which she had enjoyed 'physically', as she puts it. Now she wanted to learn the grammar of dance, and begin as it were a journey in another language. Predictably, yet perceptively, it was Baba who approved of Guru Ellappa Pillai, as Chandra's first dance teacher, who remains a vibrant presence in her memory to this day.

The 'Trinity': Baba, Guru Ellappa, Dashrath

In providing a brief biography of Guru Ellappa Pillai, a description of his *parampara* is unavoidable. In terms of his heredity, it is said that he hailed from a family of musicians from Kanchipuram, whose origins can be traced back to one Ashvadhati Pacchamuthu Mudaliar who allegedly could 'make horses dance.'[15] Guru Ellappa's immediate mentor in his youth was his maternal uncle, Tiruvengada Mudaliar, who taught him dancing and the art of *nattuvangam*, which involved the conducting of dance recitals with appropriate music and *sollukattus* (dance syllables). However, the real definition of Ellappa's *parampara* came not so much from his hereditary links as from his close affiliation to Kandappa Nattuvanar, who conducted Balasaraswati's recitals for many years before leaving for a brief stint at Uday Shankar's Art Centre at Almora in 1938. It was through this rich association with Kandappa that Guru Ellappa developed his own distinctive sensitivities as a musician and *nattuvanar*.

The choice of Ellappa as dance teacher was instinctively right for Chandra's particular sensibilities as a dancer. Though she was enamoured of most dancers whom she saw in Madras at that time, it was Balasaraswati's style that was the most inspiring, particularly the subtlety of its imaginative capacities and, as Chandra emphasises, the 'preparation' for realising these capacities in dance. Through Ellappa, Chandra had direct access to this style, though to the credit of her guru, he never once upheld Balasaraswati as a model for his young student, preferring to focus on her own possibilities as a dancer.

Strange as it may seem in the context of Chandra's 'contemporaneity', it should be remembered that she has derived her basic lessons and principles of dance from a tradition that can be traced directly to the Tanjore Quartette.[16] (Kandappa Nattuvanar was a direct descendant of the Quartette through the women descendants of Chinnaiah, the eldest member of the Quartette.) Though one should guard against mystifying the 'continuities' established through such a lineage, it cannot be denied that in the study of any traditional discipline like Bharatanatyam, the actual transmission of the art through the *guru-shishya parampara* is a valuable, if not essential, component of the dancer's education. Perhaps, one should also add that one could speak of the vibrancy of a particular *parampara* with greater conviction in the fifties than today, when most *paramparas* are either dead or dying or, worse still, manufactured to accommodate contemporary fashions and tastes.

Apart from Kandappa's distinctive heritage, it should also be remembered that he was responsible for some major innovations.[17] It was during his time as an accompanist for Balasaraswati's performances that the musicians began to sit on one end of the stage instead of standing behind the dancer and moving back and forth in accordance with her movements. In addition, he replaced the *melaprapti* (the pre-performance playing of *mridangam* and cymbals) with an 'invocatory prelude.' He also substituted the *mukhavina* for the flute. All these 'innovations' coexisted along with his commitment towards enriching the musical component of dance — a commitment that was amply recognised by the legendary Dhanammal, Balasaraswati's grandmother, who entrusted him alone to 'carry her *vina* to and from her Friday soirees.'[18]

Despite his exposure to Kandappa's 'innovations', Guru Ellappa's method of imparting Bharatanatyam, according to Chandra, was entirely 'traditional.' He showed the movements and position of feet with his hands accentuated by the movement of his eyes. Very rarely were there elaborate demonstrations of movement. Above all, there was no theory. Today, Chandra seizes on this fact and elaborates on it in the larger context of a dancer's consciousness: 'I was not taught any theory at all. That area is for the individual to enter when he or she is ready for it. The guru takes you to that level when you can experience dance. He facilitates your area of freedom, but you have to define it for yourself.'

Though Chandra would share the growing resistance among feminist performers to the authority wielded by gurus — and it is significant in this regard that she totally rejects any attempt to be viewed as a guru herself, preferring to remain a 'seeker' — the point is, that her own feelings for Guru Ellappa remain very warm and respectful. In this regard, it is the human dimension in the relationship that she emphasises most of all in her reminiscences of his tutelage. As for the one-to-one learning/teaching process, she regards it as nothing less than a luxury: 'You learn about so many things besides dance. The guru's entire experience and conditioning become part of your learning process.'

At times it is true that what a dancer may be imbibing need not correspond to the drives and desires of her own consciousness. This disjunction, which can and frequently does become very painful, is confronted only later in the learning process when the dancer consciously works against the directions of her guru. This process of 'freedom' generally begins once the 'grammar' of a particular dance tradition has been imbibed. At still later stages in a dancer's career, as in Chandra's case, there may be a total separation from the initial learning process when the dancer may be motivated to reject or redefine her basic grammar as a performer. At the beginning of a dancer's training, however, Chandra acknowledges the value of 'imitation', so long as the guru in question is worthy of being called a guru, a 'storehouse of knowledge', and is not just another dance-master.

Today Chandra remembers her first lessons with Guru Ellappa with a very perceptible warmth. His criticism could be sharp but was invariably accurate. So close was the tuning in this *guru-shishya parampara* that Chandra is capable of acknowledging that, 'If you went out of *tala*, it hurt him physically. It was from being sensitive to that hurt that you learned to discipline yourself. Your own lapses became a kind of corrective.'

This is not to deny that after Chandra's dance career was established she continued to have the same kind of uncomplicated relationship with Guru Ellappa. As her own attitude to dance culture became increasingly critical, she found herself questioning the power wielded by gurus. What needs to be emphasised is that she never saw Guru Ellappa as an antagonist: 'In the performance, he knew when you were going to make a mistake even before you made it. He knew your strength and your weakness. He protected you.' One should also point out that Guru Ellappa continued to support Chandra when she began to choreograph her own productions, contributing substantially to her productions of *Devadasi* and *Navagraha* with his rich musical repertoire.

One other important factor about Chandra's early dance classes is that she always had an audience for them. In his spotless white dhoti with *vibhuti* smeared on his forehead, Guru Ellappa would arrive early in the morning and teach for two to three hours. Sitting on one side of him was Baba. On the other side was one of Chandra's oldest friends, a 'constant in a floating population' as he likes to describe himself, Dashrath Patel, who was the third member of Chandra's intimate audience.

Dashrath is yet another creative, child-like person in Chandra's life who, at some level, refuses to grow up. At approximately the same time that Chandra came to Madras, he too travelled south to study with Debiprasad Roy Chowdhury at the Madras School of Art. Santiniketan was 'too feminine' for him, *'dhila-dhala'* as he puts it. Once again, it was Harindranath who served as a go-between. As a friend of Roy Chowdhury, he brought Dashrath and Chandra together. They had at least one thing in common. Both had families back in Nadiad, Gujarat, and they even shared a common surname. Chandra had dropped hers by this time preferring to be known as 'Chandralekha.'

What does Dashrath remember of Chandra at this time? He responds with a characteristic bubble in his voice: 'She was always very clear about her values. She never had a facade. Everything she did, she did seriously.' For instance, in addition to her study of dance, Chandra was also by this time deeply interested in painting. Unlike Dashrath who freely confesses that he resisted formal studies by the time he was in class two, preferring to explore his considerable visual talent, Chandra was capable of conceptualising the history of art. If she talked about Picasso, Braque, Miro, she had entered their work and vision as Dashrath himself discovered when he eventually developed a closer understanding of these masters while studying at the Ecole des Beaux Arts in Paris.

The other thing that Dashrath remembers about Chandra in the early fifties was her 'abundant creative energy'. and her 'ability to relate.' Few people, he emphasises, have both these capacities to 'create' and 'relate.' At one level, listening to Dashrath about Chandra is to be in the presence of a man in love, who has never ceased to be fascinated by a woman who has served as his 'reference point for seeing.' He also acknowledges her as his most 'sincere critic', the only one, I may add, who is really and truly capable of puncturing his ego. Their relationship is a life-long companionship in which Chandra has scrupulously guarded her own space as an artist and woman. We will dwell on it further as this book progresses, because Dashrath is very much part of Chandra's ongoing work. He is truly the 'constant'. in her life.

For the moment, let us leave him, a much younger man, sitting alongside Guru Ellappa, watching his friend Chandra dance in the company of one of the 'giants' of the Indian cultural scene, Harindranath Chattopadhyay. Together these three men formed the unofficial 'Trinity' in her work not only as her earliest spectators but also as the chief members in the production team that made her *arangetram* possible.

The 'Contradiction' of Life and Dance

Arangetram, the formal debut of a young dancer, has become commonplace in Madras city today. More and more families (and fathers in particular) are keen to see their daughters on stage, regardless of their individual interest or talent. At one level, the *arangetram* serves as an advertisement not only of the family's wealth and social prestige, but of the potential of the girl in the marriage market.

Chandra's *arangetram* in 1952 at the Museum Theatre in Madras City was a rather different affair. Here there was no family in attendance. As Dashrath recalls,'Most dancers have mothers and sisters dressing them and attending to their make-up and hair. I did that job for Chandra.' I should also emphasise that Dashrath displayed yet another of his many talents in the *arangetram*, which has now become one of his trademarks: ironing saris to perfection. Needless to say, while he was helping Chandra backstage, Baba was handling the PR and front-of-house. Guru Ellappa, of course, was the *nattuvanar* who accompanied Chandra in her first public performance.

It appears that the performance was received very well by a 'select audience of musicians, aesthetes, and intellectuals.'[19] At some level it cannot be denied that Chandra had a tremendous advantage in having what has come to be known as a 'backer' in Harindranath. What needs to be emphasised, however, is that this 'backer' was also a close friend. Therefore the question of Harindranath exhibiting Chandra for mercenary or selfish reasons did not arise. Baba was genuinely interested in her creativity and growth as an artist. Chandra, on the other hand, was fully aware of his influence but also wary of being seen as his protégée. In this context, she was particularly embarrassed by his introduction and the sound of his booming voice intoning 'Chandralekha.' It took time, however, before she learned to speak for herself in public, which was a long and occasionally painful journey.

Already in her debut something happened to Chandra that was distinctly a consequence of her own critical alertness. She has now confronted this 'experience' in public, most significantly at the first East-West Dance Encounter in January 1984 at the National Centre for the Performing Arts in Bombay. Here in the midst of a wide range of dancers and artists, Chandra revealed the 'contradiction' between life and dance that had emerged during her *arangetram* even while she was dancing.

> (My first public dance recital) was a charity programme in aid of the Rayalaseema Drought Relief Fund. I was dancing *'Mathura nagarilo'*... I was depicting the full-flowing Yamuna, *gopikas, jala krida* or the water-play of the *sakhis*, the sensuality, the luxuriance and abundance of water.
>
> Suddenly, right in the middle of the performance, I froze to a stop with the realisation that I was dancing and depicting all this profusion of water in the context of a drought. I remembered photographs in the newspapers of cracked earth, of long, winding queues of people waiting for water with little tins in hand. Guru Ellappa was singing *'Mathura Nagarilo.'* Art and life seemed to be in conflict. The paradox was stunning. For that split second I was divided, fragmented into two people.[20]

To the best of my knowledge, this could be the first reflection on classical Indian dance from the experience of a dancer that confronts what feminist performers and theorists are beginning to problematise as a 'split' in performance.[21] Chandra chooses to speak of it as a 'contradiction' both emerging from within the artist herself and as part of a larger 'social contradiction.' Though Chandra admits that she has not been able to resolve this 'contradiction' as an artist, her recent attempts to struggle with its demands (and the vulnerability emerging from such a confrontation) have resulted in some of her most reflective statements, which I would like to discuss in some detail.

Let us begin with the concrete problem of dancing in a country where acute water scarcity coexists with numerous myths about the abundance of water. A realist strategy of representation would be to focus on the 'waterlessness', which could result in a predominantly didactic exposure of the social problem devoid of myth and fantasy. Another possibility (almost *de rigeur* in classical performances) would be to surrender to the myth of 'abundant, free-flowing water', oblivious of, if not consciously indifferent to larger social considerations. For Chandra, the first option is devoid of any life-sustaining capacities that can enable us to confront, and hopefully transform our reality. The second option, on the other hand, runs the risk of succumbing to a vacuous and dishonest aesthetic.

So how does a dancer consciously intervene in such a situation? It is significant in this regard that Chandra refuses to dichotomise the 'contradiction' between life and dance, preferring to hold on to the possibility that they can be engaged in a vibrant dialectic rather than juxtaposed in black-and-white opposition. Though she has as yet no 'solution' to the problem, she is 'learning', in her words, 'to cope with it, learning to see the beauty of one reality ('water') and the truth of another ('waterlessness').'

This is how Chandra attempted to explain her position to me:

> I would perceive the extremity of the problem something like this. You can show 'reality' directly or you can aestheticise it in a different mode or juxtapose the two. In all these modes, the context is lost. The challenge would be to... (silence) see the area which is so nebulous where you don't know what to do. How to bring art and life together: what are its joineries? The main thing is not to show the fist by imagining that you can change the world. The true area of reality is your own insignificance, your own limitation, your despair which is real, your love for life.

Clarifying her position further through the actual process of thinking it aloud instead of articulating a position already 'worked out' — this is what made listening to her so moving — Chandra added:

> The thrust of our creative work should be to see our impotency, to face it, and through that to confront those little truths through which one can make a gesture to reach out towards change.

It could be argued that this 'vulnerability' moving towards a tentative gesture of 'change' is not particularly evident in the most famous of Chandra's productions. As we shall examine in much greater detail in the book, the distinctive quality of her choreography lies in her affirmation of the life-sustaining elements of the body and universe. It would be wrong, however, to assume that she is oblivious of those forces and realities which counter or negate these elements.

Significantly, it is in her work dealing more specifically with women such as *Request Concert* and *Sri* that Chandra has come closest to exposing her vulnerability as a dancer and choreographer. Here, as we shall describe later, we can actually see a confrontation of those 'little truths' and the beginnings of a 'gesture' reaching out towards 'change.'

Art and Survival

Continuing to probe the 'vulnerability' of the dancer, I think it would be useful to situate Chandra's thoughts on the subject in a still larger context of the 'purpose' of her art. Put so directly, it can seem pompous and even misleading as if every artist is bound to have a mission that can be spelled out. In a less formal way, we could ask: 'Why dance? What does it mean to dance?' These are the 'basic' questions that Chandra has confronted with, perhaps, a greater degree of self-reflexivity and critical consciousness than almost any other performing artist in India today.

Once again, when we arrive at these basic questions in our discussion, Chandra's intervention is startlingly honest: 'We need art only to the extent that life dehumanises us. We need art to survive.' Not to recognise the humility of this statement is to miss out on understanding Chandra's strength, which emerges out of a confrontation of her vulnerability and not (as it would appear) through a denial of its existence.

If Chandra appears to have what some women have described as 'armour', a 'tough exterior', it is because she has been compelled to work out ways of asserting her freedom in conditions that are increasingly hostile to the exploration of creative work in general and to the interventions of women in particular. Recalling what could be one of the most painful and frightening periods in her life, when she was falsely charged with sedition along with her companion, Sadanand Menon, (details of which will be examined in the section on Skills), Chandra confronts the liberational possibilities of dance in the larger context of survival:

> I have been wounded many times. The attacks in my life have been very real. I know what it means to feel that chill in your spine. I know what it means when you can feel that your eyes are losing their light and lustre. The power of the eyes is capable of making holes in space. But then you see the dimming of your eyes. At that time you have to pick yourself up from the debris as it were and ask yourself: Can art save me? What can art do for me? Does it have any meaning? Can it heal? Can dance give me back my spine? This is my real quest as an artist.

Hearing Chandra articulate these questions, sitting (I might add) with her spine absolutely straight, there was no doubt in my mind that she had *tested* these questions through struggle and intense reflection. Seemingly rhetorical questions like 'Can art save me?', which may seem melodramatic in print, or permeated with a false anguish if taken out of context, had an immediacy in the way she confronted the 'wounds' in her words. As always, there was no self-pity in her statement. The tears, if any, were held back. Countering the rhetoric of resistance, Chandra was content to uphold the simple truth that art helps us to cope with life. Nothing more, but also, nothing less.

Spontaneously, Chandra breaks her thoughts and listens to the wind that sounds in the background of our discussion, stirring the trees in her garden and ruffling the waves on the sea. 'Why do we need to organise sounds when we can listen to this? Just tuning to the hush of a forest or the flapping of a coconut leaf ... you cannot duplicate these sounds in art.'

For a moment, we are back where we started with a girl who sensed an 'entire education' in nature, falling asleep under trees. But the reality is that art becomes necessary in the actual process of growing up and confronting the social and political pressures determined by family, education, religion, and culture. For Chandra, these 'collective institutions' place 'limits' on our freedom by compelling us 'to conform, to adhere, and never to question.[22] Over the years these 'limits' are internalised through a series of 'blocks', even as 'that small, very small spirit at our centre, craves to break away.[23]

In response, therefore, to the question posed at the beginning of this section and the end of this chapter — 'Why dance?' — one could say that for Chandra it is the strongest way of freeing herself from some of these 'blocks' and learning to cope with life not through a derived militancy, but by learning 'how to stand', and thereby, affirm the power of the spine. This process is valuable not just for oneself but for the people and the space around us, which can be energised through concentration. Chandra's 'contemporaneity', therefore, is affirmed at one level through the seemingly 'small', yet crucial attempt, in her words, 'to hold herself together.' 'From being broken up, divided, alienated, I have to learn how to stand.'

This insight, expressed in a dancer's language rather than the rhetoric of resistance available in the social sciences, has a specific discipline and struggle which we shall discuss in the analysis of her training process. It is worth keeping in mind at the very start of this book as we explore her life-in-dance centred in her understanding of the body.

4

5

6

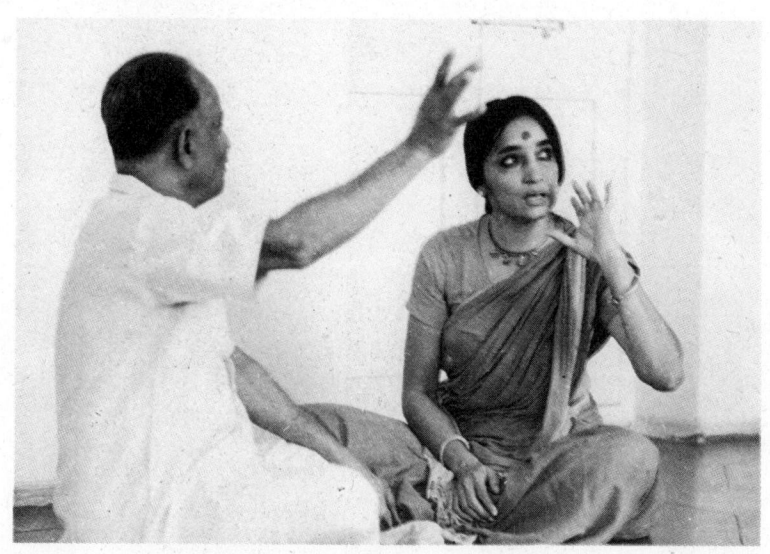

7

2

8

Early Career

After her *arangetram*, Chandra 'blazed into the dance world' as she laughingly acknowledges, giving solo performances in important cultural centres throughout the country. Significantly, this is a period in her life that she rarely talks about today. If anything, she tends to dismiss it as part of a youthful dalliance with dance that she had not yet recognised at the start of her career. The reception she got as a young dancer was clearly flattering judging from the eulogistic reviews of important critics like A.S. Raman, G. Venkatachallum and Charles Fabri. Occasionally, Chandra was described as the youthful successor to Balasaraswati, and more glibly, as the 'rising moon' to the 'descending sun' of Shanta Rao. Predictably, Chandra refused to be entrapped by these comparisons and epithets, preferring to think of herself as a dancer in her own right. 'I did not want to be anyone but myself', she asserts today, adding mischievously that most critics had already begun to typecast her as 'vivacious'. That tag remained with her for a long time.

It could be argued that Chandra's career was, to a large extent, facilitated by the wide literary and political contacts of Harindranath. Jawaharlal Nehru and Martin Luther King were just two of the eminent personalities for whom she had danced early in her career. Already between 1952-54 she had visited the USSR and the Peoples' Republic of China as part of the first Indian cultural delegations to these countries. Baba's influence was also clearly perceptible in her introductions to Uday Shankar, the poet Vallathol, Ustad Vilayat Khan, among other eminent personalities.

This combination of patronage and friendship that Chandra received from Harindranath was accompanied by an increasing resistance on her part to 'being endorsed.' In a few years, she would free herself entirely from the male-dominated world of sabhas and cultural organisations by opting out of dance for almost eleven years. In the early fifties, however, she experienced the 'glamour' and 'excitement' of a successful dance career without seeming to question the contradiction between 'art' and 'life' that had surfaced in her *arangetram*. All the tensions relating to the representation of Indian social realities were submerged in her 'quick-spirited' performances, where as Dashrath recalls, the bells attached to her feet would be invariably scattered on the stage floor after every performance.

After five to six years of her 'whirlwind' career, Chandra's thoughts about dance deepened. More specifically, she began to question Bharatanatyam itself, which was both the 'language' and the 'structure' within which she attempted to define her 'freedom' as a dancer. Unlike her most inspiring role model, Isadora Duncan, the founder of modern dance who had 'freed' herself radically from puritan American culture, both as a dancer and political activist, Chandra had a different 'tradition' to deal with and dance within. Unlike Isadora who almost fetishised the freedom of the dancer as a state of pure spontaneity without any specific discipline, Chandra realised that her *parampara* to which she had surrendered had its own rigour and demands. Without being questioned, this 'storehouse of knowledge' could easily become a prison. Its 'embarrassment of riches' could be stifling.

It is in this context, therefore, that Chandra undertook the important task of 'historicising' Bharatanatyam through her first piece of choreography, *Devadasi* in 1960, which she may not remember very well today, but whose conceptual implications enable us to view the 'tradition' of Bharatanatyam within its larger political, social, and economic constraints. In this chapter, I shall work towards a brief description of *Devadasi*, and more specifically, the *Tillana* which concluded the production, by narrating those aspects of Bharatanatyam that are relevant to our understanding of its 'tradition' today. This will necessitate a somewhat extended background on the subject leading through the Devadasi tradition and the luminous career of Balasaraswati to Chandra's first intervention as a choreographer.

Bharatanatyam: An 'Invention' of Tradition?

One of the ironies about Bharatanatyam is that it continues to be regarded as an 'ancient' tradition despite the increased acknowledgment among some of its practitioners that its heritage is barely 300 years old.[1] The term itself — Bharatanatyam — which is possibly one of the most presumptuous, all-subsuming categories assumed by a single dance tradition, was invented in the early thirties. There is some confusion as to who used the word for the first time. The redoubtable scholar, V. Raghavan, has implied that he was responsible for it, but the names of E. Krishna Iyer and Rukmini Devi, have also been associated with the early endorsement of the term.[2] Together as the most illustrious representatives of a Brahmin elite based in the city of Madras, these luminaries proselytised the art of Bharatanatyam in opposition to its more 'degenerate' antecedent in *sadir*. This earlier dance tradition was associated with *devadasis* ('servants of god') who had, increasingly in the eyes of respectable society, been reduced to *dasis*, mere prostitutes. All this is common knowledge in the dance world today, but the historical processes by which *sadir* was transformed to Bharatanatyam have yet to be fully confronted in the context of an 'invented' tradition.[3]

Traditionalists would argue, of course, that Bharatanatyam is not an 'invention' (something made up), but rather is very much part of 'what has been handed down' through 'tradition' over the centuries. That diminutive figure of a so-called 'dancing girl' from the archaeological remains of Harappa has once again been used to authenticate the 'ancient' origins of a particular art. The fact that this girl might not be dancing at all or that she could be more cogently associated with the Grama Devata, the 'ancient ever-young Earth Mother of village India',[4] has yet to be recognised by some of our major dance scholars.

Though he was possibly aware of its nebulous associations, it is significant that V. Raghavan included the figure as one of the earliest representatives of dance in his authoritative study of Bharatanatyam. Later, this source became essentialised through more derivative readings of his scholarship in popular 'histories' of dance in which it is unquestionably assumed that the 'antiquity' of Bharatanatyam can be traced to 'the Rigvedic hymns and to the figurine of a dancing girl of Mohenjodaro statuette.'[5] It is through such casual errors of judgement and perception, that the history of Bharatanatyam has been authenticated.

On slightly stronger ground, scholars have also affirmed that Bharatanatyam can be traced back to a particular 'form' called Lasya described in at least three different places in the *Natyasastra*. Here again it would seem that too much has been read into the twelve-part scenario of a Nati, a solo dancer, who waits for her lover with a range of *bhavas* inspired by *shringara*.

For V. Raghavan, once again the most articulate proponent of the theory, there is no doubt that this gamut of feelings relating to separation in love contains 'the origins of the essential themes of the *Sabdas, Varnas,* and *Padams,* and even of the *Alarippu,* of the Bharatanatyam recital of modern times.'[6] One wonders what is gained through such verification which, at a purely thematic level, can be related to so many other dance situations and traditions in India. It is one thing to view Lasya as a classification, a generic type of drama which has inspired many manifestations and regional variations in performance, but it is quite another thing to uphold it as the 'oldest classical form' of Bharatanatyam itself.

Such judgements deny the possibility of other dance forms possessing their own connections to these allegedly primary sources of our culture contained in texts like the *Natyasastra*. It would seem that Bharatanatyam alone has the credentials to affirm a direct line as it were with 'tradition' itself. It is this kind of assumption that enables Rukmini Devi, for example, to state: 'Other forms of dancing, like Kathakali and Manipuri, are obviously variations of Bharatanatyam.'[7] The fact that these forms could have their own origins not necessarily mediated through Bharatanatyam or linked to traditional sources is a possibility that is not even acknowledged.

Besides, the very generality of terms like 'Manipuri dance' reveals a total lack of consideration for the variations within the multicultural context of Manipur itself. This kind of cultural categorisation is almost as shallow, if not downright condescending, as V. Raghavan's reference to Assam as a 'cultural outpost' where the 'Nati style of dance' can also be viewed.[8]

The entire thrust of building up the 'ancient' and necessarily 'sacred' origins of Bharatanatyam was not made for entirely programmatic reasons — in other words, to give Bharatanatyam the 'requisite status' (to use V. Raghavan's phrase) at a time when its immediate heritage in *sadir nautch* was being condemned by 'respectable' members of society. At some level, the sanctification of a classical genealogy was strategically necessary, and no one was better prepared to construct (and verify) it than Brahmin scholars like V. Raghavan, E. Krishna Iyer, and Rukmini Devi. But it would be inaccurate (or at least incomplete) if we simply accepted their intervention in the larger context of reviving a 'dying' art.

Sadir, after all, was not just being revived; it was being consciously adapted, crafted, and advertised as the 'national dance-art *par excellence.*'[9] Though this could be dismissed as hyperbole, it is significant how V. Raghavan chooses to elevate Bharatanatyam within the larger context of the 'nation'. This is ironic, to say the least, because the makers of Bharatanatyam also affirmed an aesthetic that would seem to transcend the realities of politics.

Indeed, Rukmini Devi would go so far as to say that, 'Like the *Vedas,* the *Upanishads,* the *Bhagavad Gita, Dhammapada,* and other scriptures, Bharatanatyam is a method of spiritual learning for human ends. Therefore, it is not to be expected to reflect modern life and its ways, which are based essentially on surface expression and are thus artificial and base.'[10] If such is the case then one can only question how such a dance could be regarded as one of the greatest creations of 'the artistic genius of the nation', unless, of course, the 'nation' itself becomes an ethereal category in the spiritual tradition of the *Vedas* and the *Upanishads.*

The 'nation', however, is a political category despite its propensity to be 'imagined' in different ways. Cultural figures like Rukmini Devi and V. Raghavan were also official representatives of a larger cultural movement in which 'national identity' was celebrated. This was a different kind of movement from the later emergence of the Indian Peoples' Theatre Association (IPTA) in which Harindranath Chattopadhyay, for example, had participated. Here nationalism was also advocated not just through an affirmation of 'traditional' and 'indigenous' cultural sources but, more specifically, as a critique of imperialism.

It could be argued, of course, that for all its mass appeal, the activities of IPTA were ultimately constrained by the largely urban and middle-class moorings of its leaders. But the attempt to organise a cultural movement at a national level cutting across regional, linguistic, and class differences has not been surpassed for the sheer scale of its activities. In contrast, the kind of 'movement' that seems to have been generated around the propagation of Bharatanatyam in opposition to what came to be called the Anti-Nautch movement, was ultimately restricted to a small coterie of aesthetes and art lovers.

Predominantly Brahmin and upper class, their constituency was centred around that most august of cultural institutions in India, the Music Academy of Madras founded in 1928. Significantly, this organisation was formed after the First All India Music Conference was held in Madras in 1927 in conjunction with a session of the Indian National Congress. The conflation between the promotion of Bharatanatyam and the propagation of values associated with the Brahmin-dominated Congress lobbies of the Indian elite was becoming increasingly apparent.

For and Against Devadasis

It was at the Music Academy that E. Krishna Iyer, one of the foremost crusaders of Bharatanatyam sponsored a performance of two *devadasis,* Jeevaratnam and

Rajalakshmi, better known as the Kalyani daughters. Held in 1931, this performance was apparently not well attended because of the social stigma associated with *devadasis* whose art Iyer had attempted to propagate earlier by dancing female roles himself in public. The next year in December 1932, he used his rhetorical skills as a lawyer to engage in a verbal battle with Dr. Muthulakshmi Reddy, the first woman legislator in British India who was also one of the earliest members of the Women's India Association, founded in 1917 to 'organise women on an all India basis with the objective of social and legal reforms.'[11]

Their much-advertised 'battle' conducted in the columns of *The Madras Mail* and *The Hindu* was precipitated by Dr. Reddy, who had reacted sharply to the presence of *devadasis* at an official function honouring the Chief Minister of Madras, the Raja of Bobbili.[12] Reddy's repugnance for 'these Devadasis' was scarcely concealed by her excessively self-righteous condemnation of their 'unwholesome practice'. Iyer, on the other hand, invoked the 'Muses' in his advocacy of an 'Art minus Vice'. Much was written around this controversy with contributions ranging from Gandhiji's condemnation of the *devadasi* system as 'a blot upon those who countenance it' to the intervention of social reformers like one Miss Tenant from London who conducted a signature campaign against the 'evil' system.

In all this furore, it would seem that the *devadasis* themselves continued to be marginalised, apart from a few sporadic forums in which they attempted to represent themselves. For the most part they were represented by others. Ultimately, it would seem that Iyer's position proved to be victorious after the Kalyani daughters presented a highly successful concert at the Music Academy on January 1, 1933. This was followed by Rukmini Devi's formal debut as a Bharatanatyam artist at the International Convention of Theosophists held at Adyar, Madras. Originally groomed by Annie Besant and the Elders of the Theosophical Hierarchy as the chosen Vehicle for the World Mother, Rukmini Devi was now formally backed by the Theosophical Society as one of the primary representatives of India's cultural renaissance.[13]

Needless to say, with such a strong nexus between the Brahmin Congress elite and the Theosophists, the 'battle' in favour of reviving Bharatanatyam was won. And yet, one could hardly say that the rights and dignity of the *devadasis* had been served. What emerged through the promotion of Bharatanatyam was the affirmation of a new kind of 'national culture' that endorsed the religious and social aspirations of a predominantly Brahmin elite. By the time the Madras Legislative Assembly passed the Madras Devadasis (Prevention of Dedication) Act in 1947, almost seventeen years after Dr. Reddy had introduced the Devadasi Abolition Bill in the same Assembly, Bharatanatyam had already severed its ties from the '*devadasi* system' and was hailed by at least some of its supporters as 'the national art *par excellence*.'

Much more can be said about the 'devadasi system', but I will limit myself here to a brief account of how the 'nation' was inscribed in the debate surrounding *devadasis*.[14] It would seem that the chief proponents of the Anti-Nautch movement spearheaded by Dr. Reddy were regarded as 'progressive nationalists' as opposed to 'conservative nationalists' like S. Sathyamurthy of the Madras Congress, who persistently opposed the passing of the Bill in the Madras Legislative Assembly.

Sathyamurthy's opposition, however, was not motivated by any real concern for the *devadasis* themselves despite his attempts to mobilise their opinion. What became eminently clear at least to one section of the *devadasis* in Mayuram town was his concealed attempt to preserve a Brahmanic hegemony in matters of religion and culture. It was obvious that he feared that the abolition of *devadasis* could precipitate a non-Brahmin demand for 'the abolition of temple priests, who were Brahmins.'[15] Thus, in the guise of preserving the *devadasi* system as part of 'the indigenous Hindu/national culture', he was merely safeguarding his community's vested interests sanctified through religion.

If the 'conservative' position, therefore, upheld the sanctity of the 'nation' within a larger Hindu framework, the 'progressive' stance was no less 'Hindu' in its propagation of an alternative to the *devadasi* system. For Dr. Reddy, who considered the saving of 'one girl's honour and purity' greater than the 'feeding of millions of our people', the rehabilitation of *devadasis* necessitated enforced marriages (with employment benefits for the husbands). Only then could these 'objectionable' breed of women become 'legal and chaste wives and loving mothers and useful citizens.'[16] Within this context, the middle-class norms determining Dr. Reddy's 'progressive' reformatory zeal become only too evident.

Where does one place the champions of Bharatanatyam within this spectrum of attitudes to the nation? On the one hand, they are linked through their class affiliations and predominantly western education to the 'progressive' politics of reformers like Dr. Reddy. On the other hand, in their overt divinisation of dance, there is a close affinity to the 'conservative' upholding of traditional values. It would seem that the promoters of Bharatanatyam in the thirties imagined themselves to be 'progressive' while they were essentially 'conservative'.

Thus, the 'sacred' dance had to be 'purified' of its 'baser elements.' *Padams* with licentious undertones had to be bowdlerised. *Shringara* had to be doctored through *bhakti*. In essence, dance had to be made respectable. Its aesthetic had to conform to the dominant norms of decency upheld by the elite society of that time.

In such a scenario, it is telling that Bharatanatyam ultimately catered to both the 'conservative' and 'progressive' representatives of nationalism, the Sathyamurthy and Reddy camps in our political culture. Under the leadership of Rukmini Devi, whose Kalakshetra founded in 1936 became the premier institution for the teaching of Bharatanatyam in India, the dance was associated with a certain 'aristocratic' aura, exemplifying the highest standards of artistic excellence to be found in our burgeoning 'national culture.' Along with this aristocracy of spirit, there was also an etherealisation of dance, or more specifically, of the female dancer, whose model was 'the ancient temple dancer, who is a pure and holy, chaste woman', the very antithesis of the 'living *devadasi*.'[17]

Over the years, this model has been increasingly secularised through a steadily proliferating elite whose understanding of Bharatanatyam is less determined by a 'spiritual Yoga' than by the more crass aspirations associated with the promotion of social position and rank. Now the *devadasi* is no longer marginalised, she has been ruthlessly eliminated by a system ultimately controlled by politicians and the leading members of *sabhas* to whom deference is almost obligatory if a dancer wishes to advance in her career. As Balasaraswati, who herself was born in a family of *devadasis*, put it caustically: 'They (the Brahmin elite) have taken away our dance and our profession.'

Balasaraswati's Parampara

It is in the legendary example of Balasaraswati in which, I believe, the distinctions between *sadir nautch,* the 'devadasi system' and Bharatanatyam can be most meticulously studied. No one brought together the different strains of the *parampara* with greater depth than this extraordinary performer, who was at once steeped in tradition and yet capable of transmitting it to diverse audiences both at home and abroad in predominantly modern conditions of representation. At once worldly and deeply spiritual, she was able to see the ironies of the so-called 'transition' of *sadir* to Bharatanatyam with a combination of knowledge and pain which has yet to be studied seriously by dance scholars. It is too easy to rhapsodise about Balasaraswati and thereby reduce her to a 'phenomenon'. What is harder, I believe, is to see the multiple strains that constituted her complex personality which enabled her to 'travel' a greater distance *imaginatively* than almost any other performer in our dance tradition.

Almost like a fiction, her connections to the court tradition of *sadir* can be traced through six generations descending from mother to daughter beginning with Papammal, who is said to have danced and sung in the Thanjavur court in the 18th century, leading to her grandmother Veena Dhanam and mother Jayammal.[18] Balasaraswati (one could say) had *sadir* in her blood. Connected to the *parampara* through her knowledge not only of dance but of music and literature as well, she was schooled at home in George Town, Madras, which was regarded by many connoisseurs as a 'seat of music.'

From the absorbing interview with Balasaraswati conducted by N. Pattabhi Raman and Anandhi Ramachandran, we learn how her teachers were in and around the family. Her 'goddess' of a grandmother, as Balasaraswati described Veena Dhanam, interpreted legendary *padams* for her. Her mother on the other hand stimulated her profound understanding of *ragabhava* through song. Kandappa Nattuvanar was her relentlessly stern dance-master; Radhamma, a neighbour and scholar, taught her Tamil, Telugu and Sanskrit; Chinnaya Naidu would quiz her about particular *nayikas* (heroines) by singing short phrases relating to their attributes; Kuchipudi Vedantam Lakshminarayan Sastri, who instructed her in the art of improvising *varnams,* would occasionally ask her to 'cast the horoscope' of a particular *varnam.*

Not only was Balasaraswati's education wide in the sheer scale of its areas of knowledge, it was intrinsically creative. Thus, along with the rigour of her discipline to which she dedicated hours of work, she also had the extraordinary privilege to explore improvisations in which she performed entire songs only through facial expression, both with and without music. Such details fill one with awe about her *preparation* as a performer for transmitting the innermost subtleties of her tradition.

Along with her thorough grounding in the *sadir* repertoire, which enabled her to select from 13 *varnams,* 97 *padams,* and 51 *javalis,*[19] Balasaraswati was steeped in the devotional aspects of her dance. This is what enabled her to link the court heritage of *sadir* to the '*devadasi* tradition.' For her, *bhakti* and *shringara,* which are so often dichotomised, could not be separated: '*Shringara,* which is considered to be the greatest obstacle to spiritual realisation, has itself become an instrument for uniting the dancer with

Divinity.[20] Therefore the question of 'purifying' *shringara* becomes a redundancy, if not an impertinence.

Affirming the significance of Bharatanatyam as an 'artistic yoga', she had once imagined the passage of a dance recital within the structure, contours and inner space of a temple. Though her statement has been quoted on many occasions, it is worth quoting at length for the sheer radiance of its conviction:

> The Bharatanatyam recital is structured like a Great Temple: we enter through the *gopura* (outer hall) of *alarippu,* cross the *ardhamandapam* (half-way hall) of *jatiswaram,* then the *mandapa* (great hall) of *sabadam,* and enter the holy precinct of the deity in the *varnam.* This is the place, the space, which gives the dancer expansive scope to revel in the rhythm, moods, and music of the dance.... The *padams* now follow. In dancing the *padams,* one experiences the containment, cool and quiet, of entering the sanctum from its external precinct.... Dancing to the *padam* is akin to the juncture when the cascading lights of worship are withdrawn and the drum beats die down to the simple and solemn chanting of sacred verses in the closeness of God. Then, the *tillana* breaks into movement like the final burning of camphor accompanied by a measure of din and bustle. In conclusion, the devotee takes to his heart the god he has so far glorified outside; and the dancer completes the traditional order by dancing to a simple devotional verse.[21]

Such is the density of thought and emotion in the passage that one can sense the intensity that Balasaraswati was able to bring to her immortal rendition of *Krishna nee begane, baro.* The preparation for such intensity, I believe, could not come entirely from her technique and discipline as a dancer. It was enhanced by her devotional faith that occasionally inspired her to dance within the sanctum of the temple itself. At least one such clandestine homage to Lord

Murugan at the Tiruttani temple (clandestine because dancing in temples was illegal with the passing of the Devadasi Act of 1947) convinced Balasaraswati that her 'career began to prosper again', and that her dance was essentially a 'religious offering' to which Lord Murugan had responded.[22] Such faith can only be ascribed to that of a 'believer.'

Responding to this aspect of Balasaraswati's dance, Chandra (who is not a 'believer' in an orthodox sense) acknowledges:

> For Balasaraswati the act of worship was real, which has not been so for anyone else I have seen. For her, the gods were real, legends were real, ritual was real.

This sense of the 'real' was conveyed in performance itself, where the *parampara* came alive with a depth of emotion. Recalling one such performance where Balasaraswati played Nandanar, the social outcast who seeks a glimpse of the Lord from outside the temple, Chandra remembers:

> Bala could make us cry while depicting the story of Nandanar. She was able to create the scene of a massive crowd in the temple. She was able to show the attitude of a Paraya in Nandanar's body. Through the interstices between the people in the crowd, she showed us Nandanar trying to see. She showed us his pain. And on feeling this pain, people would cry. Today, if someone had to imitate exactly what Bala did, the experience would not be the same. The dramatic level could be sustained, but not the human.

In this perceptive account, we begin to sense how Balasaraswati's 'traditional' art nurtured through *sadir* and temple-worship could be 'transported' to secular spaces and audiences. Today, however, when we see Nandanar performed by some of our leading Bharatanatyam dancers, the effect is, more often than not, hypocritical. The dancer, bejewelled and 'winsome', alternating between fixed smiles and expressions of pain, rarely succeeds in 'becoming' Nandanar. Standing outside his body and state of consciousness, she 'exhibits' him rather than 'enters' and thereby 'transforms' his state of suffering. In the process, she merely affirms her own class and caste priorities, appropriating his world-view with the support received from the predominantly elite members of her own society for whom she performs.

I shall deal with the problems afflicting the contemporary Bharatanatyam 'cultural scene' at greater length in the course of this book. For the moment I would like to situate Chandra's attitude to the 'history' of Bharatanatyam within the larger framework that I have explored so far concerning the 'invention' of its tradition, the distinct (yet conflated) traditions of *sadir* in court and the temple, and the positions of dancers like Balasaraswati and Rukmini Devi in whom the *parampara* came alive in different ways.

Chandra's 'Devadasi'

Chandra's need to 'historicise' Bharatanatyam in the late fifties came out of a very different consciousness from the kind represented by Balasaraswati. Understandably, much has changed in Chandra's articulation about Bharatanatyam since that time, but the basic premises underlying her attitude to dance were already being formulated.

Like many reflective dancers, she had reached a point early in her career when she asked herself: 'Is the audience looking at my dance or at my appearance? I realised that they were actually seeing me as a "vivacious" and "attractive" woman. I questioned their appreciation. What satisfies the male mentality in the audience?' At one level, therefore, Chandra began to rebel against her dance career because of the way in which she was perceived. This perception in turn was determined by the larger 'culture' supporting Bharatanatyam as a refined embodiment of 'traditional' and 'national' culture. It was this immediate questioning of her own role as a dancer that compelled Chandra to view Bharatanatyam in a more critical context.

Yet another impulse that contributed to Chandra's inquiry of her dance tradition emerged from her ideological resistance to its *parampara*. As I have examined earlier, she had access to Balasaraswati's school through Guru Ellappa Pillai. In her formative years, she dutifully learned a significant variety of items from the traditional repertoire, including full-length *varnams* lasting two hours. Even at that stage of 'submitting' to the tradition, it was clear to Chandra that its 'religious' context could not be entirely accepted.

She herself was not religious. Her 'life-style' (as we put it so glibly these days) was assertively 'modern', if not 'radical'. Resolutely, she denied traditional 'Hindu' values relating to marriage and child-bearing, and to her credit she did not merely intellectualise her position through rhetoric but actually implemented it in her assertively independent life and relationships with men.

At a more general social level, she was exposed to the cultures of the world, to the murals of Ajanta and the paintings of Picasso, the philosophy of Marx and Patanjali, Isadora Duncan and Balasaraswati. With such a cosmopolitan world-view, it is not surprising that Chandra could not immerse herself in the *parampara* with the kind of 'devotion' that Balasaraswati assumed.

Once again, it is to the credit of Chandra that she never deceived herself about this fact, unlike so many dancers today who masquerade a homage to the gods on the stage while living a totally different kind of life off-stage. Early in her career Chandra knew that 'art' and 'life' had somehow to go together. The 'contradiction' that she had confronted in her *arangetram* was now beginning to manifest itself, if not in performance, then certainly in the desire to 'historicise' her art more rigorously.

Today Chandra's stand in relation to the *parampara* is much clearer. She prefers to tune into its principles and energies through levels of abstraction rather than narrative. When she does deal with a 'text', she either responds to it ironically (such as the direction of the 'male gaze' in her representation of the *varnam* in *Angika*) or through a totally different kind of 'secular' narrative such as Bhaskaracharya's mathematical riddles posed to his daughter, Lilavati. In short, she has found her own ways of relating to the *parampara* which may still be too 'traditional' for some feminists, but as Chandra would put it: 'You don't throw away your culture when you reject some of its taboos, codes, rhetoric, and clichés.'

On the other hand, Chandra is clear about what needs to be rejected. While acknowledging the 'levels of expressivity and experience' assumed by *devadasis* in the past, she is, nonetheless, compelled to emphasise:

> Today it is not possible to endorse all these skills and values. Women today are seeking out different areas of relationship devoid of male control. You have to be tuned to the consciousness of your time and space. This does not mean that we should give up sensuality. Rather, we should shed religiosity.

It is this position which has guided Chandra over the years in adopting a selective attitude to material with strong religious overtones. Already in the late fifties she was searching for new material in dance where 'religion' could be contextualised in a secular frame of thought rather than assumed as the foundation of dance.

Thus, by 1959, Chandra began to conceptualise her first piece of choreography, a full-length production called *Devadasi*. This was her attempt to see Bharatanatyam in the larger context of its history, and thereby provide a critique (however veiled) about the divine origins of dance: 'I felt that dance doesn't belong to the temple or to the court or even to one's country. It must go back to the people, to the body.' Though the vigorous thrust of this statement may not have been fully embodied in the choreography of *Devadasi*, which continued to rely on traditional items from the Bharatanatyam recital, the attempt to make a personal (and political) statement about Bharatanatyam through dance must be regarded as one of the first ventures of its kind contrasting sharply with the celebrated dance-dramas performed in Kalakshetra which relied predominantly on mythological themes and stories. In Chandra's *Devadasi,* the content of the production came not so much from a story as from an examination of the historical continuum of dance itself.

Not much is remembered of the production today which was staged only four times, on two occasions each in Madras and Bombay between 1960-61. Most of the details of its choreography (apart from the concluding *tillana*) have been forgotten. What Chandra remembers, or perhaps, chooses to remember today is the overall framework of the production. Already in this frame one realises Chandra's early ability to conceptualise dance which may be one of her strongest points as a choreographer. No longer entirely dependent on the directions provided by Guru Ellappa, Chandra was now more free to make her own statement about dance not in the context of a solo performance but through an ensemble of six dancers. Indeed, *Devadasi* marked the beginning of a total departure from the 'solo tradition' of dance performance to which Chandra has never returned.

Structured in a somewhat linear manner, *Devadasi* attempted to trace the evolution of Bharatanatyam through its manifestations in the temple, court, and the modern stage. While the context of the temple was created through the performance of a *pushpanjali* with traditional *sollukattus* (rhythmic syllables), this demonstration of faith was contrasted with the more erotic performance of *varnams* specifically addressed to the rulers of the Thanjavur court.

Then followed sequences depicting the gradual decline in the dancer's status, her social ostracism, the consequences of the Devadasi Abolition Bill, leading to the 'revival' of dance in the thirties. Breaking the chronology was a somewhat contrived 'flashback' evoking the art of legendary dancers like Ambapali and Madhavi (from *Silappadikaram*). Concluding the production was a rousing *tillana* with four dancers in which Chandra's 'statement' probably came through with the greatest vigour: the need for dance to be centered in the primary energies of the body, resistant to the larger constraints imposed on dancers through the temple, the court, and the state.

Despite the seeming clarity of this overall structure, it is, perhaps, necessary to acknowledge that the production is a blur today, almost as hazy as the gauze drapes that were used in the background to enhance its very rudimentary sense of design. Instead of attempting to 'reconstruct' the production from non-existent clues, it would be more useful, I think, to examine the concept of the production, and at a later stage, to provide a more detailed account of the *Tillana* which concluded it. Fortunately, this piece was revived as an independent item in 1984 and has also been recorded on video, enabling us to study some of the most basic principles of Chandra's choreography.

Conceptualising 'Devadasi'

Regarding the concept of the production, I think one needs to question the linearity of Chandra's narrative which has also been duplicated in her later work *Angika*. Here, too, a clear historical continuum is assumed in depicting a dancer integrated within the ritualistic context of the temple, then gradually demeaned and eroticised through the 'male gaze' of spectators in court, followed by her degradation as a prostitute.

Historically, this kind of chronology is simply too neat a reading of a dancer's status and subsequent decline. Even a perfunctory reading of the lives of court dancers and *devadasis* in the temple reveals that they were simultaneously 'honoured' and patronised by the kings. They were at once distinctly subsumed within two separate contexts, yet related through a common system of patronage. Therefore the question of viewing the *devadasi* as somehow preceding the role of the court dancer is misleading. What would be more pertinent would be to examine how the dancers in the temple and court were discriminated within the overall patriarchy.

The more problematic aspect of locating the *devadasi* at the very 'beginning' of the 'history' of dance unavoidably enhances a mystification of her role. To show her declining from this 'imagined' status through her cosmetic objectification in court to the degraded status of the prostitute, somehow essentialises the 'purity' of the *devadasi,* as if her dedication to god was more 'wholesome' than her eventual capitulation to men.

The scenario is charged with all kinds of contradictory possibilities of interpretation which Chandra would be only too prepared to deal with today, and go beyond. In 1960-61, however, it is obvious that she was still subscribing to the dominant 'progressive' norms of her time by viewing the *devadasi* as a victim of historical tendencies.

This position could have been more effectively problematised had it not also subscribed to the euphoria surrounding the 'revival' of dance in the thirties. Here Chandra's position does become complicated because she openly demonstrated her 'support' for the movement by honouring the figures of Rukmini Devi and Balasaraswati. Indeed, in the first performance of *Devadasi* at the Raja Annamalai Manram Theatre in Madras, both these legendary figures were seated in the audience, while the dancers on stage garlanded their portraits as part of the overall performance.

At some level, this sequence can almost seem like a publicity stunt, bordering on sycophancy. It would have been an entirely different matter if Chandra had chosen to honour Rukmini Devi or Balasaraswati without eulogising them unconditionally. But I am also compelled to accept that she respects both these women in their own right. Today, if Chandra had to revise *Devadasi,* it is likely that she would continue to honour the memory of these great dancers, but I think she would also contextualise the so-called 'revival' of Bharatanatyam in a more critical framework. In all probability, she would link it to her increasing distrust of the 'pan-Indian nationalism' that has determined the 'official culture' of India in the last decade, particularly its control of dance activities.

Like all early productions, *Devadasi* needs to be placed within the context of its historical moment. The late fifties we should remember, were among the most buoyant and hopeful years for the majority of Indian artists. As yet art had not been bureaucratised through a surfeit of cultural institutions. The attitude of the government towards the arts was also somewhat more 'concerned', perhaps because it had yet to formulate its policies. As such, the early 'national' seminars on dance, theatre, film held in the mid-fifties opened up all kinds of possibilities, even though some of the problems afflicting Indian artists today were already being raised in these early forums.

The point is that it was still possible in the fifties to hope for a vibrant, secular culture in India by drawing on a diverse range of languages and performance idioms. Though the 'regionalisation' of 'Indian culture' had already begun to surface, it was still possible for artists to 'meet' through an exchange of differences. 'Territorialities' were far less defined. Also there was a greater camaraderie among the performers, much less competition and backbiting. This is what made it possible for two seeming 'rivals' like Rukmini Devi and Balasaraswati to honour the 'opening night' of a young dancer's choreography with their gracious presence.

Perhaps, it should also be remembered that Harindranath Chattopadhyay was personally known to both these artists, and as master of ceremonies for *Devadasi*, his invitation to attend the performance must have carried additional weight. Though Chandra's autonomy in conceptualising and mounting the production was undeniable, Harindranath continued to provide his suggestions. While Guru Ellappa was Chandra's 'point of reference' for matters concerning the selection of music in the temple and court sequences, Harindranath was her sounding-board for the historical framework of the production. It is only inevitable that his own rhetoric coloured the commentary for the production, which he narrated in counterpoint to the dances performed on stage. Though the text of his commentary no longer exists, it undeniably played a vital factor in holding the production together, and perhaps, authenticating it through the sheer force of his personality.

From this use of commentary, we encounter a recurring

feature in Chandra's work as a choreographer: her need to introduce or even interrupt the performance through speech. In each of her productions, Chandra's *vacika* (as I like to call it) is absolutely vital for both our understanding and enjoyment of her work. The significant difference in *Devadasi*, of course, is that the commentary was Baba's. It was *his* voice that connected, substantiated, and verified her particular way of seeing the 'history' of Bharatanatyam. Today, it would be simply unthinkable for Chandra to allow anyone to speak for her during the performance. In fact, her vocal contribution is so vital that Sadanand, her close friend and critic, dismisses the possibilities of a 'ghost voice'. To hear Chandra necessitates that we *see* her on stage, articulating her philosophy of the body with a presence that is inimitably hers.

When Chandra remembers *Devadasi* today, she does so sparingly. It is obvious that she has left the production behind. What she does remember, however, are the numerous problems she faced in holding her small company together, and most of all, the 'detested' system of mothers chaperoning their daughters to rehearsal. Unbelievable as it may sound, it appears that Chandra even learned how to drive a car to provide an alternative escort service for her dancers. Among the most reliable contributors to the production were Vidya Shankar, a seasoned *veena* player who is one of Chandra's most trusted friends even to this day, and an American dancer called Robin Squire who stimulated Chandra's emerging ideas about choreography with her own first-hand perspectives on the work of Martha Graham and Merce Cunningham.

It should be remembered that choreography was a relatively new concept in the world of classical Indian dance in the fifties. While most Bharatanatyam dancers continued to elaborate on traditional items with stylistic changes associated with different schools of *nattuvangam*, there was little attempt to view the 'science of organising movement in space' (which is how Chandra defines choreography) within new narrative structures and ensembles.

The one notable exception was Rukmini Devi who

created her own dance-dramas at Kalakshetra based on Sanskrit classics like *Gita Govinda, Kumarasambhavam, Kurmavatara* (based on *Shrimad Bhagavata*), and several episodes from the *Ramayana* including *Sita Swayamvaram* and *Rama Vangamanam*. Needless to say, these productions (which are still revived with ageing members of the 'original' cast) upheld an image of 'pure classicism' that has come to be associated with the 'Kalakshetra style'.

In contrast with this rarefied approach to dance, which has justifiably been associated with the ivory-tower, Chandra's attempt to 'historicise' Bharatanatyam came out of a very real dissatisfaction with the existing conditions of dance. Unable to seek solace either in religion or a Brahmanic civilizational ideal, she was compelled to question not just the relationship of 'art' to 'life', but the very grammar of dance in which the mutations of its history had been inscribed.

Tillana

We now enter the most significant aspect of *Devadasi's* choreography, the celebrated *Tillana* which ended the production. This was revived as an independent item in later forums including the first East-West Dance Encounter held at the National Centre for the Performing Arts in Bombay in January 1984, and also at a special performance in Kalakshetra in 1985 which was attended and addressed by Rukmini Devi herself. The recording of the *Tillana* on video enables us to examine some details of Chandra's choreography which constitute the basic principles of her dance language.

At the very core of her principles is a profound understanding of the concept of *mandala*. For most dancers, the *mandala* is generally restricted to a standing posture, also called the *aramandi,* in which the knees and feet are turned out sideways, the waist and head held in an upright position. For Chandra, however, this posture can be more meaningfully described as a position, or more precisely, a circuit of energy in which the feet can be said to be holding the earth.

More than a movement, *mandala* is a principle in which the body is realised as the very centre of the cosmos itself.

Inevitably, in such a formulation, the 'technique' of Bharatanatyam begins to make sense only within a larger, more holistic awareness of the body in space. As Chandra articulates her position with vivid clarity:

> In terms of the body, *mandala* is a holistic concept integrating the human body with itself, with the community and with the environment. It generates a centred, tensile, and complex visual form. It is a principle of power, of stability, of balance, of holding the earth... of squaring or circularising the body and of breaking the tension and rigidity of the vertical line by a curve.
>
> This inward/outward dynamic of the *mandala,* — one spatial movement curving inward and another flowing outward, radiating into expanding circles while intensely held by the *bindu* — is its basic strength.[23]

In this inherently dynamic concept of movement, the *sharira* or body itself becomes a *mandala*. Driving home her point with the clarity of a practitioner rather than the discrimination of a theorist, Chandra asserts:

> Only when we are able to see the cosmos not as some external point of reference but something contained within us, only when we begin to see the body as *mandala,* then only can we hope to fully participate in the aesthetics of our dance tradition.[24]

It could be argued that there are many assumptions in this statement that are not viable for most contemporary performers who may 'begin' their concept of dance with a denial of the cosmos in the first place. It could also be said that Chandra assumes the possibility of a certain continuity with 'the aesthetics of our dance tradition' that has been fragmented and diffused over the years. Certainly, one would have to accept that the *sharira* as *mandala* need not be regarded as the *sine qua non* for all Indian dancers. For Chandra, however, it is central to her concept of dance, a living principle that has animated her choreography since her startling *Tillana* in *Devadasi*.

Before entering the details of its choreography, one should acknowledge that the intrinsic multi-dimensionality of the concept of *mandala* is, more often than not, neutralised if not flattened in the two-dimensional space of the proscenium. This rectangular stage space has, unfortunately, become almost the only space in which dance is viewed in India today. To Chandra's credit, her understanding of the very limits of the proscenium (which has framed all her productions) has enabled her to explore dimensions in space with an illusion of 'three-dimensionality' rarely experienced in dance or theatre today.

In this regard, her intuitive understanding of graphics (nurtured, as we shall discuss later, through her experiments with visual design) is what has facilitated her concrete representation of *mandala* in dance. In addition, of course, she has been inspired by her absorption of visual concepts drawn from texts like the *Chitrasutra,* notably the laws of perspective or *kshayavriddhi* determining principles like *rijjvagata* (frontal view) or *sachikrita* (diagonal view).

It is, perhaps, elementary yet necessary to point out that the basic configurations of energy in Chandra's choreography are drawn from her profound understanding of 'lines' of movement — horizontal, vertical, diagonal. Though they can be used in diverse ways, these lines are primarily associated in Chandra's mind with harmony, confrontation, and conflict respectively. Yet, such is the profound ambivalence of these 'lines' that Chandra never fails to marvel that an entrance from the upper corner of stage left to the downward corner of stage right, for example, is so much stronger than the same movement repeated in the opposite diagonal on stage. These are seemingly 'small' observations that have enormous implications in the world of dance, linked, perhaps, not just to the right and left functions of the brain but to solar and lunar energies as well. Chandra does not theorise about these problems preferring to incorporate their enigmas within her choreography.

She is equally attentive to yet another neglected area in choreography — the activisation of 'blank spaces' that dancers create in relation to each other: the space between bodies, but also above bodies. So meticulous is Chandra's grasp of the relation between mass and volume, body and space, that she never allows the 'blank spaces' between dancers to become 'dead' (i.e. inert, static, lifeless).

It is this close tuning to lines and directions of movement that enables Chandra to create an almost ceaseless dynamic of energies on stage. Never in her choreography, at least to my mind, does the movement of Bharatanatyam atrophy into postures. This is the surest way to create 'dead space'. In Chandra's dance, it is not just the dancers that move, but the entire space which is energised through a configuration of particular energies and inter-relationships.

One such principle evident in *Tillana* is Chandra's ceaseless need to 'break' a form as soon as it is 'made', so at no point is the dance allowed to become static. Defying any attempt to document her choreography in a series of patterns, the 'visual logic' of Chandra's dance is consciously made up of breaks which accentuate rather than disrupt the overall 'flow' of the performance.

One of the most appropriate images that could be used to describe Chandra's sense of 'flow' is the movement of waves. In *Tillana,* the *sum* of the choreography occurs on a horizontal line that the four dancers repeatedly make in the course of the dance, facing the audience at the edge of the stage. From whatever part of the stage they may be positioned, the dancers have to almost 'jump' into this position, the 'shock' of the choreography emerging from the sight of four bodies 'crashing' as it were on a horizontal line front stage.

A feeling of ecstasy is created in this movement, as the dancers seem to be stretched to their limits. Even at this 'ultimate point' in a particular cycle of movement, there is a silent prefiguring of another movement, almost like the undercurrent of a wave that compels it to ebb. The horizontal line, therefore, is not so much a 'formation' as the caesura in a flux of movements, a breathing space, and also paradoxically, the moment of maximum energy.

As the dancers 'break' the horizontal line, either to form pairs or to stand in a vertical line or dart across the stage in a criss-cross of diagonals, the space is once again activated through new configurations. Some of these are shaped through the contrary energies of dancers, dancing to and against each other.

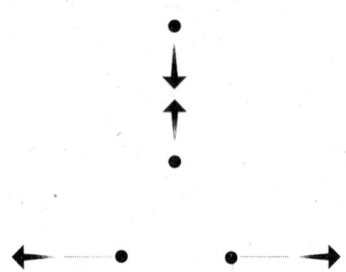

In this formation, for example, two dancers hold each other backstage within a tight orbit of energies, facing each other and almost blending into one dynamic unit, while the individual dancers on the sides throw out their energies from the back while dancing in opposite directions. It is through such contrary pulls of energy that the entire space is dynamised.

Yet another recurring pattern of energy in Chandra's choreography creates the sense of the entire space being pulled vertically in contrary directions.

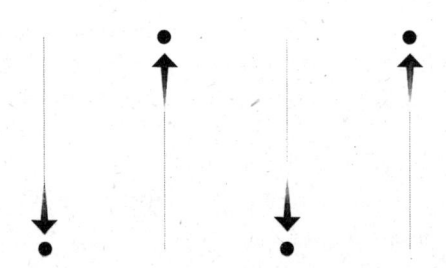

Or more startlingly, in her now classic way of 'cleaning the space' through horizontal slashes of energy across the stage:

```
                    ————————→•
    •←————————
                    ————————→•
    •←————————
```

All these particular movements 'return' to the *sum* with the four dancers neatly punctuating the horizontal line down-stage.

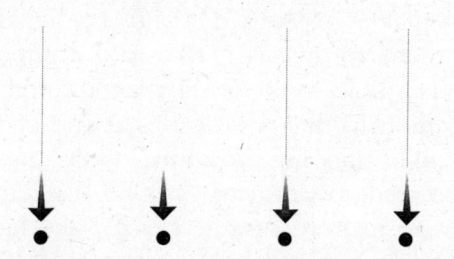

```
    |     |     |     |
    ↓     ↓     ↓     ↓
    •     •     •     •
```

Then, in a sudden shift of energy, the horizontal line could be replaced by a vertical line made up of three dancers with one dancer 'out of orbit' as it were, creating her own sense of time and space. For example:

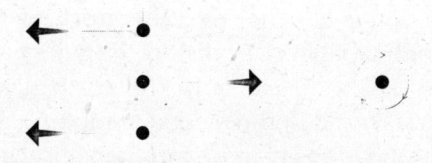

```
    ←—•
       •  →      •
    ←—•
```

This juxtaposition of 3:1 is typical of Chandra's consciously crafted asymmetries. Moreover, this idea of never entirely completing a pattern of movement, but of challenging it somehow through a recalcitrant element, is reminiscent of the musical principle of Vivadi. Here the note is somehow off-centred in relation to the *swara*.

In terms of movement, this positioning of a dancer 'out of orbit' provides a sense not just of 'resistance', of not quite fitting into the overall scheme, but also of potential, of contributing to the next possible dynamic of movement. This kind of 'off-centering' also directly challenges the audience to assume a certain responsibility in figuring out and participating in the 'logic' of dance. As Chandra puts it: 'You never make a full movement. It is the eye that has to complete the movement. This creates involvement in seeing, where the spectator becomes a dancer. Seeing should not become passive.'

In this relentless bid not to 'spoonfeed' the audience, Chandra also makes rigorous demands on her dancers. She may require them, for instance, to 'relate' entirely with back energies or else, hold multiple energies through stillness. It is not uncommon in this regard to see one of her dancers hold the simple standing position, while the others are partially concealed, yet moving, behind the dancer. In this case, the dancer in front cannot 'freeze'; she has to absorb the movements behind her while remaining still, which is not as simple as it sounds.

Also connected with this specific demand made on dancers concerns the *density* that Chandra establishes through her choreography by creating clusters in which the dancers' bodies are masked by the dancers in front of them, yet visible through deflections of hands, feet, fingers, or the elevation of a neck. The overall effect of such clusters (which are not tableaux) is one of fragmentation, where a specific mass of bodies acquires a particular density, not unlike a frieze of sculptures in a temple.

Tellingly, the density and fragmentation are enhanced not through a disparity of movements, but through the repetition of the same movement performed simultaneously in different ways. For example, in the opening frieze of *Tillana*, the four dancers stand in a vertical line with *mandala* positions at different body levels. In such a grouping, there is not only a sense of space being sculpted but of an architectural form being moulded, its depth and dimension created through a series of arched hands — arch within arch within arch.

Once again it should be emphasised that the inner energy of these forms and their dissolution into other forms is what prevents them from becoming decorative. Even when Chandra uses the familiar motif of the *swastika* created through the *hastas* of individual dancers, at first through the bodies and hands of pairs of dancers, then through the positioning of four dancers at the extremities of the stage in everwidening *swastikas*, the effect is never predictable. The point is not to create tableaux, and thereby, evoke the much mythicised 'timelessness' of classical Indian dance; rather, it is to activate a ceaseless energy through an inner and outer flow of movement in space held together by the dancers through particular combinations in time.

At one level, Chandra's *Tillana* can be regarded as a 'de-structuring' and 're-structuring' of the basic elements of the traditional *tillana* that she had learned from Guru Ellappa. What is astonishing about the 'synthesis' of such an effort — and in Chandra's choreography there is always a drive towards synthesis, never a celebration of fragmentation — is that it makes us see the 'tradition' of a particular school of dance through an altogether different angle of vision. It celebrates multicentricity while animating the idea of the 'centre' through an embodiment of the *mandala* concept within the bodies of the dancers themselves. Each is a *mandala* and is part of a larger *mandala*.

It is of considerable historical importance, I believe, to point out that Rukmini Devi did not merely approve of Chandra's 'innovative' *Tillana;* she had the grace to acknowledge its seminal contribution to Bharatanatyam at the special programme organised at Kalakshetra in 1985. After seeing *Tillana* (which was included in a lecture-demonstration along with *Alarippu* and *Suryamurte*), Rukmini Devi delivered an extempore speech which I would like to quote not least to counter the absurd 'criticism' often made by some traditionalists that Chandra does not 'know' Bharatanatyam. This is not the impression we get from Rukmini Devi.

> Such wonderful enthusiasm — I've never seen anyone like Chandralekha in this respect and she has done this work with tremendous devotion and great originality. I've never seen *alarippu* like this. I've never seen *tillana* like this. And this idea of dancing to Dikshitar's song (in *Suryamurte*). There's a saying which many occultists have said that 'God geometrises'. That's a phrase I've been accustomed to. And I think she too has 'geometrised' because there is occult meaning in dance too... I was deeply interested in her ideas and in her originality.[25]

What makes this tribute so moving is that it was made by Rukmini Devi towards the end of her life when Chandralekha was 'beginning' her dance career after almost twelve years of inactivity between 1972-1984 when she was invited to participate in the first East-West Dance Encounter held at the National Centre for the Performing Arts in 1984. At this point, it was Rukmini Devi (the most celebrated of dancers, if not the most esteemed artist in India) who responded to Chandra's tentative request for four dancers from Kalakshetra to be used in *Tillana* which was revived for the East-West Encounter. It is significant that Rukmini Devi did not merely facilitate the 'revival' of *Tillana*, she had the generosity to endorse the 'originality' of its vision.

It takes humility for a senior artist of Rukmini Devi's stature to acknowledge: 'I have never seen *alarippu* like this. I have never seen *tillana* like this.' This is quite different from saying: 'This is not *alarippu*. This is not *tillana*', which is characteristic of the kind of response Chandra receives from certain quarters today: 'Of course, she is a very brilliant artist, but she is not doing Bharatanatyam.'

Not only was Rukmini Devi able to see the 'originality' of Chandra's Bharatanatyam, she was able to connect it to 'occult sources' in which dance becomes a form of divine mathematics, the 'geometry of God'. Though the implications of this insight are varied and contradictory, as we shall examine in the assertively 'secular' celebration of 'mathematics' in Chandra's production of *Lilavati,* it indicates the depth at which Rukmini Devi could tune in to Chandra's work.

Coming to the end of this chapter, which has attempted to situate Chandra's *Devadasi* within the larger context of the 'history' of Bharatanatyam, it is only appropriate, I think, that we should conclude with a 'fast-forward' in Chandra's dance career in 1985. Rukmini Devi, who figured prominently in the 'renaissance' of Bharatanatyam in the thirties was also present at the first performance of *Devadasi* in 1960 and the revival of *Tillana* in 1985. Much had changed and atrophied in the 'history' of Bharatanatyam in the intervening years. Though Rukmini Devi and Chandra had almost antithetical views on history and politics, it is telling, I think, that they could meet through a deep love for the underlying energies and concepts of Bharatanatyam, which had nurtured them in different ways.

Their meeting becomes all the more meaningful because it breaks the dominant mystique of Chandra as an 'iconoclast' and 'rebel' who has rejected 'tradition'. If anything, I believe this 'rebel' has drawn her sustenance and even concepts of freedom from a specific relationship with and confrontation of 'tradition' itself. Her *parampara* is alive because it has been personally defined, questioned and lived.

3

Living in the Sixties

After *Devadasi,* Chandra found that she could not sustain another production in the absence of an organisation or professional infrastructure. The prospect of being linked to an agent or institution was unacceptable to her. Nor was she interested in pursuing a career as a solo dancer. She realised more and more clearly that she was being 'appreciated' for the wrong reasons. As she recalls today without mincing words: 'I had the right kind of waist, the right kind of bosom. I was being watched in much the same way as a Hindi film actress is. I felt terribly dejected.'

To sustain her creativity, Chandra decided to opt out of the dance scene altogether. At one level, there is much to regret about this choice because, if Chandra had been able to sustain the sheer choreographic brilliance of *Tillana,* the dance world around her would have been radically questioned. Instead, she 'returned' to *Tillana* as late as 1984 more than twenty years after it was first conceived and then proceeded to stage her landmark production of *Angika* in 1985. From this point on she has not looked back, adding significantly to her repertoire with daring and intensely creative productions and workshops. But between 1961-1984, Chandra staged just one production, *Navagraha* in 1972, associating herself with dance only through sporadic workshops conducted primarily abroad which enabled her to travel and to earn a living.

In these intervening years, it would be difficult to say what Chandra has not explored as a woman. Even a cursory look at her activities reveals a range of skills that are not normally associated with our increasingly 'specialised' artists. Over the years, and beginning in the sixties, Chandra embraced a certain eclecticism in her exploration of creativity. She has written poems, articles, reviews, *haikus,* and a prose-poem entitled *Kamala* (which I will describe in this chapter). Through the years she has also produced her own hand-made books on ecology, some of which are delicate art works on seeds and leaves and flowers. She has also spent years exploring the graphic formations of *kolams* (rice-flour patterns on the floor) and their abstractions through various permutations of dots on a sixteen point square grid. Literally hours and hours of her life have been spent in exploring multiple directions in this square formation.

Beginning in the sixties, she also started to travel, at times 'taking off' for a year as in 1968 to 'do *nothing*', as she puts it emphatically. This hippie-like existence was sustained through the firm belief that 'one needed to earn money only if one was broke.' Being Chandra, all kinds of things happened on these 'fantastic' journeys, primarily meetings with artists in the 'alternative sector' (when alternatives had not yet been institutionalised). She would visit the Cairo Museum, meet someone who was working on an exhibition, and then find that she had something to contribute to it. So, in exchange for board and lodging, the rudiments of a 'barter' economy, she would stay on and share her creative insights with strangers who later became friends.

The same kind of collaboration was explored in America where her hands, for instance, became the subject of a poster and experimental film. Here, too, the experiment happened spontaneously following a Merce Cunningham dance show in New York, when Chandra went up to David Tudor, whom she had earlier met at the National Institute of Design in Ahmedabad. She had imagined that he would have forgotten her only to be greeted with a warm embrace and a prompt introduction to 'a most fantastic group of people', including John Cage and Billy Kluver who were involved in an organisation called EAT (Experiments in Art and Technology). It was for this informal forum that Chandra's hands were used for a film in which 'everyone freaked out' (Chandra's lingo of the sixties resurfaces in our discussion). This was the period of Woodstock when it was almost mandatory that Chandra should explore LSD at least once ('I felt the grass growing under me and raising me in the air'). At a more political level, Chandra also had an opportunity to engage in all kinds of 'loving' acts including the distribution of apples and pumpkins to the cops during Halloween.

Friends were everywhere, in Brussels, London, New York, Cairo, and nearer home in Bombay and Ahmedabad. Chandra is not coy about the fact that many of these friends were male companions with whom she explored relationships 'at several levels — physical, sexual, sensual, emotional, sentimental.' Looking back on these relationships, she acknowledges that some of them were 'idealised' and that the 'highest state of sexuality' for her is increasingly to be found in a 'dream-state' where it is possible to cross the 'limits, borders, and boundaries of the body.' It is in this state where 'everything that happens is real, more so than when you "concretise" it,' as Chandra reflects emphatically. 'Today I would say that the strongest and most enduring relationships for me are strangely the ones which are not based on sex.'

Even in the sixties, when her thoughts were far less crystallised, Chandra's experiments with intimacy were often nurtured in solitude, where she could be in touch with herself through areas of fantasy, glimpses of which we will examine in this chapter. Her friends were dreamers as well, seekers of 'other' worlds, who hovered on the borders of their disciplines. At an artistic level, Chandra was linked to poets and designers exploring different idioms of modernism through new trends in writing (particularly in Gujarati) and experiments in graphics and architecture at the National Institute of Design in Ahmedabad.

Sharing her cosmopolitan and freethinking spirit were two of her closest women friends in Bombay — Asha Puthli, who was then pursuing a career as a jazz singer, also a model, who was known for her rejection of orthodox social norms in her embrace of freedom as a single woman. Equally passionate, but with a different orientation, was Indira Jaising, who commands respect today as a lawyer known as much for her intensity as for her ability to subvert the patriarchal premises of the law through the smallest shifts in the gestures and rhetoric of protocol. In Indu (who was Chandra's companion on a trip to Europe in the early seventies), we find affinities in the ways in which they have intervened in their respective fields. What matters is not so much their achievements as their capacities to 'humanise' their disciplines and extend their influence to a wider range of ongoing struggles and commitments.

Occasionally described as 'the three inseparables', Chandra, Asha and Indu celebrated their independence as metropolitan Indian women, fully aware that they were capable of confronting patriarchal demands and expectations in their respective fields and relationships with men. Their one 'acceptable' male friend, at once a link and a confidant, was the effervescent Sunil Kothari, who is one of the most familiar figures today in the Indian dance world as an itinerant critic and dance scholar. At once a source of intense irritation and affection, he continues to support Chandra's work, his warmth as a human being contributing significantly to the friendship.

Chandra's closest companion during the sixties in Bombay was the film director, Hrishikesh Mukherjee, with whom she shared some of her most intimate thoughts despite the obvious differences in their careers. In his house in Bombay, which was open to so many artists from the film world ranging from Ritwik Ghatak to box-office heroes, Chandra once again found that her companionship with a particular man was sustained through larger creative interactions. But the tinsel of the film world was obviously not her scene and she was compelled to go her own way. As for 'Hrishida', who has now matured into one of the 'elder statesmen' of the Bombay film world, he has never failed to appreciate Chandra's sensibility. As he once stated admiringly: 'Rarely in life does one come across such a unique personality. She has never borrowed ideas, they all spring from within her. She has the potential of being one of the finest writers in the country.'[1] And this is precisely the word to be used in recalling Chandra of the sixties: her *potential*. But for what? To dance, to write, to design, to *live*.

At one level, one could say that Chandra did not develop her potential at that time in any one direction, preferring to explore different disciplines with the intensity and directness of an amateur. Indeed, she remains something of an 'amateur' even to this day, distrusting the 'regimentation' of any kind of professionalism. If her dance productions are 'professional' today, it is despite the fact that she has no formal school or administration. Looking back on the sixties, it is possible to see that Chandra was most true to herself by not restricting her creativity in any one particular way. As she says today, 'I have never regretted what I have rejected.' And in the sixties, her rejection of dance was exhilarating precisely because it compelled her to search for other sources of creativity and relationships that have, ultimately, nurtured both her life and art today.

Unlike most artists, who at some point in their careers invariably realise that they have not lived, the same cannot be said of Chandra. The sheer intensity and joy of her living along with the struggle and disillusionment that she was to experience in later years, are inextricably linked to the energy one finds in her productions today.

Kamala

One of the clearest glimpses we have of Chandra's innerworld in the sixties can be traced in her early writings which explored a range of poetic forms. Even her critiques of art works and books were more in the nature of impressions and clusters of images. Significantly, she never thought of herself as a poet following the Indo-Anglian tradition of poetry exemplified by figures like Nissim Ezekiel, Kamala Das and Keki Daruwalla. Circumventing the derivative patterns of their rhetoric, Chandra invented a direct, yet lyrical idiom of her own. At its most evocative, her writing could be described as a choreography of words.

One of her most memorable writings of this period was a prose-poem entitled *Kamala* in which she attempted to present 'montages of Madras.'[2] The word 'montage' is, perhaps, too complex for the simple flow of narrative in which Chandra evokes her relationship with a domestic maid, Kamala, based on 'real-life' experience. The relationship is contextualised within a larger background of working-class community life which is more strongly reminiscent of the 'village' rather than the 'slum.' Within this community, Chandra presents vignettes of different kinds of workers, all of them bound through a common struggle that continues from day to day, monsoon to monsoon, election to election, as the city around them gradually expands and levels out their meagre, yet vibrant existence.

The very choice of the subject-matter is worth dwelling on because it is the total antithesis of what one would expect from a young writer with Chandra's cosmopolitan background and class. One can imagine her, for instance, writing *haikus*, which she did explore as a matter of fact with considerable skill and delicacy. Along with these crystallised impressions, however, there was also a need to confront a larger social reality, a different class of people, not in the 'scientific' terms of a derived Marxism, but more directly through a fiction based on relationships. In her own way, Chandra was responding to what most Indians from her class are generally immune: the realities of poverty and survival that stare us in the face on streets and pavements, which we walk past as if they do not exist.

In *Kamala*, Chandra engages herself in getting to know the people outside her own home. At times the women from this working-class community approach her for some water when there is none in the corporation tap. It is through such simple exchanges based at once on need and curiosity, a desire for friendship, that Chandra gets to know some of these women as individuals. Without underestimating the grind of their lives, she also observes the creativity of their daily tasks, the 'grinding of chillies with coriander seeds', the decoration of household thresholds with *kolams*.

Among the women is Chelli who 'coaxes' creepers to grow on the roof of her hut, so that it becomes 'thick with leaves/luxuriant/looking up/communing with the sun.' Gradually, flowers grow on Chelli's hut attracting birds and bees. This in turn is followed by the growth of gourds and pumpkins, 'round and tumbling', which keep Chelli busy as she 'tends her village identity farming her roof.'

In contrast to the quotidian creativity of the women in the community are the men, who are out most of the time searching for work, getting drunk, or abandoning their families for another woman. They are first introduced to us in the narrative through a naturalistic image — the hair from barber's shops that collects under the tamarind tree:

> The ground is thick with hair
> tufted or tangled
> nothing but hair
> men's hair
> from heads
> beards
> armpits
> emptied in bulk from the saloons opposite
> where towelled men
> with contorted faces
> sit soapsmeared
> before large mirrors
> under framed colour prints
> of politicians
> gods
> actors
> saints.

Despite the crudity of this male world, there is no attempt on Chandra's part to dehumanise and reduce these men to absolute villains in the course of the narrative. Instead of succumbing to melodrama, she opts for a more ironic view of patriarchal power which is most tellingly glimpsed in her portrait of Venku, 'a man of drive', who starts off with a *paan*-shop, then proceeds to own a tea-shop, which is inaugurated by a local politician. As the 'votecatcher' for the ruling party in the locality, Venku's prospects are bright. But:

> Thirty eight
> and very popular
> he died.
>
> It was a loss to the party.
> His funeral was quite a spectacle —
> the body was placed
> in a lorry filled with party-flags...
> to show Venku propped up on a high chair
> with goggles and garlands
> in silk kurta
> thumbs tied to toes
> neck to the backrest
> hair greased and combed
> with just one stylish curl on his forehead.

From this description it is only too clear that there are no tears shed for Venku, who emerges as a working-class icon cast in the *filmi* mould of Tamil politics.

Despite the anti-patriarchal biases of the text, *Kamala* ultimately celebrates the idea of the community involving men, women, children, animals and plants. With all the hardships suffered by the inhabitants of the working-class community, there is also 'kinship' and sharing of 'food and sorrow and words of wisdom.' Without idealising their suffering, Chandra marvels at the capacity of the slum-dwellers for celebration:

> Every festive day was remembered
> not the way we did
> with a semblance of celebration
> In those huts everything was real.
> There were no short cuts.

Deepening her sense of the creativity that animates the entire neighbourhood, Chandra focuses on her relationship with Kamala, in whose 'blush' the 'rice fields' of Kerala can be felt. Bordering on a certain romanticisation of feminine household tasks, Kamala's representation comes alive through her almost effortless capacity to transform work into poetry: the 'art of living' in a very real sense.

When she washes the dishes with 'ash and tamarind and coconut fibre', 'so many suns' fill the pots with light. On auspicious days she decorates the rice-paste of *kolams* with 'yellow flowers of the pumpkin.' On Fridays she tints the threshold with dots and lines of 'turmeric, kumkum and rice', decorating the door with fresh mango leaves. Then there is her art of cooking so evident in 'soft white *idlis, adais, vadais, apams,* with egg or coconut milk.' Her afternoons could be spent stringing jasmines with 'deft fingers' or narrating stories of her childhood and 'rice-paste-painted Kathakali dancers', while combing Chandra's hair.

In all these details there is a deep sense of a woman's creativity (Kamala's) that is acknowledged and appreciated by another woman (Chandra). But there is also a duality between these women that emerges less through class than consciousness about the most seemingly precious aspect of Kamala's life, which is also a primary source of her oppression: childbearing. It is at this level that Chandra attempts to intervene in her life after Kamala has produced five children with no support from her husband apart from blows and sexual demands. Abortion, however, poses legal problems and Kamala herself resists sterilisation, so there is not much that Chandra can do but observe her anguish as a mother through successive pregnancies.

This anguish is shaded through complementary (and contradictory) feelings of shame, ecstasy, fear, torture, and resolution in relation to child-bearing. Kamala could be working in the kitchen whereupon she would suddenly stop:

> amma, I must go home...
> my child is hungry —
> I looked up at her ...
> Then her head slightly bent
> a profound mystery on her face
> she showed me her blouse and said —
> look the blouse is all wet with milk.
> I know my child is hungry.

Through the narrative Kamala is almost afflicted with her 'surplus of milk.' After futile attempts to suppress her foetus through indigenous means, by eating raw papaya, herbs and rare roots prescribed by indigenous medicine men and soothsayers, Kamala ultimately attempts to end her reproductive capacities through her own means:

> i strayed into the kitchen
> sniffing
> something was burning —
> what is it Kamala
> what's wrong with you
> why are you looking like this...
> she stood before the fire
> transfixed
> a can in her hand
> in an anguished voice
> tremulous
> she said —
> i have poured my milk in the fire
> now at last
> my breasts will dry.

It could be argued here that the writing is somewhat too flat to capture fully the anguish of the moment, but it is effective in its own right. Along with Kamala's condition, Chandra presents searing images of the larger horror of being poor and pregnant in a big city. From Kamala herself she learns about the 'pandemonium' in government hospitals where babies get mixed up or lost, or more terrifyingly, eaten by stray dogs. In the garbage we can see 'women's dried menstrual blood/in the mouth of the dogs', along with scraps of food. In another scene we are shown how a slum dweller who carries tiffin carriers to many offices ekes out her living by selling the remnants of food to beggars and waifs:

> and then the tiffin carriers returned
> for the next day's meals

and the next day's —
tiffin carriers
a tradition of our times.

It is through such ironic jabs that the narrative of *Kamala* resists sentimentality just as the total homelessness of five hundred families in a slum fire ends with 'nothing to salvage/except the statistics.' Most brutally, after being 'startled' by the 'gentle push' of a girl on a bus, 'not begging' but just picking up remnants of food from the crevices and corners of the floor, Chandra adds:

They were everywhere —
expelled of womb
outflung in space
inheritors of the earth and sky.

But immediately, she also acknowledges the 'inheritance of our earth and sky', which comes alive in a 'fantasia of light and colours' that the city landscape has not yet brutalised. Even on the street in the thick of the traffic one can sense the city's 'pulse' under a 'liquid noon haze.' Later at night the street itself becomes

....a river
of columns of colour
trembling nervously
dilating
vanishing
and ephemera circling
spiralling...

It is a 'superb choreography' in its own right, tinged in the 'momentary yellows/indigoes/greens/reds' of the night, as the street 'leads to nowhere.'

Ultimately, what *Kamala* resonates is not despair but a strangely harmonious vision of dissonance and ruptures in space and time through which life continues uncertainly, broken yet held together in a tense process of struggle and survival. Much more work is needed on this narrative for its vision to be fully realised — *Kamala* is very clearly a 'youthful' work in a neo-realist mode tinged with autobiography and fantasy. However, what the writing does reveal is a very discerning sensibility that is capable of confronting the harshest realities without surrendering its capacity to dream.

An Illumination through Flowers

Dreaming was, perhaps, one of Chandra's most potent pastimes in the sixties when she was not formally attached to any particular discipline. This can be regarded as something of an indulgence though it has also provided Chandra with some of the deepest revelations of her creativity. Today she is more vocal about the necessity for dreaming which she has stressed in feminist forums, interspersing the discussion on more seemingly weighty matters with an affirmation of fantasy in any process of social transformation. Some of her views have been dismissed by activists as 'impractical', 'romantic', and 'ultrasubjective', though there is a growing number of feminists who are more open to the emancipatory possibilities of women 'finding their own spaces' through fantasy.

In this section, I shall offer just one glimpse of Chandra's innerworld of fantasy by describing an experience that began as an 'experiment' on herself which later got transformed into a creative response to another artist's work, which in turn became the source of creative energy in her own dance world as well.

Chandra's 'experiment' focused on some lilies growing in a pot in her house in Madras. She would water these flowers regularly along with many other plants that made up a kind of 'jungle' on her terrace. One evening she noticed that there were no buds on the flowers, but the next day, almost magically, new flowers were blooming in the pot. Chandra asked herself: How did I miss it? How did these flowers happen? She decided to watch their nocturnal movement by sleeping on the terrace at night. Ever so often she would wake up to see if any buds were flowering. 'Then I fell asleep for some time,' Chandra recalls, 'and when I woke up, the flowers had already bloomed.'

At one level, this experience seems to be 'made up.' And Chandra herself used it as a fable of sorts when she had the privilege of seeing one of the great masters of Noh drama perform in Japan. When she expressed her appreciation backstage, the master merely smiled in a formal way. Chandra realised that every tourist was probably paying him similar compliments, so to convey the depth of her appreciation, she recalled the movement of flowers on her terrace to the Noh master and told him that his 'walk' was as silent and invisible as their nocturnal growth. To this the master did respond with deep appreciation of Chandra's sensitivity. Once again, the story with the Noh master seems to be 'made up,' resembling a Zen parable where life imitates art. I think it also reveals Chandra's capacity to respond creatively to someone's art, thereby revealing her own sensibility.

Many years later, as I imagine it, the 'invisible movement' of the flowers continued to haunt Chandra's imagination as a choreographer. And to my mind, it has nurtured her understanding and use of *vilambit kaal* (the slow tempo) most notably in *Prana* where the dancer's yogic movements are like astral rhythms corresponding to the sustained measure that holds the production together, almost in one continuous breath. This kind of 'movement in stillness' can also be seen in her most recent experiment on herself, where she has attempted to embody the herb-goddess Sakambhari through a slow movement and rotation of the feet and legs from whose depths the flowering of trees can be imagined through the awakening of 'ancient memory.'

The 'illumination through flowers' as I would like to describe Chandra's experience and its subsequent transformation in her own work, is representative of the way she choreographs — always with intuition, drawing on what she tends to describe as 'primary experiences.' Despite her emphasis on 'conceptualising' productions (which we examined earlier in the context of *Devadasi*), it is ultimately an image, or more precisely, the memory of an image that stimulates Chandra to think in dance-language about a particular theme or movement. Without this openness to experience (as in the case of the flowers), and a need to 'experiment' with it, at first imaginatively, then more concretely through the actual shaping of a work, Chandra's choreography would be lacklustre and even mechanical.

Her strength, however, lies in her capacity to 'have a vision', as Eisenstein once put it, in the larger context of envisioning cinema, and then, more crucially, 'grasping and holding on to it.'[3] This is where, I think, Chandra scores over most performing artists of her time — she has the capacity to visualise certain images not just from the permutations and combinations of her tradition but from a certain illumination she has received from life itself. In addition, she has the drive and curiosity to sustain her source of inspiration not by 'applying' it to a work of art but by 'playing' with it through dreams, fantasies, sketches, poems, and eventually dances. All these seemingly amateur indulgences are her ways of holding on to those brief glimpses of 'vision' that flit through our lives without any attempt on our part to nurture them in our work.

It is in this context that we have to think of Chandra's numerous experiments with dots on a sixteen-point grid or the sketches in her notebooks. In their own way, they recall the impulse underlying Eisenstein's drawings, which were 'attempts to grasp stenographically the features of those images that flash through your mind.' Comparing them to 'Japanese paper toys that, when cast into warm water, unfold and develop stems, leaves and flowers of fantastic and surprising shape,'[4] these images were Eisenstein's ways of nurturing the vision that had yet to be born in cinema.

In her own way, Chandra has nurtured her vision of dance by scribbling and sketching her thoughts constantly, at times on paper, but more often than not in her mind. I can see her now sitting on her favourite swing where she can spend hours by herself radiantly in touch with the possibilities of her dance. It is through such playful dream-states, experiments 'on herself', that Chandra can be said to prepare the groundwork for her choreography.

Sources of Experience

An important contribution to the 'dreaming' of Chandra's choreography emerges from her intimate connections with a range of images and texts. I am thinking in particular of 'sacred' texts like the *Sri Lalita Sahasranama*, which (to name just one source of inspiration) has nurtured her predominantly sensuous response to 'tradition.' Here it needs to be emphasised that Chandra 'tunes' into these sources not for revivalist purposes but to enliven her imagination through a poetic idiom.

Though the metaphysics of the Sakti cult is inscribed in *Sri Lalita Sahasranama* through an accumulation of physical details, Chandra tends to separate its 'physics' from its 'metaphysics.' Defending her need to adopt a 'selective' attitude towards traditional sources, Chandra nonetheless believes that, 'You can't throw out your culture even if there are aspects of it to which you may not be able to respond or may even be compelled to reject.' Besides, the 'poetry' of texts like *Sri Lalita Sahasranama* can inspire autonomous works of art where the purpose is not to endorse any particular religion but to celebrate the act of creation itself.

One can be sure that Chandra respects the context of *Sri Lalita Sahasranama* not to use it literally as the *sahitya* or text for a production. Indeed, as I have mentioned earlier, she maintains a distance as a choreographer from using religious narratives in general. But as a source of inspiration for creating new incarnations of women *vis-à-vis* traditional iconography, a text like *Sri Lalita Sahasranama* cannot be ignored. It would be the surest way, in Chandra's case at least, of impoverishing the possibilities of her imagination.

Later in the book we will examine how Chandra uses traditional icons in her choreography not to uphold religious values but to celebrate certain manifestations of feminine power and energy. For the moment, let us turn to those images in *Sri Lalita Sahasranama* that have excited her imagination. I use the word 'images' consciously as opposed to *mantras* (which is how a 'believer' would regard the one thousand names of the Divine Mother which are to be recited with the appropriate meditation and faith). For Chandra, the experience of *Sri Lalita Sahasranama* has emerged not through worship but through a more private absorption and fantasising of the text, not unlike an actress' internalisation of a particular play or a musician's immersion in a particular *raga*. It is through such states of fantasy that we can begin to speak of the transformation of 'religion' into 'art.'

Predictably, it is not the relationship of *Sri Lalita Sahasranama* to the Brahmandapurana or the learned commentaries provided by Bhattanarayana, Shankara and Bhaskara that are of primary concern to Chandra.[5] What draws her to the work are the specific images by which the goddess is evoked in her own *swabhava*, her 'forehead resplendent like the half moon' (15), her eyes like 'sparkling fish in the ocean of her beauty' (18), 'the sun and moon suspended from her ears like earrings' (22), her breasts 'seeming to grow like fruits from the line of hair on her abdomen.'(34) For sheer sensuality of the figure, this image of the goddess cannot be surpassed. At a more cosmic level, she is the embodiment of *shakti*, the very 'root of the world' (*Visvadhika*), whose 'womb contains the universe' (*Visvagarba*). In her more militant manifestations, she appears as a demonslayer (*Raksasaghini*), the ruler of armies (*Caturangabalesvari*), the mother of warriors (*Viramata*).

All these images, one could say, have 'slumbered in the depths' of Chandra's consciousness for a long time. Twenty to twenty-five years later we can begin to see the stimulus of these images embodied in Chandra's choreography, notably in the erotics of the Shiva-Shakti interplay and union in *Primal Energy* (1984) and the bold iconography of Naravahana in *Angika* (1985), where Chandra shocked audiences by sitting astride a man with a warrior-like demeanour. If the physicality of these images is convincing, it is, to a large extent due to the sources that have nourished it, including the *Sri Lalita Sahasranama* and the numerous texts and icons of Tantra into which Chandra has delved since the early sixties.

What needs to be stressed is that Chandra does not

duplicate traditional icons, she transforms them through her own angle of vision as a choreographer. So complete is the process of transformation that the icons become 'intensely familiar' to her. In the language of performance, one could say that she has succeeded in making the images her own. Ultimately, when you see *Naravahana,* it is Chandra's presence as a performer that registers, not the religious context to which it may be linked.

To understand this process of transformation in a slightly wider context, I would recall the great example of Martha Graham, who in her own way, tuned into the Greek myths to explore much the same kind of 'primal energy' that has attracted Chandra. Here too there was a searing conviction that Graham brought to her representation of archetypal figures. Similarly, in Chandra's representation of archetypes, there is a connection with 'primal energies' that should not be mystified but which are, nonetheless, palpable in the way she holds her body as a performer. Significantly, the most iconic representations of the Shakti principle in her work have invariably been played by herself, and not by her dancers who, for all their other qualities, have not prepared themselves *imaginatively* for entering these heightened states of being.

Once again, I would say that the process of incarnating a traditional icon or mythical figure on stage cannot be learned through technique alone. It is a personal journey that every performer has to undertake not just with desire but a consciousness of what that icon or myth could mean to her as a woman and artist. Today, contemporary dancers, at times with a feminist orientation, have turned to principles like Shakti without having explored it with sufficient rigour over a period of time. The concept is either exoticised or used as a slogan to counter contemporary social realities. Merely figuring out the concept historically or ideologically is not necessarily going to facilitate its embodiment in performance. What is needed is a psychophysical process by which such a concept can be transformed within the particular resources and body of a performer. A dancer, of course, may choose to reject this confrontation with 'myth' and 'icon' in the first place, but the point is that if they are confronted, their representation in performance can become valid only if they have been tested and 'dreamed' (to use Chandra's word), crystallising slowly in the dancer's imagination through a process of hibernation, transformation, and expression.

Navagraha

In attempting such a crystallisation through performance, it would seem that for Chandra the process begins with some kind of 'experience' that prefigures the production. At least this is how she was inspired in creating her second production, *Navagraha*, (1972-73), which like *Devadasi* was performed barely four times. What remains of the production today (whose television recording by Bombay Doordarshan was unfortunately erased through a technical mishap) are a few scattered details and memories. What can be documented with more accuracy is the opening sequence of the production, a homage to Surya, which Chandra has retained in her repertoire. Most vivid of all, however, is Chandra's memory of an experience that prefigured the production, and which has continued to haunt her ever since.

It would be best, I think, to evoke this experience through Chandra's words which describe the act of circumambulating the Navagraha, the nine planetary deities worshipped in the temple. As she once recalled in an interview:

> Every time I go to a temple, I immediately go to the Navagrahas. Always there are people doing *pradakshina;* they go around nine times, and I join them. The moment you start walking, you get the vibrant sensation of the gods moving too, each one in their own space, and together, it is a whole cosmic movement, and the visualisation/installation of the Navagrahas astounds you. It's not just left to some arbitrary principle, it is a highly organised, harmo-

nious principle of space. The visualiser is not me, I'm just trying to get the inspiration from its existence. The experiences and realisations follow as I do the *pradakshina*. That whole circular movement... it is a mindblowing experience of understanding space.[6]

Significantly, this 'experience' has not been lived once and then documented in an interview. It *has been re-lived many times* through more *pradakshinas* around the *grahas*, more memories of such experiences, which have been questioned, sketched with dots on a nine-point grid, and gradually transformed into at least two productions, *Navagraha* and *Prana* (1989). The latter can be regarded as an expansion of the earlier vision, more true to the cosmic scheme than the earlier exploration of the concept.

Hailed as the 'first consciously interdisciplinary work in classical Indian dance', *Navagraha* attempted to bring together various iconographies and disciplines of thought drawing on 'Tantric forms, colours, symbologies' and the principles of Yoga in relation to dance.[7] In the iconography of *navagraha* with its nine planetary 'deities', each facing in different directions, rotating around specific centres yet cohering within a perfectly constructed orbit created through a square or 'stylised circle', Chandra found the most perfect embodiment of a *mandala*, at once geometrically precise and concentrated in its embodiment of cosmic energies.

The problem was that she had no dancers to embody the nine *grahas*. In an early experiment on the production, when she was still exploring the possibilities of abstracting its form, she had attempted to work with nine young boys. She had wanted them to create iconographical forms only to confront the horrifying reality that they could neither sit nor stand. 'The last straw', as Chandra recollects, 'was when I saw one of them yawn on stage. That was intolerable, they were constantly fidgeting. It was a most frustrating experience.' After enduring their presence for only one show which was held at the Aurobindo Ashram in the presence of the Mother (who had 'a terrific artistic response'), Chandra totally abandoned her idea of creating the planetary configurations through nine bodies on stage. To realise this vision, she would have to wait almost twenty years before *Prana* could be realised with nine disciplined dancers, who created the grid of the Navagraha with a vibrant clarity.

In the early seventies, Chandra's only real collaborator in dance was the male dancer, Kamadev, whom she acknowledges today as perhaps the only person with whom she has been able to have a dialogue in the language of dance. 'The great thing about Kama at that time', as Chandra emphasises, 'is that he only wanted to be a dancer, and nothing else.' Brought up in London, yet closely connected to various dance traditions in India, he was one of those rarities in the classical dance world: a poised and highly talented male dancer. 'Perfectly tuned', in Chandra's view, he had learned Bharatanatyam from Guru Ellappa Pillai, Kuchipudi from Guru Vempati Chinna Satyam, and Chhau from Guru Kedar Nath Sahoo. In his sensibility and sharp reflexes, Chandra found a perfect counter for her own consciousness. Their partnership, alas, was restricted to a few shows of *Navagraha* and the first performance of *Primal Energy* (1984) which was almost improvised during one of Kamadev's chance visits to India. In his tragic and untimely death in September 1992, Chandra has lost her closest male friend in dance.

Today, from what I can sense of *Navagraha* through Chandra's recollections, the focus was not so much on choreographing a composite view of the planetary deities, but on exploring the interaction, meeting, and separation of 'cosmic' and 'human' elements. While Kama would 'become' each of the *planets* with the appropriate *hastas* (as recorded in the *Abhinaydarpana*), his movement more or less centred in a specific space, Chandra was the 'human element', as she puts it, who 'danced *to* the *grahas.*' And not just 'to' but also 'with', 'against', 'from a distance', and 'at close quarters': the dynamics of the dance was created specifically through the interplay of energies that Kamadev and Chandra were able to sustain through their performance.

Inevitably, the interplay of the 'human' and 'cosmic' elements was translated more specifically into dance-language as the juxtaposition of 'male' and 'female' energies. The sensuality of the encounter was heightened through an exploration of the 'elasticity' of space. As Chandra recalls, 'We were conscious of our own individual space and the intermediate space that would at times be stretched to the limits of the stage and at times brought so close that we were almost touching each other.' While Chandra had the opportunity to use a wider space, in which she would 'throw her energy' in multiple directions, Kama was more 'centred', at once drawing on and deflecting the kinetic energy of his partner. While the proximity of their bodies enhanced by 'sheer eye-power' would at times appear 'tantalisingly sexual', the intimacy could also be cut through a kind of impersonality, almost (as Chandra says) 'as if we had nothing to do with each other.'

'In *Navagraha*', as Chandra is able to formulate today, 'the important thing for me was not to get involved in any story or narrative or even the characteristics of the *graha*. What mattered to me was colour; form; the abstractions of particular temperaments relating to space; directions — reaching out towards a dance language.'

Once again, Chandra had an opportunity to deepen her exploration of the dynamics of horizontal, vertical, and diagonal lines, which she had 'geometrised' earlier in *Tillana*. The difference in *Navagraha* was that these dynamics were more specifically investigated within the interplay of male/female energies. 'Unpredictable things began to happen', Chandra recalls. 'I would approach Kama with tremendous speed almost going into him, and then find my own bearings. In the "ring of Saturn", we literally held each other with our eyes.'

Clearly, this kind of 'electricity' was not achieved through technique alone. When Chandra has attempted to duplicate this male/female interaction in her productions using younger dancers, where her specific instruction to the female dancer has been to 'push the man against the wall', the effect is powerful, but not always sensual. As Chandra regretfully says of her dancers, not basking in memories of her own youth, but simply confronting certain home-truths about dance: 'They don't have the consciousness or sensuality to capture the kind of energy Kama and I explored in dance.'

These two factors — 'consciousness' and 'sensuality' — it would seem to me, are inextricably linked in Chandra's temperament as an artist. One could argue that there are more erotic dancers than Chandra in the contemporary dance world, but there are few, I think, who can combine sensuality with intelligence as she does. This very combination of energies is what defined *Navagraha* in the first place. Along with the male/female interplay of energies, it is significant that the production began on an austere note which must have been altogether radical in the early seventies: the invocation to Surya performed by Chandra in an adaptation of the Surya Namaskar set to Muthuswamy Dikshitar's famous composition on the sun-deity.

Homage to Sun

In her initial thoughts on the production, Chandra had wanted to use all the nine *kritis* composed by Dikshitar on the *navagraha,* but she found that it was almost impossible to dance to the 'sheer weight' of these compositions.[8] Later in *Prana,* she clarified this impulse by making her dancers perform yogic *asanas* rather than the *adavus* (dance-units) of Bharatanatyam to Dikshitar's *kritis*. In *Navagraha,* she made her first choice in this direction by exploring an idiom of movement outside the Bharatanatyam repertoire. Adapting the Surya Namaskar that she had learned from the Yoga master, Ambu, at the Aurobindo Ashram, she performed her own homage to the sun using Dikshitar's composition *'Surya murte'* as the musical accompaniment.

Danced almost in one spot at the far end of the stage, at 'vanishing point' as it were, daringly distanced from the audience, the invocation to Surya (as can be observed from Chandra's revival of the piece) begins in almost total stillness. Then with a slow, hieratic movement of the hands, the body rotates through half-circles and quarter-circles. The relentlessly slow 'flow' of the movement is punctuated with micro-rhythms, so that each turn of the body seems somewhat fragmented. It is through a series of tiny jerks that the rotation is completed.

Then with an even more sustained concentration, Chandra goes down on her knees and prostrates herself on the ground. The 'namaskar' is deeply moving in its pristine simplicity. There is no attempt to theatricalise it, or make it look more 'dynamic.' At a most basic level, it is pure dedication, an act which says through the silence of its energies, 'I am dedicating myself, my body, to you, Surya, from whom I get every particle of energy to live and perform this ritual in the first place.'

As performed by Chandra, this movement could be considered too 'simple' to be described as 'dance' in the conventional sense. It is more like a gesture of homage to the elements in which one can trace the almost infinitesimal transformation of Yoga into dance. It is a very delicate balance that Chandra maintains in her performance which is also something of a ritual. At times, the 'flow' does not quite 'work' from a distance, and the astral blossoming of the form begins to resemble a demonstration. But for most of the time, and particularly towards the end of the 'namaskar', there is an inner radiance that suffuses Chandra's being. Quite unlike *Naravahana,* where the transformation from traditional iconography into performance is complete and dramatic, the homage to Surya is more like an inner passage of movement, a yogic flow of energy.

I have described this opening section of *Navagraha* not only because it happens to be the only piece of choreography that can still be seen today, but because it embodies an austerity that counterpoints the sensuality of the male/female interactions described earlier in the section. We should keep in mind that this spare, almost minimalist choreography was created almost twenty years ago in an idiom that totally contradicted the norms of Bharatanatyam. One can imagine the impact it must have had as can be assessed from the warm reminiscences of eye-witnesses of the first production in Bombay. From the homage to sun, the production travelled through an exploration of the various planets leading to Rahu and Ketu, and eventually back to Surya, who was evoked in the closing sequence of the production with Chandra facing Kamadev while kneeling on the floor in a traditional Chhau *namaskar*.

Whether or not *Navagraha* worked cohesively as a production, one cannot be entirely sure in the absence of comprehensive documentation. What is moving, however, is the very attempt it made to break new ground in the understanding of dance by bringing it a little closer to philosophy and the abstract traditions of iconography. Chandra acknowledges today that she was still 'searching' at that time and occasionally, felt 'isolated' in the absence of any meaningful dialogue with other dancers. Dashrath once again contributed to the production by preparing different slides of graphic symbols for the various *grahas*. Musical inputs were provided by seasoned vocalists like B. Krishnamurthy and Madrimangalam Ramachandran, T.V. Gopalakrishnan (*mridangam*), Vidya Shankar (*veena*) and Guru Ellappa Pillai who guided the composition of the dances and conducted *nattuvangam*.

Once again Chandra found that she could not sustain her work beyond a couple of shows. But the production had 'triggered off', in her words, 'a tremendous understanding of space, and an opening to an entire gamut of material relating to texts, icons, and rituals.' The challenge was now to find ways of transforming this material through different cultural expressions.

Exploring the Media

a) Posters

Unable to find viable forums or collaborators in the dance world, Chandra turned her attention to the media where she made her first intervention. Her first project was to find a way of using the material that she had collated in her research on the Navagraha. Contrary to the opinion of close friends like Hrishikesh Mukherjee who emphasised her potential as a writer, Chandra was by this time more interested in investigating 'visual forms.' It is around this time that she began designing posters, which is one of the activities for which she has been recognised, along with the design of jacket-covers of books and logos connected with the feminist and environmental movements.

Among her first explorations of graphics were two companion posters that used the research from the *Navagraha* production as a 'take-off point' for their own visuals. While one poster represented the days of the week in particular bands of colour, consciously breaking the colour codes of the 'Swiss graphics colour spectrum', the other was a compilation of all the essential information relating to planetary elements and properties through a particular combination of symbols, graphics, and words. What is significant about these posters is that they were the first attempts on the part of a contemporary Indian artist with a 'traditional' base to communicate performance research through graphics. In the larger context of commercial design as well, these posters opened up an entirely new way of using the most sophisticated printing technology to 'visualise' traditional sources of knowledge.

Through these posters it would seem that we have entered a totally different kind of activity from that of Bharatanatyam or Yoga. One could say that this was Chandra's first confrontation with the market. While the actual negotiations around the posters were 'one-shot deals', Chandra was more interested in the process of working on design and crystallising her knowledge of dance through graphics. One could say that this work was a kind of 'hobby', one of her 'informal' activities from which she also managed to earn some money.

Significantly, all the posters that she designed in the early seventies were 'dance-related.' The concepts came directly from her experience as a dancer, for example, the relationship between Distance and Time. 'I asked people,' Chandra recollects, 'how they could visualise the relationship between "time" and "distance". Most of them were baffled.

They didn't know how to deal with the question.' This is where Chandra's knowledge of dance was useful. In Bharatanatyam, it is well known that a dancer can show the passage of time through the waxing of the moon from *ardhachandra* to *purnachandra,* or the distance between a lotus and a steadily darkening sun, through a few subtle changes of gesture. It was this 'non-verbal' language evoking the passage of time that Chandra attempted to incorporate in her design.

Other posters that followed 'Time and Distance' focused on concepts like Purna and Shakti (for which Chandra used a striking black-and-white still from the closing image of *Navagraha.*) Her work on design also enabled her to collaborate with Dashrath who by this time was one of the most experienced designers in India, whose work on exhibitions in major international forums like the World Fairs had necessitated a close contact with the most recent developments in technology, computer design, and even holographs. In 1969, he and Chandra had collaborated on an exhibition in honour of Mahatma Gandhi's birth centenary entitled *The World is my Family* which was introduced provocatively with one of Gandhiji's statements: 'Let these lines serve as a warning for those who want to honour me by erecting statues and having portraits of my figure, that I heartily dislike these exhibitions.' In the very questioning of the idea of an exhibition on Gandhiji, Chandra had attempted to present a 'non-establishment' view of the Father of the Nation, focusing as much on his ironies and contradictions as on his greatness.

Later in life, Chandra and Dashrath once again collaborated on another intensely reflective exhibition, *Stree: Women in India.* In the late sixties, however, what needs to be kept in mind is that Dashrath had already begun to explore 'spectacles' which he was later to develop in his design of the Festivals of India in France and the Soviet Union. Chandra, on the other hand, constantly attempted to subvert his 'big' visions through a radically different kind of content. So when she began to design posters in the early seventies, she challenged Dashrath to explore his own creativity through seemingly 'smaller' means.

One such challenge was to photograph her hands which she had wanted to use in two posters representing friendship and altercation. 'I wanted to show that hands are not stumps', says Chandra, 'as they so often appear in dance photographs. I asked Dashrath if he could photograph hands that retained a quality of life.' And much to her appreciation, he was able to do so, confirming the faith that their mutual friend, Henri Cartier-Bresson, had in Dashrath's 'eye' as a photographer.

Over the years, Chandra has continued to design posters increasingly connected with women's issues, and more specifically, with myths and symbols celebrating fertility and female power. We shall address these images and the ways in which they have been perceived and occasionally criticised by some feminists in a later chapter. For the moment, it would be more appropriate to document Chandra's exploration of yet another media in the early seventies — cinema. This exposure was initiated by the film director, Kumar Shahani, who invited her to choreograph a dance sequence for his first feature film, *Maya Darpan*.

b) Cinema

It is significant how in the early seventies, Chandra found herself immersed in multiple idioms: dance, graphics, photography, cinema. Though a cultural history of the period has yet to be systematically documented or assessed, one could say that all kinds of shifts were beginning then to manifest themselves in cultural activities. On the one hand, one can discern a growing institutionalisation of the arts manifest in the increased power of official and cultural organisations centred, for the most part, in New Delhi. There is also the assertion of new commercial pressures embodied in the film industry, which was probably at the peak of its power during this period, monopolising 'mass culture' without the serious threat posed by television or video, which dominate the cultural scene today.

There was also a significant isolation from the earlier

national cultural movements such as IPTA, with an increasing depoliticisation of the arts which can be studied in the commodification of the 'folk', among other urban trends. Yet, along with this scenario, or perhaps because of it, there was also the emergence of an *avant garde,* totally unstructured, poorly financed, yet fuelled by individual and intransigent visions, which brought artists like Chandra and Kumar together in the first place.

When they first met, as Chandra recalls, there were immediate affinities of belonging to a 'minority' community of artists, searching for alternative languages both in their media and beyond, holding on to their still-unrealised visions with a total lack of compromise. The one particular affinity that Chandra shared with Kumar was a modernist response to 'tradition', where the purpose was not to illustrate, or to decorate, or to deify 'tradition', but to open up its contradictions and life-sustaining principles through a process of questioning. If both Kumar and Chandra were drawn in their own ways to the dialectical thought-process of a Marxist historian like D.D. Kosambi (whom Kumar has acknowledged as one of his gurus), they were also concerned about the cultural sources that informed this process. More specifically, both of them were drawn to certain possibilities of expressing sensuality in art. Indeed, this is possibly what attracted Kumar to Chandra in the first place. As she puts it: 'He was searching for someone who had explored sensuality.'

At that time Kumar had just come back from abroad where he had assisted Robert Bresson in the making of *Une Femme Douce.* For Chandra, Kumar was still something of an 'outsider' at that time. More precisely, she felt that he 'tended to look at the bodies of Indian women with a sense of wonder.' Along with this seeming rapture, he was also intensely cerebral. In their first discussion, he had attempted to explain the kind of 'break' in an individual that he was attempting to explore in his film against a larger canvas of 'social change.' And then, as Chandra states candidly: 'He floored me by wanting a dialectical interpretation of Kali.'

Placing that moment within her own response to Kali,

Chandra says:

> Now when he mentioned Kali, he had entered my area. An area with which I was familiar. The dialectics of class struggle and social change — all that was more abstract. I asked him: 'Have you seen Kali?' He said, 'No'. 'Have you any preconceived ideas of Kali? Any image?' I realised that he was talking about Kali intellectually, rather ideologically.
>
> I told him that I had seen Kali in the Kalighat Temple in Calcutta. What struck me was the power of colour — red, black, and white. Colours of earth, body, blood. It had a very strong impact. What I saw was a jet-black stone image of Kali, white eyes, white sari, red border, white skulls, and red hibiscus flowers. I was able to see through the crowd of worshippers. In between the movement of the people, I saw the movement of colours. And for me that was Kali — the movement of colour.
>
> When I came out I saw the women making marks on their foreheads with the blood of the sacrifice.

Predictably, this statement appears to have 'made sense' to Kumar, who 'responded strongly' to Chandra's experience. Later he attempted to connect the 'movement of colour' specified by Chandra with larger political associations of colour. Out of these discussions emerged a search for the appropriate dance idiom to be used in the film. At first Chandra thought that she would use Bharatanatyam, but Kumar, it appears, was not impressed by any of the dancers. Chandra herself did not want to dance in front of the camera. Indeed, she continues to be camera-shy despite the considerable publicity she has received in recent years. Even in the recent television broadcast of *Lilavati*, one senses stiffness, even artifice in her introduction, before she relaxes in front of the camera.

Rejecting Bharatanatyam, Chandra and Kumar decided

to attend a Chhau festival in the company of K.K. Mahajan, the gifted cameraman, for whom Chandra has a deep regard. After watching Chhau in the village of Baripada in Orissa, they decided that the idiom of Mayurbhanj Chhau was what they were looking for. Somewhat arbitrarily, and with some uncomfortable echoes of the kind of borrowing of 'folk' sources with which we have become so familiar today, Chandra claims that, 'we decided that we would take what we wanted out of it.' Indeed, the seeming arbitrariness underlying this spontaneous decision to 'use' Chhau is reflected, to my mind, both in the choreography and its location in the film itself.

It would seem that the actual process of conceptualising the dance, however, was more valuable than its eventual execution. For one thing, Kumar and Chandra were able to exchange notes on the basic dynamics of movement in dance and cinema through an exploration of circular, horizontal, vertical, and diagonal lines. Another area of inquiry concerned colour and its abstraction in relation to energy and content. By now the 'theme' of the dance sequence in *Maya Darpan* was more or less focused on 'archaic movements of struggle and confrontation.' The challenge was to work out a scheme of colour in relation to the dynamics of this struggle in the language of cinema.

'We started', as Chandra recalls, 'with a lot of black. Slowly red is introduced. Then white dominates black. Slowly red gains strength while white steps sideways; red grows; still a lot of black. Then white moves uncomfortably, jerkily out, red asserts itself slowly and purposefully — till the white becomes red and vibrant, full and rounded and coordinated.'[9] Within this interpretive scheme, black represents forces of darkness and doubt, white those of reaction, while red of change and life. It was through the movement towards *rajas* by surmounting the elements of *tamas* and *sattvika* that Chandra attempted to conceptualise her choreography with a specific use of colour.

Unfortunately, it becomes almost impossible to assess the 'effect' of this colour given the current state of the film, whose print has blurred considerably. What does register, however, is the abruptness with which the dance is inserted in the film, with no apparent thematic or auditory connection to what precedes it. Here one is at a loss to find either a 'dialectical interpretation of Kali' or, at a more concrete level, a mythic embodiment of the change in consciousness that the heroine is supposed to have internalised. Indeed, I would have to regard this sequence as one of the most self-conscious uses of dance in film that I have seen, and while accepting the logic of non-causality within the larger framework of the film, it still appears contrived, if not mystifying.

As abruptly as it begins, the dance is 'cut' with the closing images of the film focusing on the pellucid waters of a lake from within the interior of a cabin in a launch. Gradually, the camera moves with the imperceptibly slow movement of the launch towards the steadily darkening green of the bank facing it. This expanse of water and the movement towards the green attempt to evoke a process of revitalisation and fertility. If the images fail to transcend their artifice, it is because the film itself seems more concerned with making a statement about art rather than 'being' itself.

While being hailed as far ahead of its time by a coterie of artists, *Maya Darpan* received a predominantly 'hostile' reception, as Chandra remembers it, both from the critics and the public at large. Though the film needs a far more detailed critical inquiry than I am able to provide in this study, its value, I believe, may lie in its priorities concerning abstraction and non-linearity in the construction of narrative and image. While this results at times in acute mannerism, most evident in the deadpan delivery of dialogue in which the actors indulge as part of their 'non-acting', the film asserts its aesthetic without compromising at any point with the pressures of existing norms in the Indian cinema.

It does make sense that Chandra should have been involved in the film in the context of her own resistance to the dance establishment. While her own grasp of the Chhau idiom in the dance sequence of the film is not entirely convincing, it does reveal the tremendous distance that she has covered in her understanding of the use of disparate physical traditions in productions like *Angika*. What appears jumbled and 'ethnic' in the film sequence (despite the use of 'real' Chhau dancers), has now been replaced in Chandra's recent choreography by a more rigorous attitude to 'folk' and 'traditional' elements.

Today, however, it is not so much the dance in *Maya Darpan* that Chandra remembers but the experience of exploring movement through the lens of a camera. At the New Theatre Studios in Calcutta, Chandra had the opportunity to discover the 'vertical energies' of dance in an altogether different idiom. Through the use of a crane, she discovered how a group of dancers could be made to disappear as it were into a darkened space, almost descending like primordial images into a state of *tamas*. Then, once, again, they would reappear from this state to reassert their energies on a stage which the camera made no attempt to conceal.

Regardless of the ultimate result, the process of exploring dance through a different medium was a rich experience for Chandra, and the opportunity to collaborate with gifted artists like Kumar Shahani and K.K. Mahajan was additionally rewarding. It was becoming clear to Chandra that her potential collaborators were to be found in disciplines outside dance. With the death of Guru Ellappa Pillai in 1973, she felt even more distanced from the world of performance. Apart from keeping in touch with the basic *adavus* (dance-units) of Bharatanatyam, which she began to reinvestigate through 'personal research', her dance activities were confined to holding a few workshops.

Increasingly, she felt a need to engage in activities that could somehow resist the commercialisation of art as she perceived it, and the centralisation of political power to which it seemed to be linked. Already by the Emergency in 1975, Chandra's process of politicisation had crystallised. Along with her need to explore different media of expression, she was also beginning to formulate her political instincts. Now she was learning to articulate her thoughts in public forums. This 'finding of her voice' was a painful and slow process which corresponded to a different kind of social activity involving the communication of 'skills' like print-making, design, and even street theatre, to individuals and groups committed to non-governmental cultural and political interventions.

Today, this kind of work has been institutionalised through the rhetoric of 'development.' But in the seventies, it was still possible to think of viable alternatives to the established modes of education and communication controlled by the government and the elitist sections of society. Joining her in this search for alternatives was her closest collaborator, a journalist called Sadanand Menon, who along with Dashrath Patel formed an organisation called Skills, whose history will be narrated in the next chapter.

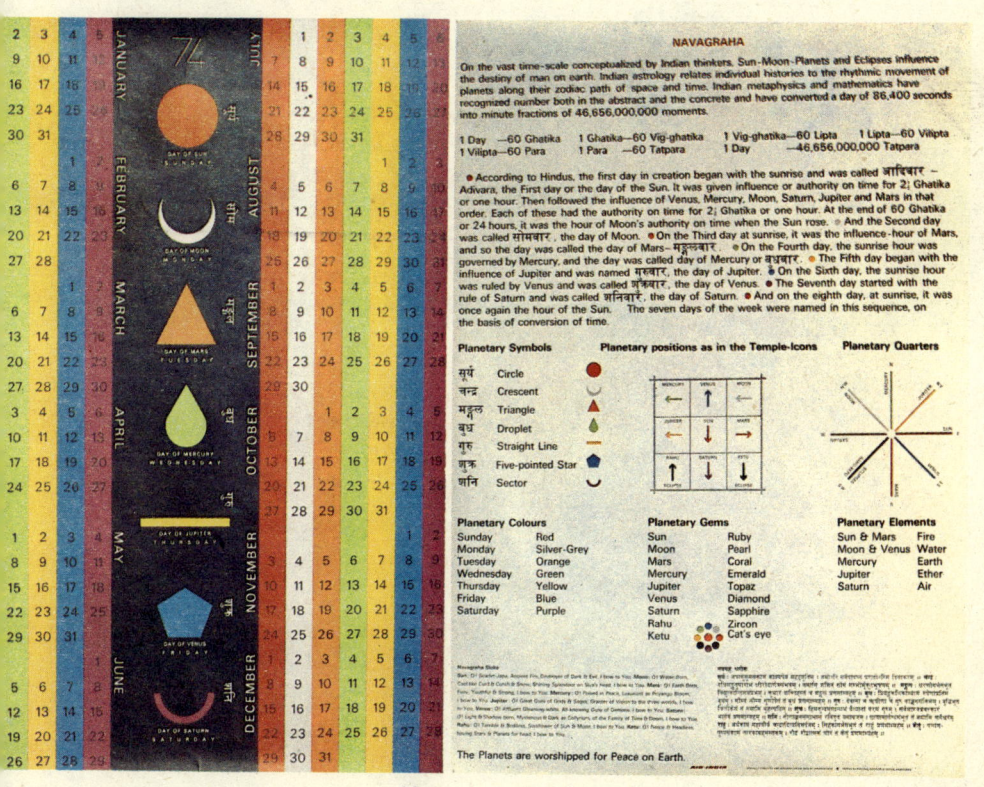

4

The Politics of Friendship

Before we begin to discuss the activities of Skills, which will be the focus of attention in this chapter, it is necessary to study the relationships that have made its organisation possible. Here it is necessary to introduce the third person in the narrative, apart from Chandra and Dashrath, who has contributed substantially to the formation of Skills in 1979, and who is an inextricable part of Chandra's world today.

Sadanand Menon, or just Sadanand as he is known to most people, is not the kind of man one normally associates with dance. A big, burly, gruff fellow, he is affectionately called 'Sado' by Chandra's dancers who know, perhaps more clearly than other observers, how much he has contributed to the group. At once the stage manager, lighting designer, transport coordinator, public relations officer, pacifier (during moments of tension), instigator (during moments of complacency), at once the strongest defender of the group and its most relentless in-house critic, Sadanand is an indispensable part of Chandra's work today. Though he has recently moved to New Delhi to focus his attention on journalism as the Arts Editor of *The Economic Times*, his links with the group remain strong.

In Sadanand, one finds yet another 'urban nomad' whose early life was even more peripatetic than Chandra's. Since his father's job was transferable, Sadanand found himself living in a quick succession of places including Koni (near Bilaspur), Aundh (near Pune), then New Delhi, Bombay, Bhopal, and eventually, Madras where he first met Chandra in the late sixties. At that time he was still an undergraduate at Loyola College closely associated with a student magazine called PACE. While collecting advertisements for this magazine, one of his colleagues had bumped into 'that incredible storm' called Chandralekha, whose writings Sadanand had read in the *Illustrated Weekly of India*.

'Practically the next day', as Sadanand puts it candidly, 'a gang of us went to meet her and were promptly swept off our feet.' They were 'zapped' by this free-thinking, free-living woman, who made no apology about being single. 'In our discussions with her', as Sadanand remembers, 'we could see that she was cutting through our preconceived notions of politics. She made us see how derivative our thinking was.' In her company, Sadanand discovered an 'immediate learning process', something that continued through the years in which they eventually lived together.

As friends they shared a growing concern for the shaping of 'alternatives' through non-governmental forums of social action. The pre-Emergency years between 1974-June 1975 were a particularly 'fertile' period for such organisations, as they began to establish links with various alternative groups in the country. As yet, the seminar circuit had not been bureaucratised. In fact, Chandra and Sadanand were connected with various Marxist study groups functioning outside the party framework, which had emerged out of the radical students' movement of the late sixties. By 1974, there was a more concrete agenda to be confronted in these forums through the movement initiated by Jayaprakash Narayan, which is justifiably viewed as the first significant resistance to the political hegemony of the Congress Party since Independence. This was the closest that Chandra and Sadanand in particular came to supporting the immediacies of the *realpolitik*.

When the Emergency was declared in 1975, Chandra's resistance was not compromised at any point, as unfortunately was the case with some of our most socially concerned artists who imagined that a 'new India' was in the making. Her attitude was characterised by a total rejection of the existing system, and in this case, even her strongest critics would have to accept the efficacy of her alleged 'iconoclasm.'

It was around this time that she invited Sadanand to look after her house while she was conducting a dance workshop abroad. Indeed, what makes the relationship between Chandra and Sadanand so special is that it is totally open, known to people around them. It is the absolute antithesis of the kind of 'affair' in which a dancer may be involved, which is at once the source of gossip and endorsement by 'respectable' society. Chandra and Sadanand have never seen themselves as a couple. If the relationship deepens even as they no longer live together, with Sadanand's recent relocation to New Delhi, it is because they have always felt free to be themselves.

The elusive quality of this friendship is that it exists outside of the norms assumed by 'marriage' and 'romance.' If I were psychoanalytically inclined, I might have made much of the fact that Sadanand lost his mother when he was three, a death that he remembers vividly. It would however be crude to read a substitute mother-son relationship in his friendship with Chandra, if not laughably contrived, because their friendship is so free from familial dependency and sentiment. Within the neo-Marxist framework of ideas that brought them together in the first place, it would be more accurate to describe them as 'comrades.' But there is something archaic, if not misleading about this description, given their mutual distrust of the patriarchal and puritanical codes determining relationships in a communist context. I suppose it is best to describe them as 'friends', who have supported each other in the deepest crises by being open to, yet critical of each other's vulnerabilities and defences.

It is a small, yet telling detail from their early life together that Chandra's hair began to fall by the mid-seventies. Amusing as this may seem, this was not an easy situation for her to handle as a woman and dancer. Her experiments with henna only resulted in her hair turning peculiar shades of red and purple. Finally nature prevailed, as her hair turned prematurely white, the most distinctive sign in her appearance today, and which totally contradicts the traditional norm that dancers must have black hair. As for Sadanand, he was becoming bald while Chandra's hair was whitening, which was one of the ironic coincidences that contributed to the laughter in their lives.

Significantly, dance was not a major issue in their

relationship at that time. Indeed, Sadanand had never seen Chandra perform in public though he would occasionally listen to her thinking aloud on the subject and observe her demonstrating *hastas* and militant forms of Devi in conversation. What brought them together was not a concern for the arts but a somewhat restless, yet passionate search for emerging modes of political resistance outside the party system.

In this regard, their life together was constantly interrupted by a wide range of social workers, activists, and drop-outs who were connected at various levels to voluntary groups, non-governmental agencies and anti-poverty forums. For the most part, these were Sadanand's friends and acquaintances who later became known to Chandra as well. For the first time in her life, one could say that she was consciously addressing the contradictions and possibilities of political praxis in an altogether different context from the one she had speculated on as an 'artist.' Her own instincts about 'freedom' and 'rebellion' which she had investigated personally and through relationships were now being juxtaposed with political forums focusing on 'civil liberties', 'alternative technologies' and 'neo-Gandhian' modes of protest.

Indeed, after the Emergency was lifted, it would seem that a period of alternative platform-building had been initiated. The Janata government itself sponsored welfare and adult literacy programmes in the villages on a wide scale. Autonomous, people-oriented development activity was encouraged. Unfortunately, in the absence of an adequate infrastructure to implement these programmes as well as the inner dissensions within the Janata Party, the initiative for alternative platforms merely opened up new avenues of corruption. Significantly, it was after the fall of the Janata government that Sadanand and Chandra began to realise the need for some organisation in which they could mobilise their resources and commitment.

Still functioning without any party affiliation, they decided to channelise their freewheeling affinities to 'human rights', 'Chipko', and the 'women's movement' through a more concrete expression of social and political action. It was at this time that both of them focused their attention on organising workshops in which certain 'skills' could be imparted to non-profit social and political groups and individuals concerned with alternative methods of communication. Within such a context of 'informal education', it was only natural that they should have invited Dashrath to participate in the work-process by contributing his own insights as a teacher of design and visual concepts. Their need to incorporate his talent within the larger enterprise of Skills also coincided with his own doubts about the National Institute of Design to which he had been linked since its inception in the early sixties. At this juncture we need to digress a little into Dashrath's career before documenting the activities of Skills.

Dashrath's Dilemma

At an external level, it would seem that Dashrath had nothing to do with the political ideas that concerned Sadanand and Chandra at that time. His position at the NID, which had been initiated through the enlightened patronage of Gira and Gautam Sarabhai, seemed quite remote from the realities of 'alternative' politics. And yet, the NID had started off with its own 'alternative' vision of design. Set up in 1961 as an autonomous institution following the recommendations of Ray and Charles Eames, who had been invited by the Indian government to suggest guidelines for a training programme in design, the NID embarked on one of the most ambitious educational programmes in the country. Inspired by the radical model of Bauhaus and the Ulm School of Design, its purpose was to influence industrial design by adapting some of the most modern, if not *avant-garde* western concepts of technology, architecture, and space in an Indian context. Le Corbusier, Buckminster Fuller, Louis Kahn were among some of its early advisers, in addition to visiting 'experimental' artists like Robert Rauschenberg and David Tudor, who set up the first Moog synthesizer in an electronic music studio at the Institute.

With such multidisciplinary inputs, it is not surprising that Dashrath has experimented over the years not just with painting and photography but with ceramics, graphics, industrial design, environmental design, and exhibition design (for which he is, perhaps, best known). While the NID facilitated his creativity in the early years, it was gradually bureaucratised by administrators who were essentially policy-makers rather than artists or teachers. More critically, the larger vision of the Institute was not, in Dashrath's view, realised by the government:

> The hope was that the input of design would contribute to the growth of the industry, but the merchant-mentality of Indian industrialists soon had them running for second-hand technologies from the West. Our Ministry of Industry was not interested in developing a long-term philosophy of industry or design. It was interested only in short-term monetary gains. Consequently, the inevitable happened: the rejects of the West became our primary imports. Since the vision of the Institute was not realised, it became an elitist, redundant institution. The industry was not using it, so in walked the advertising agencies and bureaucrats who took over.

However, it could also be countered that the NID's vision itself was elitist in its inception and that its advocacy of 'innovative' concepts had no bearing on the immediate realities of Indian life. No one has pointed this out more trenchantly than V.S. Naipaul, who in his otherwise simplistic condemnation of India as a 'wounded civilisation' has nonetheless made some sharp observations about NID as an 'imported idea, an imported institution', that has ultimately been 'reduced to its equipment': a technology divorced from the needs of people.[1]

Tellingly, it was a mindless use of 'technology' that eventually compelled Dashrath to leave the NID when he was urged by Chandra and Sadanand to join Skills in 1979. The immediate cause of his resignation is worth recalling.

It appears that a particular kind of thresher was being sold in the market without adequate safety measures. This had resulted in some fatal accidents in which the hands of young peasants had been chopped off. When Sadanand brought this to Dashrath's attention, Dashrath, in turn, raised the issue at a Policy and Planning Board Meeting at the NID where he was strongly criticised by his colleagues. 'I was told', Dashrath remembers vividly, 'that technical failures have nothing to do with design. We cannot blame the machine. It is the training of the worker which is at fault.' Needless to say, this resulted in some kind of crisis for Dashrath. For the first time, he was compelled to admit that there were at least 'two sides in his life: the visual and the social' which did not necessarily meet. Rather movingly, he admits: 'I realised I was a media person, but what were my messages?'

It was at this point that Sadanand and Chandra challenged him with a totally different set of principles and goals. The very inadequacy of their finances became the source of the challenge. Was Dashrath capable of teaching basic visual skills to non-design students within a budget of one thousand rupees rather than one crore? Could he adapt his knowledge to address the needs of social activists? Was it possible to have an 'institute' of design at a grassroots level?

All these questions 'sparked him off', as Sadanand recalls. Yet there were vacillations about his 'security', which were valid in the context of his familial obligations. For all his bohemianism, Dashrath (unlike Chandra) remains closely linked to his home and to his mother in particular, whom he continues to support. It was inevitable that some kind of financial compensation would be needed by Dashrath after he resigned from the NID. In addition, money would be needed for the purchase of basic materials relating to the workshops at Skills, apart from paying modest stipends to the participants from rural and suburban areas. All these considerations ultimately resulted in Chandra and Sadanand making the difficult, yet necessary decision about accepting a grant from a German organisation called 'Bread for the World.'

Before Skills could begin to function as an 'alternative organisation', for teaching drawing, painting, sketching, screen-printing, poster-making, and book production, it was necessary to have a *space* which could accommodate so many activities. For this to materialise Chandra would have to confront her long-standing decision not to 'settle' in any one place. The time had come for her to confront her 'urban nomadic' ways by basing herself in a cultural complex at the corner of Elliots Beach in Madras, where she presently lives and works.

The Space of 'Skills'

In what would seem like 'a long time ago', in 1963 to be precise, Chandra had bought a plot of land on Elliots Beach. The foundation of a building structure was laid in 1970 with a five-foot wall and no roof. Not surprisingly, given the sheer isolation of the place — and Elliots Beach was almost totally deserted in those days apart from a few fishing villages — Chandra's land was taken over by some rowdies who used it as a den for distilling illicit liquor. Chandra was aware of the problem but was unable to set it right. She was also fervently opposed to the idea of settling down in a permanent place.

However, by the late seventies, when Skills began to materialise as an organisation, she was compelled to acknowledge the exhaustion of moving from one rented apartment to another. The 'landlord menace' was as much of a deterrent to her freedom as the prospect of settling down in her own property. Besides, the rental of halls in Madras, which would have been necessary to accommodate the activities of Skills, was so prohibitively high by the late seventies that it made sense for her to work in her own space.

Ultimately, it was Dashrath who made the decision by simply moving into the barracks-like enclosure on Elliots Beach which was now, officially, Chandra's 'home'. Sadanand and Chandra herself moved in soon after, and together they started to plan and supervise the building of a small house. Needless to say, Dashrath's considerable experience as an architect came in handy. Most of Chandra's energies were spent in planting trees and driving away the cows and goats from eating the scant vegetation. It is difficult to believe that barely ten years ago there was not a single tree on Chandra's property, which almost merged with the beach. Now after considerable effort, this seeming wasteland has become a sanctuary with a wide variety of trees including *neem, banyan, peepul, badam, gulmohur.* No one who has worked, lived, or even visited Skills can fail to be inspired by the fertility of its surroundings.

Chandra, however, while acknowledging the privilege of living and working on Elliots Beach, still continues to have misgivings about owning space. For her, this is like being 'married', tied down against one's will to certain legalities and power structures. Most recently, she was compelled to erect a concrete wall around the far end of her property. This became necessary after repeated thefts of the granite blocks which had been used as a fence, and from which the sea could be seen in strips of blue. 'Now there is a wall', Chandra states, with a combination of sadness and anger: 'You have to pay a price for freedom.'

By the summer of 1980, the ground floor of the house had been constructed and was ready to be used for the first workshop. Following the model of a working commune, the large living space of the house was also designed with a work-space in mind. The bedroom could duplicate as a storage space and studio, the kitchen could be used for cooking food and also for preparing the various inks and colours to be used in the workshops. Even the toilet could be used as a darkroom for developing photographs. These were the basic components of the space of Skills which has now been extended to include more rooms, some other shacks, and an open-air theatre called Mandala.

So much has been achieved in this space in the last ten years that one has every right to dispute Chandra's alleged loss of freedom. Even she would not deny that this 'loss' has also resulted in her most creative and productive phase as an artist beginning with *Angika* in 1985. The space has also provided the site for a range of workshops and interactions that have made 1 Elliots Beach a very special place attracting a wide range of people participating in the shaping of alternatives within the larger spectrum of contemporary art practice in India.

Workshop

Before documenting the first workshop held at Skills between July 1-September 30, 1980, it will be necessary to examine the *raison d'être* of the organisation within the larger range of development groups and voluntary associations that had emerged in India since the early seventies. Some attempts have been made to trace the origins of these groups to the social and religious reform movements from the late nineteenth century which were motivated by the principles of 'philanthropy', 'charity', and 'relief.'[2] As yet, there are many voluntary associations and social groups linked to religious organisations like the Church and the Ramakrishna Mission, but they have modified their priorities in accordance with the changing political conditions and the emergence of new philosophies like 'liberation theology' and 'development.'

So far as Skills is concerned, it is important to stress that it was not part of the larger 'charity-philanthropy-relief' type of organisation. Nor did it structure its ethos around a particular ideology as is the case with Gandhian and Sarvodayaite groups. Nor was it at all faintly interested in any kind of proselytising, even though its initial funding came from a German Church organisation called Bread for the World. Skills was distinctive in so far as it opened up the relatively unexplored area of cultural praxis — forging new relationships between communities through the dissemination of particular skills relating to visual communication and the arts. This focus on 'culture' was what differentiated Skills from almost all the development groups functioning in India in the late seventies. Even today its explorations have not been sufficiently confronted or extended.

In addition, another distinguishing characteristic of Skills was its affirmation of a metropolitan base. Though some of its participants came from mofussil and rural areas, many were drawn from the metropolis itself — in fact, the core group including many of Sadanand's friends were attached to different disciplines centred in and around the city. The 'skills' imparted in the workshops were indigenous derivations and transformations of 'modern' techniques and modes of expertise. There was no attempt on the part of Skills to disguise its urban moorings or to romanticise its connections with the 'oppressed' and 'rural poor', categories of 'development' which have been increasingly valorised over the years.

At the same time, there was a keen awareness at Skills of the disparities in the availability of different modes of knowledge, particularly in relation to visual communication. Consequently, in the very first workshop, an attempt was made to confront this disparity in a highly original and creative way. The participants of the workshop included seven representatives of an organisation called MERG (Medical, Educational, Rural and General Development), a voluntary association based in the Chingleput district of Tamilnadu.

The purpose of the workshop was to facilitate the existing projects of the participants which included night-schools for children, leadership training programmes for the village youth, and the production of education aids through books, posters, and puppet shows. At a very basic level, the responsibility of the 'project leaders' (which is how Chandra, Dashrath, and Sadanand were designated) was to contribute to these grass-root activities by imparting the technique and knowledge of certain skills: the use of stencils, block printing, the transformative possibilities of recycled newspapers, even more seemingly 'impossible' tasks like setting up a field dark-room within Rs.600 and developing slides without the use of a camera.

Apart from these technical skills, a vital aspect of the workshop was devoted to the actual process of imbibing skills in a wider social context. The 'trainees' (as the participants were called) were made to confront the values underlying the use of particular skills. As stated in the detailed log book in which Sadanand has documented the entire process of learning so caringly:

> A lot of ideological issues were raised in our discussions. For example, the origins and manifestations of formal concepts in the media and art; the relationship of formal space to social space; objects to objectification; coordination to alienation; perspective to consciousness; objective relations to relations of production; colour to caste system; gradations to hierarchies; scale to value — both economic and social.[3]

Clearly, this is a dense framework of ideas which could easily have become very abstract if the learning/teaching process had not been concretised through human exchange and a predominantly informal atmosphere of 'research.' It was Dashrath who set the tone by facing the participants with their first challenge: 'Let's see if you can introduce yourselves through drawings. I would like to see your village, workplace, house, what you like most in your village.' At one level, this 'visual' introduction was able to cut through some of the linguistic barriers in the group; only three of the trainees were comfortable in English. While the bilinguists in the group translated much of the discussion into Tamil for the benefit of others, the visual medium of 'drawing' was one language that transcended the difference in words.

Another purpose of the 'visual' introduction was to make the participants realise the necessity of confronting the basic 'grammar' of visual communication without which no message can be transmitted. It is one thing to conceptualise a problem in theoretical terms, quite another to communicate it to people in a language that is both intelligible and vivid. Needless to say, the 'visual' has a particular potency in areas of work where the people being addressed may be illiterate, yet open to the larger process of education through 'visual thinking.'

While the actual act of 'documenting' their environment enabled the trainees to view their lives more critically, it was enlightening for the 'project leaders' to question their own metropolitan assumptions of 'development' and perspective on how the 'rural poor' live. It was through such exchanges that the distinction between 'teachers' and 'students' broke down and a process of self-questioning was initiated for everyone in the group. It is, perhaps, not surprising that after the workshop was over, the trainees initiated their own workshops in villages inspired by their experience at Skills.

Learning Through Posters

After the first workshop, which had lasted for three months, it was decided that more intensive workshops lasting three days to a week would probably be more effective and easier to organise. Skills' most successful intervention in this regard was a one-day, 'open-to-the-public' poster workshop, which was held in the District Central Library in Madras city. The concept was at once original and bold. In connection with the local state assembly elections to be held in nine states, Skills invited concerned citizens to paint posters reflecting their own perspective on a particular theme: 'Parliamentary democracy has become a mechanism for subduing citizens.' While this statement was part of the rhetoric in 'alternative' political circles, no one had used it so far to elicit individual responses from the citizens themselves. Once again, by concentrating on a visual medium (posters), Skills was able to cut through the rhetoric of politics by eliciting personal statements through images.

Whether the novelty of the workshop was the essential source of attraction or whether it appealed to peoples' needs to express themselves politically, the fact is that by 6 p.m. on the appointed day close to 380 people participated in the workshop, including the late film director G. Aravindan, a close friend of Chandra and Sadanand, and many artists from Cholamandalam. The method of displaying the posters was also ingenious: clotheslines hung across the walls, on which posters dripping with paint were pegged. Discussions were initiated around each of the posters, with the 'artist' being questioned about his or her choice in relation to the larger realities of politics. In this process of questioning, a dynamic process of learning developed in which criticism, praise, and suggestions combined in a friendly discussion where no one was a guru or even a 'project leader.'

After this forum, it was decided that something should be done with the posters. Once again a meeting was organised which was attended by about fifty participants from the previous workshop and a few new faces. A collective decision was reached on holding a mobile exhibition of some of the posters, which could be shown in different parts of the city a few days before the election. Apart from questioning the criteria to be used in selecting the most 'effective' images, the group also began to reflect on how they differed from the more mainstream political images. As the content of each poster became more sharply delineated, it was decided that the participants in the 'exhibition' would also serve as commentators attempting to engage spectators in a discussion on the images.

Using bamboos and palm leaf mats (*thattis*) as the base for setting up the posters, the participants travelled to at least six public spaces in Madras displaying the posters in busy locations on Mount Road and near the railway station. Since the *thattis* were light, they could easily be carried by hand or on rickshaws. Hanging them on pavement railings was also not much of a problem.

Still later, when it was decided to create a fresh group of posters, which would attempt to present an 'abstract' as it were of the earlier posters, the *thattis* were replaced by collapsible cartons of refrigerators. All that was needed were four such cartons with posters placed on four sides with images relating to communalism, the atrocities committed on *harijans*, electoral malpractices, among other political realities. For these posters, Dashrath also used an ingenious method of screen-printing, where the photo-process was substituted by a more rudimentary use of blocks and stencils. Flour and hand-made dyes provided a cheap, yet effective alternative to printing ink.

Directly related to the effectiveness of these images was the discussion generated around them. From Sadanand's log we learn that the spectators initially acknowledged their inability to intervene in the electoral process apart from voting mechanically for this or that party candidate. 'What can we do? We know politicians are crooks. All of them. But how can we ordinary people participate in or determine political processes that seem remote from us?' Instead of dismissing the question or haranguing the spectators with Marxist rhetoric, the strategy adopted by the Skills members was to initiate a discussion on the following lines: 'If one cannot join politicians, then how can we as citizens organise our own forums? How do we regulate the power assumed by the government, the very power that they claim to have received from the people?' Consistently, there was an attempt to counter defeatism or cynicism among the spectators with simple, yet strong resolutions: 'Let us express ourselves. Let us resist passivity.'

Street Theatre

The critique of the State was possibly most trenchant in a street play organised by Skills in connection with electoral promises and malpractices. No medium, to my mind, has greater political effectiveness than theatre. This is particularly true of street plays where the message is rendered with total immediacy in a potentially volatile situation, where the action of the play can be interrupted at any point. This can be fatal as in the case of Safdar Hashmi and other street theatre workers who have been killed while protesting their right to perform on the street.[4] While the activity of street theatre has now gained a new respectability through appropriations by cultural groups, it continues to pose a threat to the political establishment.

In the documentation that exists of the street play organised by Skills, one can sense its effectiveness, both theatrically and politically. Reduced to a bare eight minutes, the play began with an actor clarifying the basic position of the group: 'We do not represent any party or faction. We are interested in asking questions.' This was followed by an impersonation of various politicians accompanied by snatches of their rhetoric. While one politician would describe himself as 'a servant of the people', another would promise to provide jobs to the unemployed youth. Yet another would claim that his party was capable of abolishing poverty, and so on. This spectrum of political promises would then be cut by a Kattiyankaran, a Vidushaka-like figure, who would sing a song: 'Now that the elections are over/Let's see who gets power.'

In the next sequence, an empty picture frame would be dangled in the performance space whereupon all the 'politicians' would rush to seize it. Eventually one of them would place the frame around his head and pose as the 'victorious' politician. Around him, placards would be then be raised representing coveted objects like a bungalow, a car, a plane, a moneybag. These placards would be placed in such a way that they would seem like the extremities of the politician's hands.

This striking 'visual' would then be disrupted by a song, which was Chandra's contribution to the piece, a Tamil protest song containing the insistent refrain: 'We are cheated, we are cheated. Over and over we are cheated.' Following the song, a large banner with 'DEMOCRACY' painted on its surface would be stretched in the background, while a few actors would turn to the spectators and sing: 'People will be ruled by laws, police, jails, MISA, torture, emergencies. And almost as a logical process, democracy will languish and die.' At this point the banner would be clapped together with a banging sound, and it would be transformed into a funeral bier. This was the closing image of the piece — the death of 'DEMOCRACY' — which was accompanied by a vigorous Tamil death-dance along with drumming and singing.

Even this cursory description of the piece reveals its subversive comment on electoral politics. One can understand why the play was disrupted in one particular show by members of a political party who claimed that 'they would not allow anyone without political backing to come on the streets and question all parties.' At yet another place, it appears that the 'police muscled in with their rules and regulations.' From these interventions, one can sense a more direct critique of the party system in this play than the earlier poster campaigns organised by Skills. In these earlier ventures there was at least the possibility of 'regulating' the power assumed by the State. Now there was a more clear-cut denial of such a possibility.

Reading between the lines of Sadanand's log, one traces a political transition in Skills' activities beginning with an endorsement of a 'pedagogy of the oppressed' (very much on Paulo Freire's lines), leading to an organisation of open forums made up of concerned citizens, developing into a more critical interaction with the general public on political matters, culminating in a militant rejection of the system: 'There are no choices anymore. People are only asked to endorse. Parliament is made out to be an organ of the "entire people" instead of being what it is — an instrument of class oppression.' Taken out of context, this kind of statement could easily be misinterpreted as an endorsement of 'ultra Leftist Naxalite activity' or 'anarchism' or any philosophy that could be conveniently categorised as 'anti-State'. This, unfortunately, is what happened.

The Raid

In August 1982, the police raided the property of Skills and charged Sadanand and Chandra with sedition under Section 124A. What followed was a nightmare that continued for eight long months. Their phones were tapped, their letters intercepted, their friends harrassed and investigated, their passports impounded. Worst of all, their mobility was restricted since they were compelled to present themselves in front of a magistrate every fortnight. This is one period in Chandra's life that has possibly left the deepest scars and tensions. While she and Sadanand were ultimately to be cleared of any association with sedition — indeed, the police themselves withdrew their complaint after eight months with the judge adding a piquant note to the final hearing by asking the 'accused' how he should word the order — the entire experience was profoundly debilitating and violent.

And yet, the case did open up all kinds of unanswered questions about 'sedition' itself, which has been (and continues to be) grossly misused by the police, legitimising all kinds of raids and invasions of privacy. In a larger historical context, one was unavoidably reminded of Gandhiji's pertinent statement: 'If working for the freedom of people is sedition, then I am seditious.' Sadanand himself believes that the law should be declared null and void in a free society. Apart from legitimising paranoid reactions towards modes of protest, the charge of sedition also vitiates the basic right of freedom of speech in a democratic society.

At a more immediate level, it is very likely that the case itself was instigated by some ill-wishers of Skills, and more specifically of Sadanand and Chandra. 'Interpersonal tensions' have been responsible for the destruction, if not demise of more than one development group, and Skills was no exception. Significantly, both Sadanand and Chandra were charged specifically as individuals. The organisation itself was not accused of 'seditious practices.' Nor were the other members, including Dashrath, singled out for their involvement in Skills' activities. Predictably, this was a time when Chandra and Sadanand were able to differentiate between their real supporters (the ones who stood by them through the crisis, wrote about it in newspapers and attended the court sessions) and their fake supporters and alleged friends who advised others to stay away from Skills.

Regardless of the crisis, the fact is that for all the seeming 'smallness' of its scale of operation, and after barely two years of work, Skills had obviously unnerved the complacency of certain powers. Sadanand puts it accurately today when he says that, 'At the very root of the discontent was the antipathy to the idea that different classes of people should move and work together like a composite group.' It was this ability of Skills to mobilise public support cutting across caste and class barriers that posed the real threat to the 'law.' Sadanand's 'inflammatory' articles in *Indian Express* and *Tughluq*, allegedly causing 'disaffection among needy sections of society', were merely pretexts for the charge of sedition thrust on him. As for Chandra, she was an obvious target for her general outspokenness and radical flair. The fact that she was a single woman associating freely with men must also have stirred the patriarchal prejudices that invariably surface in confrontations involving dancers and the police.

Just one detail is sufficient to describe the uncouth intervention of the police, which can more accurately be described as an invasion of privacy. In searching for incriminating evidence among Chandra's letters, they seized on one with a callous display of power. 'Who is this Aurobindo?' they demanded, addressing one of Sri Aurobindo's letters written to Harindranath Chattopadhyay, which Chandra happened to have in her treasured collection of personal letters. Today this kind of *asuric* ignorance on the part of the police is almost ludicrous, if not grotesque. It was however no laughing matter for Chandra when it actually happened, and she is unable to forgive or forget it, to this day.

After the Raid

In the immediate aftermath of the raid, both Chandra and Sadanand were physically numb for some time. The experience had been shattering for Chandra in particular, and she had lost much of her effervescence. To regain her spirit, she began to hold regular dance sessions for herself with Udupi Lakshminarayan, one of Guru Ellappa's most trusted students. In the meantime, Sadanand went back to writing about politics and culture. Gradually, it became clear to both of them that Skills would have to shift gear and focus even more sharply on cultural activities. The strategies of 'development' in cultural forums were slowly changing by this time with the increased use of video and television as the dominant media for communication. It was necessary to rethink the possibility of shaping cultural alternatives within the changing context of voluntary organisations.

Today these groups are better known as non-government organisations, many of which are lucrative businesses receiving support both from foreign funding agencies and from the government itself. What had started off as an essentially grass-roots movement, consciously opposed to governmental and party affiliations, has gradually institutionalised itself with its own hierarchies, internal bureaucracies, competitive relations with other groups, and capitulations to 'codes of conduct' formulated by the 'experts' of the 'development' world.

Particularly problematic today is the open invitation by the government to non-government organisations (NGO's) to facilitate official policies in the name of development. Not only has this depoliticised the movement, it has even, perhaps, intensified the process of misrepresenting and exploiting the rural poor. While it may not have been ideologically inappropriate in the mid-seventies to link the early non-government organisations with the opposition parties, the problem emerged when these parties came into power. Now it would seem that NGO's have been recognised by all political parties as potential vote banks, and it may not be long before the majority of them get totally identified as government organisations in their own right.

Confronting the changes in the attitudes to 'development' in the early eighties, Chandra and Sadanand decided to opt for greater autonomy by reaffirming one of the most marginalised areas in 'development work': culture. This emerged more out of Chandra's instincts as an artist rather than Sadanand's more militant consciousness as an activist. For a long time after the raid he continued to brood. Often he would argue with Chandra: 'What have we done wrong? Let's fight it out openly. Why are you afraid?' And it was at this point that Chandra was compelled to admit that she was afraid. As she puts it so honestly: 'Though you may be a rebel, though you have the strength to fight, yet you have this fear of vulgarity, of *bibhatsa* which demeans you.'

Chandra's choice was to return to dance. In her first days with Lakshminarayan, she admits 'feeling like a rag.' But she soon started restoring her energies, returning to the very sources of movement that she had learned from Guru Ellappa and finding a different energy in them not just to create, but to fight and live. Slowly through an inner process of realisation, she learned that 'there is a way of coping with brutality through creativity', and that the body is at the very centre of this process of renewal.

> Within the body there are resources on which you can draw to get back your spine. It is like the earth which has the secrets of 'reviving' itself. When there is a crisis in life and a crisis in the body — when the spine feels chill — you can become 'normal', accept 'security', submit to 'norms' that are not your own. It is only through creativity that you can resist the brutalisation. You learn to confront. You don't 'cope'. A 'fight' emerges within yourself, not with the other. A fight with the other will further brutalise you.

At this point Chandra breaks her reflection and looks in the direction of Sadanand who has been participating in our discussion with profound silence. More than ten years have passed since they were both charged with sedition. And it would seem that while Sadanand's profession as a journalist compels him to continue the 'fight with the other', he has also learned the lessons of the 'inner' fight that Chandra has embraced in her life. Already by 1984 there must have been some realisation of how they could continue to live and 'fight' together. The activity of Skills continued but in close association with its sister organisation and *alter ego*, the Cultural Centre, which had been registered in 1976. It was under this banner that Chandra produced her landmark production of *Angika* which established her return not only to dance but to a new awareness of the possibilities of the body as a source of resistance.

5

The East-West Dance Encounter

Chandra returned to dance when she was invited to participate in the first East-West Dance Encounter organised jointly by the Max Mueller Bhavan and the National Centre for the Performing Arts (NCPA) in Bombay between January 22-29, 1984. By this time most people had almost forgotten her work as a dancer. She herself was vaguely associated with a radical life-style determined by anti-establishment values. Not only did her participation in the Encounter establish the originality and power of her conception of dance, it even stimulated her to create her first major production in years, *Angika*, which was produced at the second East-West Dance Encounter a year later.

From this point on, Chandra has not looked back as a dancer and choreographer, adding significantly to her repertoire with new productions almost every year. Indeed, her most prolific and productive period as an artist can be traced back to these last nine years beginning with the first East-West Encounter in which she revived *Tillana* (from *Devadasi*) and *Surya Namaskar* (from *Navagraha*). For the Encounter, she also created a special piece entitled *Primal Energy* in collaboration with Kamadev, who through sheer coincidence happened to be visiting India three weeks before the Encounter. This was the first time that he and Chandra had danced together since *Navagraha* in 1972-73.

Undeniably, the Encounter was a breakthrough for Chandra. The ugly experience with the raid had been left behind and she was dancing in public after twelve years. Almost everyone around her was supportive, notably Rukmini Devi, who had graciously allowed her to use four dancers from Kalakshetra for the revival of *Tillana*. At the NCPA itself, Chandra was greeted with much warmth and cheer by a range of artists who welcomed her back to the world of dance. Sadanand, who was interacting with dancers for the first time, remembers the celebratory mood backstage involving friends like Sonal Mansingh, Protima Bedi, Bhupen Khakhar, Sunil Kothari, Astad Deboo, Rohinton Cama, among other artists. Since Chandra was an 'unknown quantity', people were genuinely curious about what she was going to do. Consequently, there was a total absence of competitiveness and backbiting, which changed somewhat after Chandra's presentation became one of the highlights of the Encounter.

While the dances themselves were warmly received, it was Chandra's voice at the seminar which really made an impact. The writer-journalist Anees Jung put it well when, in an interview with Chandra following the Encounter, she wrote: 'Generating passion, the color of a wild flame, was Chandralekha. Commitment and fervour dazzled in her words. Her irreverence commanded attention.'[1] The point is that Chandra's voice rang true in the seminar. She was speaking from experience, not just of dance, but of her life itself. And this could not fail to be contrasted with the artifice of established dancers, who almost flaunted their *prima donna* ways. At least one of them began her presentation with the priceless words, 'The day I was born, I knew I was going to be a dancer.'

Such affectation characterised most of the Indian dancers' responses which contrasted sharply with the more questioning and socially concerned attitudes of their western colleagues, most notably Susanne Linke, in whom Chandra found a soul-mate. Part of the problem had to do with the very nature of the forum which had invited dancers to share some creative work and personal statements about dance with other dancers. This was altogether different from the forum of solo performances that classical Indian dancers have perfected over the years. In these programmes, dance items are invariably interspersed with the obligatory commentary on the microphone, which almost becomes a performance in its own right with the dancer advertising her art in impeccable English with a smattering of Sanskrit.

At the Encounter, there was more debate and critical inquiry into areas of life, history, and politics that most Indian dancers had never addressed. Indeed, one can justifiably regard the Encounter as a catalytic event in the largely moribund dance scene of India. Significantly, the vacuum in the cultural scene was addressed not by official cultural organisations like the Sangeet Natak Akademi and the Indian Council for Cultural Relations but by a 'foreign' organisation, the Max Mueller Bhavan in collaboration with the National Centre for the Performing Arts. As much as one has reason to be wary of intercultural interventions 'from outside', it would be both parochial and inaccurate to deny the efficacy of the 'foreign' intervention that made the East-West Encounter possible in the first place.

This is not to deny that the Encounter was free of problems. One obvious difficulty in establishing a vibrant dialogue had to do with the very selection of the dancers, with the 'West' being represented predominantly by 'modern' dance practitioners still in the process of defining their idioms, the 'East' almost totally equated with 'classical' dance traditions from India. It is not surprising therefore, that the western participants were more vocal and analytical given their predominantly self-conscious and reflexive search for valid expressions of dance within the context of our times. The Indian dancers, on the other hand, sequestered within the imagined securities of their respective traditions, maintained a more 'dignified, if discreet silence' (as Anees Jung describes it), their presentations being questioned primarily by western dancers studying Indian dance forms. Predictably, it was the western representatives in the forum who questioned the western presentations as well, the Indian participants continuing to maintain their silence in the absence of any critical inquiry, or perhaps even curiosity about 'other' dance idioms.

In this context, the power of Chandra's intervention was palpable in so far as she was able to break this silence, and not just discreetly, but explosively. Her presentation on 'Contemporary Relevance in Classical Dance — A Personal Note', which has been published and documented on film, was stirringly bold and self-questioning. In her articulation about dance one could see how her years away from performance had helped her to gain a critical perspective on its 'contemporaneity.' Quite simply, Chandra was perhaps the only Indian participant who was in a position to deal ideologically with the problematics of classical dance in a contemporary context. She had both the language of the activist and the experience of a dancer to make her own synthesis about the possibilities of dance in the Indian context. And therefore, it is not surprising that she was able to negotiate the larger categories assumed by the organisers of the seminar by defining her position through them, and at times, in spite of their assumptions, by affirming her own language as a dancer.

Problematising the Encounter

In this context, her own stance *vis-à-vis* the categories of 'East' and 'West' are worth examining in a wider historical context. One of the ironies of the revival of classical Indian dance is generally attributed to the interest shown in our 'traditional culture' by foreign artists. It is well known in this regard that Anna Pavlova had personally advised at least two great Indian dancers, Uday Shankar and Rukmini Devi, to rediscover their own dance heritage. Equally influential was the vicarious interest in 'the East' shown by Ruth St. Denis and Ted Shawn from the United States, whose 'imagined versions of Indian dance'[2] in a celebrated tour to India conducted in the early decades of this century, had apparently inspired the metropolitan elite in Indian cultural circles to rediscover their 'tradition'.

Earlier, St. Denis had been regaling audiences in America with her spectacular representation of oriental vignettes in productions like *Radha, Incense, Nautch, Yogi,* and *The Cobras* (in which she had played a snake charmer, using her bejewelled hands to represent a ritualistic dance of the snakes). What needs to be emphasised here is that this naive evocation of the Orient was far from 'innocent' politically. In the close reading of St. Denis' aesthetic provided by Doris Humphrey, one of the great pioneers of modern dance in America, one learns of the racist, anti-semitic, and blatantly commercial drives underlying the enterprise of St. Denis and

Shawn.³ This has yet to be studied in depth with particular relation to the 'orientalist' images of India that our own dancers have endorsed and indeed, elaborated on in their 'discovery of India.'

Though this historical background was not addressed at the East-West Encounter, some of its implications were possibly in Chandra's mind when she admitted the 'mediation of the West' in determining our very perception of the 'traditional arts' in the first place.⁴ Clarifying her own position by refusing either to 'reject the West' (and thereby valorise 'the security of our little islands') or 'accept the West' unconditionally (without beginning a confrontation of our 'wealth of traditions'), Chandra advocated an understanding of 'the East' on its own terms. Less categorically, she emphasised the need to make 'linkages' between the interdisciplinary principles underlying the various arts in India, which are central to the concept of *rasa*.

This is where, I think, Chandra's intervention is strikingly 'modern' in impulse. Refusing to reject the framework of principles provided by 'traditional' disciplines of thought and expression, she nonetheless assumes a right to interpret them according to her needs. *Rasa*, therefore, that most obscure of concepts which has been rendered almost inscrutable by generations of commentators, becomes, in Chandra's more down-to-earth language, the 'capacity of an individual to be integrated with herself, with society and nature.' Countering its overtly aestheticised aura, Chandra chose to emphasise the liberational possibilities of *rasa* through its capacity to 'recharge' human beings. In an 'epoch of social fracture', where the human body is no longer a 'centre' in its own right but a 'target of attack', this drive towards 'regeneration of the human spirit' is nothing short of 'radical.' It is obvious that in such an interpretation, *rasa* is not just an aesthetic experience, but an energy that animates not just the performance but the world around it. While affirming the possibilities of generating *rasa*, Chandra also acknowledged the struggle involved in realising it in the first place.

All this was expressed in so direct a manner that it

enhanced the credibility of Chandra's position, even if one did not agree with it. Few could deny that she had *tested* what she was talking about. Particularly moving in this regard was Chandra's choice to 'begin' her discourse with a critical scrutiny of her *arangetram* (described in Chapter 2) in which she had experienced a momentary split between 'art' and 'life'. Here again, instead of wallowing in some kind of self-conscious angst, Chandra used it as a starting point to speculate on how fragmentation can be resisted in a continuing quest to 'remain sensitive and whole.' In this regard, what reinforced her polemic was her recognition of the transformative possibilities of our 'tradition', so long as it is open to being questioned, experienced, and if necessary rejected at certain levels to meet the inner necessities of one's creative work.

Yet another aspect that contributed to the articulation of her position at the Encounter had to do with her focus on the 'material' base of dance 'rooted in the soil, in the region, in the community, in the society, in the work rhythms, habits and behaviour, food patterns and social relations and in racial characteristics like noses, skin, eyes, hair — a whole lot of accumulations that go by the name of culture.' In spelling out the 'material' constituents of her concept of 'culture', Chandra was consciously taking a stand against the divine origins and manifestations of dance. Once again this differentiated her from most of the other classical Indian dancers whose deification of the gods on stage did not necessarily correspond with their social behaviour and beliefs off-stage.

No one was more scathing about these apparent double standards than Georg Lechner, one of the chief organisers of the Encounter representing the Max Mueller Bhavan, who criticised the metropolitan Indian dancer's failure to respond to the contradictions of a changing world:

> They continue to dance as if nothing had changed. God has taken on new dimensions of terror. Don't depict him in the old way. Depict him including the new way. Or if you don't believe in God anymore

then say so.... The question in India now is whether this sacred element is honestly felt and is deep enough to carry on the dance in the next millenium. Either India goes back to the depths of its mythology or is honest enough to admit that we no longer have the temple dancer's view nor can we live that life. It needs to reflect on the new reality and evolve an appropriate language.[5]

In addition, Lechner focused on contradictory behavioural traits exemplifying the double standards of Indian dancers:

> One of the dancers said off-stage that she hated gurus. The next day she was on stage going through the ritual of bowing and touching the guru's feet. So the tradition goes on but the feeling of real respect no longer exists.[6]

More problematically, Lechner had to deal with artistic tantrums. Some dancers, for instance, refused 'to accept the challenge', in his words, of dancing for one hour or less, and more specifically, of sharing the programme with other dancers. One of them, it appears, wanted to dance an entire number the day after her performance was over, while another danced only half her programme.

So far as the general vanity of the classical dance world in India is concerned, he was certainly right in pointing out the *prima donna* attitudes of some of its leading practitioners. In this regard, he was simply substantiating the earlier criticism of luminaries like V. Raghavan and Balasaraswati who were pained by the superficiality of performers more interested in changing their saris at least twice in the course of a steadily diminishing *margam* instead of concentrating on the inner journey of their performance.[7] Lechner merely extended this criticism by addressing the off-stage vanity of the performers which resulted in at least one of them demanding a deluxe suite with provision for ten musicians rather than four.

Reflecting on the vanity of the classical dance world, Chandra attempted to contextualise it within the larger realities of the 'social isolation' faced by most dancers. In this respect, she pointed out Yamini Krishnamurthy's somewhat disdainful attitude towards establishing 'linkages' with other artists, which was only too evident in her remark: 'I am open if they work under me.'[8] For Chandra, this attitude was 'archaic', and it is to the credit of the East-West Encounter that such exchanges between dancers, however painful, were actually possible for the first time in a cultural forum.

Thus, when probing the inner logic of choreography, the forum at the East-West Encounter also questioned Yamini Krishnamurthy's decision to make her dancers repeat the same movement in unison: 'Yamini, tell us, if six Yaminis are dancing exactly the same thing, how does it enhance the show? What is the rationale for such a quantitative statement?'[9] Such a 'statement', equally visible in the mechanistic 'group choreography' of the other productions in the Encounter, compelled Sadanand in his critical retrospective of the event to question:

> How will we ever grow out of all these clichés of the spectacle, all these conspicuous quantities of effects, all these frozen tableaux, to something that is dynamic and alive and capable of not just seducing the eye, but energising the body?[10]

It was Sadanand also who reflected critically on the issue of 'contemporaneity' in dance *vis-à-vis* the social and political realities of our time. While many dancers at the Encounter made an issue of the fact that they danced because they 'liked' dancing 'for themselves' (which was Sonal Mansingh's position) or that they were not going to 'hold up flags for any cause' because, as Kumudini Lakhia put it, they 'needed their hands to dance',[11] the point is that the dancers had no reason to be entirely coy about politics. Stating his position unequivocally, Sadanand wrote:

> Anyone who has seen the contributions of Yamini Krishnamurthy and Padma Subrahmaniam to the

Emergency exercise — quite voluntarily and without being prompted by seminars and encounters — knows pretty well how 'contemporary' they can be when they want. Yamini, subsequently, even protested in genuine surprise when a *Times of India* interviewer questioned her on this and said: 'I have not deviated from tradition. It has been our tradition to praise our rulers.'[12]

This extreme naivete could be ignored were it not for the fact that it endorses *status quo* values affirmed by the political establishment.

When questioned herself about the social relevance of dance, Chandra had the foresight to confront the question without adopting a pamphleteering position. Unlike the other dancers, she was in a position ideologically to protect her autonomy as an artist without subscribing to the norms of 'relevance' determined by politicians and social scientists. Thus, her way of confronting the question was to analyse its premises: 'When people say "why don't you portray social realities" they are invariably trying to transfer their feelings of guilt (about the way things are) on to the artists.'[13] This, however, does not mean that a dancer should function without a social consciousness. Rather, what needs to be emphasised is that this consciousness has to be embodied in the language of dance itself within the 'unexplored wealth of its form.'

In addressing the 'social relevance' of dance, therefore, it is both unfair and crude to expect any dancer to translate the 'ugliness' of social realities directly into dance. The language of dance operates at many levels of abstraction and psychological complexity, drawing on principles of 'inner space' and 'alchemy' that have their own logic. It is only by delving into the principles of this logic that a dancer can begin to shape a language that can 'recharge' human beings, and thereby, facilitate a resistance towards the mechanisation and violence of our times.

Primal Energy

In addition to Chandra's talk at the Encounter, the participants had an opportunity to see her principles in action. Along with the revival of *Tillana,* the audience was also able to witness a very different exploration of 'inner energy' in *Surya Namaskar,* which provided yet another glimpse of Chandra's early attempt in *Navagraha* to explore 'linkages' between dance and Yoga. The *cause célèbre* of the evening, however, was Chandra's new creation, *Primal Energy,* set to the *lingashtakam* attributed to Shankaracharya. In this work, which was performed with Kamadev only once, Chandra created something of a sensation, with the audience at once enamoured and shocked by her bold representation of the *yoni/lingam* interaction and assertion of the 'female energy principle' as 'primary' to the act of creation.

Among the sources of inspiration for *Primal Energy,* Chandra recalls her long-standing fascination for a particular sculpture in Kanchipuram depicting the goddess Kamakshi embracing the *lingam.* This image moved Chandra at many levels and served as a stimulus for her own response to the *lingam* in the dance language of *Primal Energy.* At another level, Chandra recalls the inspiration received from the ornate rhetoric of the *lingashtakam.* With her inimitable candour, which has often been dismissed as iconoclastic, Chandra admits that she was 'amused' by it: 'The soft, sensual feelings evoked by the language seemed to be totally remote from the reality of the *lingam* as I perceived it. What drew me to the verses was its combination of the sacred and humorous.' Though this attitude does not manifest itself directly in the choreography, which seems devoid of irony, it undeniably contributed to the modernist idiom of *Primal Energy.*

The juxtaposition and celebration of male/female sexualities in *Primal Energy* was drawn specifically from Tantric sources. As I have mentioned earlier, these sources had become intensely familiar to Chandra over the years through her imaginative exploration of texts and icons associated with the Shakti cult of worship. Once again it needs to be emphasised that it was the 'sensuous' and 'poetic' aspects of these sources that had roused her curiosity and visual sense as an artist, particularly in matters relating to colour and graphics. In dance language, it was the 'physicality' of these images that inspired the dynamics of movement in her choreography, and not the 'mystification of religion' associated with these images.

This has always been the crux of the problem in assessing Chandra's work: while, for some spectators, this conscious separation of the 'sensual' and 'religious' context of the image is either arbitrary or not particularly credible, for other spectators (and particularly, for those shocked by *Primal Energy*) the separation borders on a kind of blasphemy with the *lingam* and *yoni* being reduced to sexual organs rather than symbols of a divine order.

In *Primal Energy* there is neither *shringara* nor *bhakti,* acceptable contexts of male/female interaction within the sacred auspices of a larger Reality. There is instead what Pria Devi, one of the most sensitive commentators on Chandra's work, has described as a return to 'the older, more powerful ambivalence of the *tantras*.'[14] This is Chandra's 'take-off point' for her conceptualisation of the piece. Situating the 'Tantric tradition' within the context of a larger, 'anti-Brahmanic, protest movement', Chandra made no attempt to disguise her challenge thrown to middle-class sentiment and respectability in her 'homage to the *lingam*.' It is this very sentiment and respectability that have contributed to the 'brahminisation' of Bharatanatyam in the first place.

At a very obvious level there was reason to be 'shocked' by the stark visualisation of the *yoni* and *lingam* on stage. No one to date had actually attempted to represent these icons through the human body. While they could be invoked, poeticised, worshipped, suggested through *mudras,* no one had actually dared to represent them through the presence of a man and woman on stage. This was no adaptation of a Tantric ritual, but a conscious, personal artistic attempt to represent 'primal' energies within a contemporary choreographic structure. Through the very intimacy of the performance space, the erotics of the piece was defined, enhanced through a relentlessly spare idiom which has now become identified with Chandra's choreography. Instead of catering to voyeuristic sentiments, she settled for starkness in which the dynamics of male/female energies could be at once enjoyed and scrutinised.

Responding to the erotics of the piece and the possibilities of its misinterpretation, Pria Devi wrote:

> Nothing that Chandra does is ever in bad taste. Nothing she does lacks vitality and a sense of reverence. She returns to source.... But for audiences accustomed to the watered-down flirtatiousness of cinema heroines under the name of minor godesses, it may be more dangerous.[15]

It is precisely this sense of 'danger' that lies at the heart of the continuing objections to *Primal Energy* on 'moralistic' grounds. What makes the danger perceptible is the very directness of the eroticism where the audience is compelled to confront its own response to sensuality. It is the very denial of titillation, therefore, that makes the 'thrill' of experiencing the piece so challenging and joyous. Titillations are, however, what most audiences have become accustomed to, particularly through the intervention of the mass media, where entire families can watch the most blatant objectification of women on television commercials, without confronting their assimilation of this material. Countering this phenomenon, *Primal Energy* compelled its spectators to confront the erotics of its idiom and thereby question their own assumptions of sexuality in life and art.

The piece itself was structured in four parts that were subtly punctuated through variations in sound and rhythm, yet held together through a continuum of energy that built to a climax. In the opening sequence, which was accompanied by the invocatory verses of the *lingashtakam*, Kama would represent the total stillness of the *lingam* in a sitting posture. Chandra, on the other hand, would represent the activising female principle through predominantly vertical movements by which she attempted to suggest the 'embrace' of the *lingam* with her entire body. The intimacy of the sequence was generated as much through the close proximity of the two dancers as from the minimal distance that separated them.

In the second sequence, the roles were reversed with Chandra remaining still in what she describes as an 'open *yoni*' sitting position, with Kama building a cycle of energy through a series of movements from Bharatanatyam, Kuchipudi, and Chhau, culminating in jumps. Focusing on some of the leg movements and positions from these traditions, notably the 'interlocking of toes' position from Kuchipudi and the *ghora* movement from Chhau, Kama attempted to visualise the erection of the *lingam* in a burst of ecstasy. His movements were accompanied by a sustained chant concentrating on a single word '*Shiva*', which was sung on each note of the scale on an ascending octave at three different speeds. This musical choice, which was provocative in its own right, was part of Chandra's concept. It required considerable persuasion on her part to get Udupi Lakshminarayan and a group of singers to contribute to the vocal score.

Predictably, the third part of the piece built on what had preceded it with both Chandra and Kama dancing together, revolving around each other to suggest the 'unity' of the *Purusha-Prakriti* principle. As in *Navagraha*, Chandra recalls that 'there was a most fantastic involvement with the eyes', a vibrant dynamism that she has not experienced with any other dancer apart from Kama. This part of the dance was accompanied by the preceding chant of '*Shiva*' but in ascending and descending order on distinct scales.

During the rehearsal process, *Primal Energy* would culminate with this celebratory 'unity' of male/female energies. Sadanand, however, who saw it during this stage felt that it was a 'weak ending' and one that seemed to counter Chandra's own position regarding the 'primacy' of the 'female principle.' Noting his observation, which was possibly his first critical intervention in her choreography,

Chandra composed a final section for the piece. In this sequence, Kama would return to the still position with which he began the piece while Chandra (as *Prakriti*) attempted to evoke a sense of 'forging ahead and becoming one with everything.' It was on this expansive dilation of energy that the dance ended.

One deep source of regret is that Chandra had an opportunity to perform the piece with Kamadev only once. Immediately after the performance, he was compelled to return to his own dance assignments in Europe. Thus there was no opportunity for the piece to evolve and be tested in different forums for a wider range of spectators. This has resulted in a certain mystification around the performance itself which was harshly criticised when *Primal Energy* was revived for a more official performance in New Delhi in 1986 with Chandra partnering one of the martial arts performers in her group, Ashok Kumar.

Understandably, this was an altogether different performance with Ashok demonstrating the power of martial movements but without establishing the close intimacy and interrelatedness Kamadev had been able to establish with Chandra. Judging from the very negative critical reception, and some guarded self-criticism from Chandra and Sadanand themselves, one senses that the piece 'misfired.' Here one has no option but to acknowledge the primacy of *performance* in the realisation of any concept in dance. Without a perfect understanding and tuning of energies between the two performers, a piece like *Primal Energy* can be 'dangerous' in quite another respect from the context discussed above by failing to represent the dynamics of its vision.

In retrospect, one can only reiterate that there is a tremendous risk in performing *Primal Energy*. At one level, it is almost 'amateur' in the sheer immediacy of its vision, and I use the word 'amateur' not in the sense of a lack of 'professionalism' but as something 'raw', 'bold', *not afraid to fail*. In this context, one may question the idiom of the performance, but as a gesture affirming feminine sensibility and consciousness, the power of the piece cannot be denied.

Mandala

After her successful return to the dance world at the first East-West Encounter, Chandra had to confront new responsibilities and challenges. It was one thing to polemicise about the artifice and conceptual bankruptcy of the classical dance world, it was quite another matter to produce work that could make a counter-statement in the language of dance.

Among her admirers at the Encounter was an old friend, Soli Batliwalla, a Trustee of the Bhulabhai Desai Memorial Trust, who was affectionately known as Soli-*bhai* to hundreds of artists. He renewed his interest in offering Chandra a grant, which she had earlier resisted because she did not want to be affiliated to any institution. At the Encounter, however, Chandra was compelled to think more pragmatically about her future work which would necessitate some basic support for the dancers and martial artists whom she wanted to involve in her work. This time she herself pursued the grant offered by Soli-*bhai*. As she reflects retrospectively on this choice: 'Money always creates obligations. Once I received the grant I knew that I was obliged to produce something.'

Before Chandra could assemble a group of people to start preliminary work on *Angika* (which was, as yet, unformulated), the most major infrastructural development at Skills was the building of an open-air theatre called Mandala. For anyone who has danced in or simply visited this dreamspace, one can understand why it has served as the major source of inspiration for Chandra's work. Silently, yet eloquently, it has provided the ground and perspective for her holistic vision.

Once again it was Chandra who provided the architectural concept for Mandala, but the realisation of this concept would not have been possible without the active collaboration of Dashrath and Sadanand. They were the overseers of the entire construction in which they participated as craftsmen. Once it was built, Mandala marked the beginnings of the creative phase in the development of Skills.

Drawing on her own research and work, Chandra chose to crystallise her concept of a theatre space around the square grid of the Navagraha. The basic dimensions of the theatre are 54 feet by 54 feet, with its proportions determined around a unit of 9 feet. Such is the intimacy of the space that whether there are ten spectators or a hundred, it never feels empty. The 'centre' is established from almost any point in the space, whether one sits on the sand or on the stone benches that run along the walls which enhance the 'flow' of the space. The stage itself which has a sloping tiled roof, *cuddapah* stone floor, and mud wall, is just 1½ feet above the ground, which is the ideal height to view the dancers at eye-level. Such is the proportion of the overall space that it neither reduces nor accentuates the human scale of the dancer.

As for the elements, Mandala is always in touch with nature. Its eternal spectators are the sun and the moon. And there is not a single rehearsal or performance, in my experience at least, where the sky has not heightened the dance on stage. Somehow there is a continuum between the principles of movement on stage and the passing of clouds and the appearance and disappearance of stars. In the background, as always, there is the sea with its ceaseless ebb and flow of waves, which fluctuate so strangely from night to night.

It is a magical space no doubt, and yet so 'ordinary' that it is almost 'not there.' Its only 'embellishment' is a *mandala* of *cuddapah* stones in the centre of the courtyard which somehow seems to 'stretch' the space in opposite directions. This is obviously an optical illusion at some level, but it often feels as if the space itself is a dancer with two arms outstretched in a state of absolute poise.

At a more mundane level, it should be pointed out that Mandala was built with a budget of barely Rs.65,000 in 1984, which is an almost ludicrous amount of money when one considers the exorbitant sums that are spent on 'modern' theatre edifices. Most of the materials used for its construction were second-hand and recycled. Granite was used for the walls thereby minimising expenses on bricks and cement. In addition, Chandra's own hobby of collecting odds and ends from demolition sites including doors, beams, rafters, and knobs, came in handy. Today it is with pride that Sadanand and Dasharath as the master craftsmen of Mandala can claim: 'Practically everything in Mandala is from waste material.' Here one notes yet again the combination of talents that has facilitated Chandra's work. Mandala is not just the 'vision' of an artist. It has been realised through a knowledge of 'alternative technologies' while rejecting ethnicity and what Dashrath describes as 'visual noise' in so-called 'indigenous' architecture.

Having contructed Mandala, Chandra now had a space in which to work. As yet, she had no fixed plan for staging any particular production. In fact, she was not interested in producing anything. What concerned her was to involve a group of people in exploring their bodies through disciplines acquired by means of different physical traditions — dance, martial arts, Yoga, theatre. Characteristically, Chandra did not advertise for recruiting dancers in a formal way. The people who wanted to work with her approached her individually, or else she got in touch with them after chance meetings or through word of mouth. One of the first dancers to approach Chandra was Sumitra who had graduated from Kalakshetra. She in turn introduced Sujata, who was till quite recently one of the principal dancers in Chandra's company. In addition, there were two male dancer, Raghu from Pondicherry and Navtej, the only Sikh male dancer trained in Bharatanatyam at Kalakshetra.

Along with the dancers, Chandra got in touch with martial artists, notably Ashok Kumar, who had studied Kalarippayattu and massage at the C.V.N. Kalari in Kaduthuruthy, Kerala. Other martial arts practitioners, some of whom were also practising Yoga, included Nandakumar, Nagin, and Shekhar, who were known to each other primarily as students of Sri V. Pandian, the chief instructor of martial arts to the entire group at Skills. Apart from studying basic principles of martial movement from Sri Pandian, the group also explored a series of theatre games conducted by Bhagirathi Narayan, an actress based in Madras.

Through six months of arduous work involving the inter-relationships between Bharatanatyam, Yoga, and martial arts, Chandra began to concretise her landmark production of *Angika*, which will be described in the next chapter. Mandala was at once the site and the inspiration of the work, compelling its participants to discover new connections between different physical disciplines in their own bodies.

13

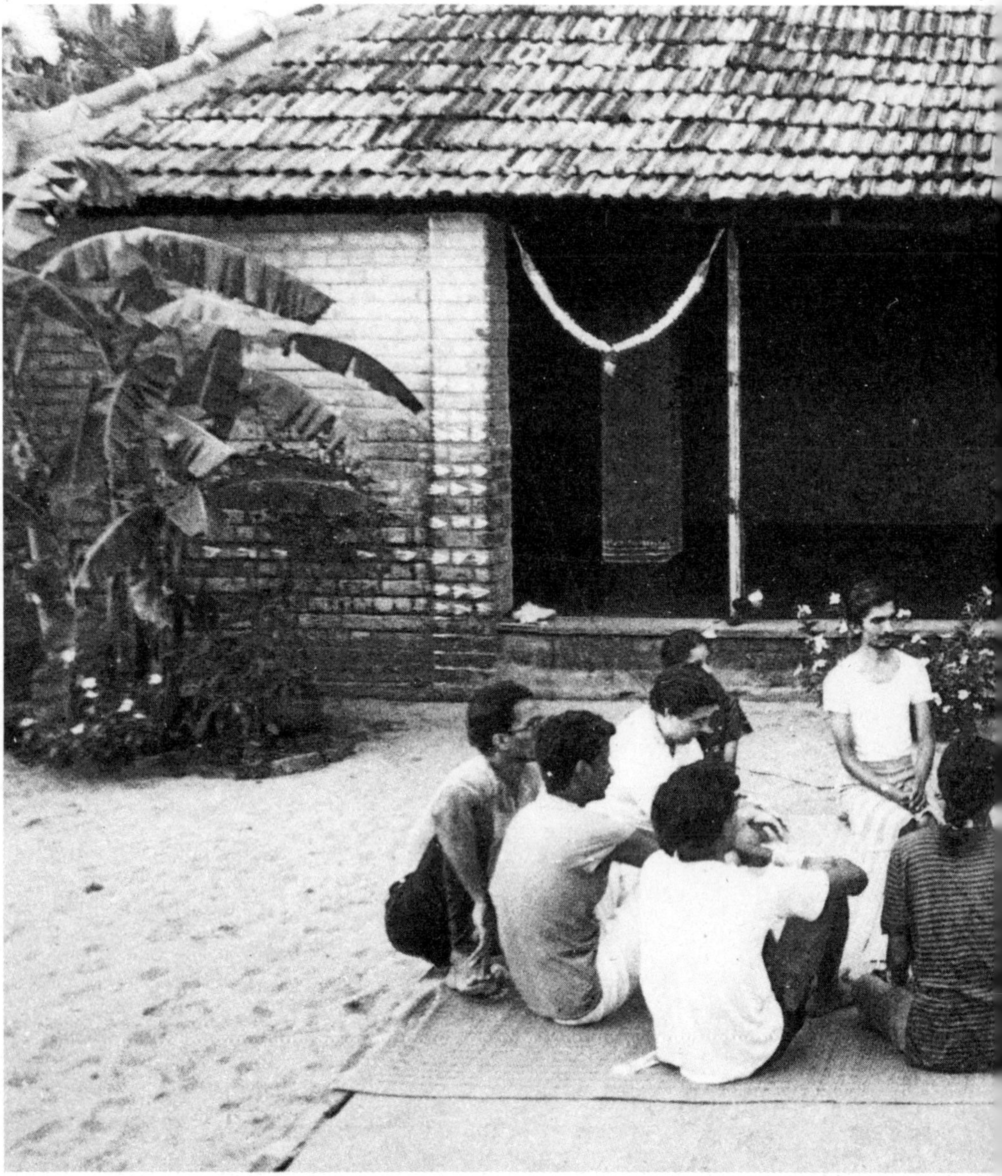

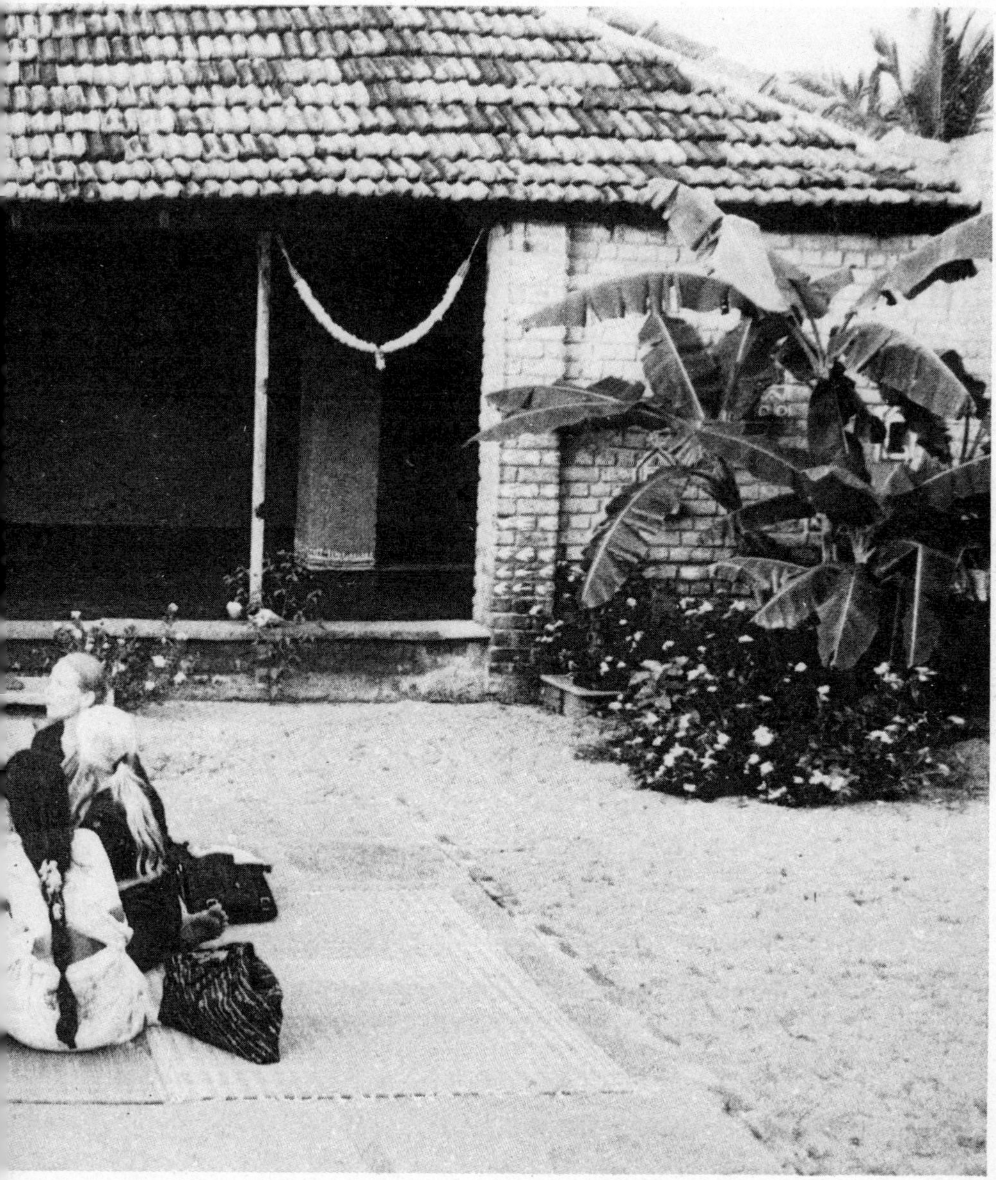

14

15

Angika

Angika can be regarded as Chandra's manifesto of the body in dance. It presents the turbulent, yet joyous evolution of dance through its origins in the 'cosmic energies' of prehistory, the warrior and animal movements of our protohistory, which are eventually crystallised in the primary movements of dance. Confronting the more recent developments of dance, which she had earlier thematised in *Devadasi,* Chandra traces the socialisation of dance through its appropriation by various patriarchal systems dominated by gods, priests, kings, courtiers, and men. Breaking this process of dehumanisation, *Angika* recalls earlier myths of women, notably the Naravahana, which radiates a power out of which a renewal of energies in dance is possible.

Undeniably, this is a broad sweep of history, which would seem to lend itself to the dramatic structure of a 'spectacle.' And yet, that is precisely what *Angika* resists through the sheer economy of its structure and the visual starkness of its choreography. Indeed, though the production is now most brilliantly realised, it can be more meaningfully viewed as a process which continues beyond the production itself. At no point can Chandra's dancers afford to forget *Angika*. They have to constantly return to it because it provides them with basic principles of movement, a total work-out of the body without which their dance could become decorative and even meaningless.

Significantly, *Angika* has gone through so many changes in its brief performance history that it is almost impossible to 'fix' a definitive choreography. Though the narrative scheme is more or less intact, the 'items' within the structure are constantly being restructured and edited. When it was first staged at Skills and later at the National Centre for the Performing Arts in Bombay in 1985, it was still a work-in-progress involving three women (including Chandra) and seven men. Now there are many more women whose participation in the martial sequences is getting increasingly active. In the earlier production, there were also sequences relating to the demonstration of *hastas* (which were silhouetted in the background); some very gymnastic *akasha bhramaris* (in which the dancers leap in the air with their legs and arms parallel to the ground); and a commentary in which Chandra would narrate the conceptual background of the entire production rather like a contemporary *sutradharini*.

All these sequences were edited in one of the more recent versions of the work which was staged in West Germany in June 1988 as part of the prestigious International Dance Festival, NRW. More recently, the *bhramari* and *hasta* sequences have been reinstated in an altered form in the production of *Angika* which travelled to Berlin in October 1992 as part of a festival organised by the House of World Culture and later to England as part of the Vivarta Festival. What I offer here is a description of some of the central elements in the production more in the nature of an evocation rather than a detailed documentation. The text is accompanied by some striking photographs of *Angika* by Dashrath Patel, who has been the 'travelling eye' of the production since its inception in 1985.

Cosmic Energy

For a long time Chandra did not know how to begin her 'history of the body.' At one level, there was a possibility of dramatising the opening chapter of the *Natyasastra* dealing with the origins of *natya*. It was also possible to evoke earlier myths like the *amrita-manthana* or 'churning of the ocean.' All these obvious beginnings with their religious overtones seemed to work against Chandra's critique of religiosity in dance. What she needed, therefore, was to find her own 'beginning' which would charge the production that followed with a particular energy and significance, apart from being arresting in its own right.

Quite accidentally, during a break in a particular rehearsal, Chandra saw Nandakumar exploring a trance-like movement in which he almost seemed to be suspended in space. As she recalls today, 'I saw the figure of primeaval man in the shape of his body. An inscription with which I was familiar: ⌗ : It so happens that this 'dynamic suspension' was Nandakumar's instinctive response to a movement from *Tai-chi* called *Neri-neri*. It served as a spark not only for his own movement in the opening sequence of the production, but for the very concept of the 'beginning' itself: Cosmic Energy.

In the opening image of the production, we see a 'grid' of nine bodies on stage in the process of exploring distinct *asanas*. Each performer is in his or her own space, yet connected to the other performers on stage through a transmission of silent, yet potent energies. Indeed, there is not a sound, not even the drone of a *tanpura* in this opening sequence, as the performers do not merely 'perform' the *asanas*, but explore it over a five-minute duration, holding a cluster of iconic and subliminal forms.

It is important to stress that the *asanas* are not presented as poses or gymnastic feats. They are processes of an inner movement that each performer discovers for himself or herself, contributing to a larger continuum of energy on stage. So powerful is the impact that the sequence evokes memories of a mythical past that encompasses 'the three levels of the universe—sky, earth, and the underworld.'[1] From the outer extremities of the grid where we see suspensions in space created through the one-legged aerial forms of the *Garudasana* and *Vrksasana*, through the earthbound forms in the middle row, to the *bindu-like* presence of Chandra sitting in the centre in the front row, there is an entire cosmos of archetypal forms presented on stage with dynamic stillness.[2]

If one does not wish to interpret the sequence within a specifically mythical framework, one also has the option to tune into its energies at a more abstract level, almost in the nature of a visual *alaap*. At an even more down-to-earth level, it is possible to view 'Cosmic Energy' as a meditative warm-up which prepares the entire company (even those feeding its energies from the wings) with a concentration for the entire production leading to the final *Tillana*. The secret of Chandra's work — or at least one secret that accounts for its vitality and power — is directly related to the fact that she never rushes anything on the stage. She knows the value of 'taking one's own time' in order to 'hold' time and thereby transform the surrounding space.

Martial Sequences

In the blackout following 'Cosmic Energy', we hear the opening *sloka* from the *Abhinayadarpanam* set to music by Udupi Lakshminarayan in *Nattai raga*. This most familiar *sloka* invokes 'the *sattvika* Shiva whose *angika* is the world, and whose *vacika* is the entire language, and whose *aharya* is the moon and stars.'[3]

> *Angikam bhuvanah yasya*
> *Vacikam sarvavangmayam*
> *Aharyam chandrataradi*
> *Tam numah sattvikam shivam*

The deep and ethereal chanting of the Sanskrit verse is interrupted by one of the performers leaping on to the stage with a martial energy. Gradually, after being joined by other martial performers, the entire group performs a *vanakkam*, a traditional salutation to 'guru, god, and earth' in the northern *kalari* style.

One startling quality about this sequence is the articulation of the *vayttari* or verbal instructions in Malayalam, which are spoken by the leader in the group with a matter-of-fact immediacy. They are accompanied by a most fluid combination of symbolic gestures which are performed by the entire group with meticulous coordination. To ward off evil forces and negative energies, the dancers rotate their hands, then offer flowers to the deity with a sudden splaying of their fingers above their heads. The ritualised rigour of these gestures is broken by a dip of the bodies in which the dancers lie supine on the floor from where they survey the world warily. Then gradually, they raise their heads and bodies with a stealthy motion, radiating a collective vigilance.

This *vanakkam* is followed by *Angika's* signature — a visual sign which is repeated like a leitmotif through the first half of the production, punctuating the martial episodes. It was Pandian who referred to this movement as *sarukku*, which is a Tamil word meaning 'to glide.' As performed by the group, it is an exceptionally nimble, quick-footed movement in which the feet hardly seem to touch the ground. Chandra's visual perception enabled her to see the power of this movement in a predominantly lateral direction on stage, even though the martial *sarukku* can be broken or diverted to surprise the enemy. Moving sideways, yet looking outwards, the dancers dart past one another, charging the entire space with slashes of movement.

As suddenly as it appears to the sharp, drumming sound of the *thimila*, the *sarukku* also stops. And the space is cleared for the next martial sequence, which is a *vanakkam* in the southern *kalari* style as taught to Pandian by Mammukutty Gurukkal. Here, too, as in the earlier *vanakkam*, the movements are intercepted by verbal commands in Tamil.

In this *vanakkam*, Pandian sees a combination of all the basic laws that a martial artist needs to know: 'how to defend, how to attack, how to defend and attack at the same time, how to defend without attacking, how to attack without seeming to defend, how to attack the *marmas* (vital nerve centres), how to lunge and attack, how to turn and attack, how to chop and attack, how to block with the hands crossed in *swastika banda*.'

A microanalytical look at this sequence of movements would reveal the coalescence of principles relating to attack and defence. For instance, the martial artist may need to protect himself by bringing his knees together with the hands bunched over them, and in that very instant, he could be preparing to lunge forward. Therefore, what one learns from such a combination of movements is the *organicity* by which one movement is already flowing into the next even while it is being performed. This is, perhaps, one of the most important principles of an essentially dynamic process of movement that Chandra has learned to embody in her own training of dancers.

Without spelling out these connections, which become visible in the course of the production, Chandra once again breaks the *vanakkam* with the *sarukku* which 'clears the space' once more for the next martial sequence. And in this manner, the first sequences of *Angika* are built with different martial movements in different combinations with varying numbers of dancers, who are grouped in triangular forms, diagonal clusters, and finally, a mass-like structure that evokes an entire forest of fighters. The most striking stances and gestures used by the performers relate to the images of *swastika, dwarapalaka, garuda, vajra,* and a 'house' with four 'chambers.' These forms are animated with kicks, lunges, jumps, blocks, hops, leaps, strides, splits... in short, an entire gamut of primary movements which have later been abstracted in the more rarefied vocabulary of dance.

It is important to stress that the martial sequences never petrify into mere demonstrations: they are fully performed as ensemble pieces transfiguring the space with their multiple energies. In addition, the constant interruption of the *sarukku* which appears at least five times and the voicing of the martial instructions (in Tamil and Malayalam) punctuate the sequences with a theatrical immediacy. The very directness of the presentation also compels us to question what we are seeing, inducing an alertness that is altogether rare in dance performances today. In this sense, *Angika* can justifiably be described as a vibrant *lehrstücke*, a production in which we can learn about the history of the body with our senses.

The Animal World

From the principles of martial movement, we confront their concrete embodiment in a series of 'animal walks' from the southern *kalari* and Tamil martial arts traditions. Once again, the movements are performed in total silence so that we get to *hear* every movement — a sliding of the foot, a stamp of the feet, a hop on the ground, as well as the rustle of the women's cotton saris which accentuate particular steps.

Stealthily, with claw-like hands placed slightly below the waist, the entire group of dancers appears from one side of the stage with their backs to the audience. As they evoke the dodging motion of the 'tiger', they occasionally accentuate the crouching motion of their bodies with a slight sway of their shoulders. This is followed by the 'snake' which darts across the stage with abrupt spasms of movement, the hands of the dancers positioned in a hood-like shape that suggests the striking 'eyes' of the serpent.

Then follows the 'horse' with a group of dancers striding across the stage on a diagonal, their legs outstretched, their hands thrust forward. More mischievously, there are the side-hops of the 'rabbit', aerial and spring-like, which are counterpointed by the slow, measured stalking motion of the 'cockatoo' in which the hands of the dancers are shaped like beaks, with their knees locked into one another.

Breaking the measured continuum of this movement are the seemingly random springs of the 'frog', at first in the southern *kalari* style in which the dancers leap in the air with their heels touching the buttocks, and then in the northern *kalari* style in which they land on all fours. These oddly menacing springs never fail to surprise with their sudden shifts in direction and combinations of movement.

Needless to say, these 'walks' are hardly naturalistic representations but abstractions of physical principles relating to energy, coordination, balance, lightness, and stamina. Very stark in presentation, yet arresting for that very reason, we are alerted to the connection between the human musculature and animal reflexes, a knowledge that is almost negated in our world today through the 'denaturing' of our bodies.

Following the animal walks is a display of the *ashtavadivu* or eight postures of animals in the northern *kalari* style. What distinguishes its performance in *Angika* as opposed to its demonstration in a *kalari* has a lot to do with the flow by which one animal posture metamorphoses into another. These are punctuated with precisely determined leaps, turns, and splits. Normally these postures are performed separately or in the context of specific fight-sequences. In *Angika*, however, they are transformed into a continuum of energies in which the varying forms of animals appear and disappear into each other. In the flow of movement we note the physical identities of the *gaja* (elephant), *simha* (lion), *ashva* (horse), *varaha* (boar), *mayura* (peacock), *kukuta* (cock), *matsya* (fish), and *sarpa* (serpent).

Significantly, Chandra does not close the sequence of the 'animal world' with the bravura of the *ashtavadivu*. Rather, she includes two more 'walks' which are among the most difficult to accomplish — the 'crocodile', which requires nothing less than a suspension from the ground supported by feet and hands, rather like a mobile push-up; and the 'camel', which proceeds through a kind of shuffle with the palms of the hands touching the ground and thereby resembling two extra feet.

The point is not to 'master' these movements and project an illusory perfection, but to show the struggle that goes into their realisation. This is what makes the audience participate in the process more attentively. The visibility of the performers' vulnerabilities and limitations enhances what Chandra has so perceptively described as the 'distances in our bodies' that can be covered only through ceaseless effort. Watching the dancers make this effort teaches us a new humility about the potentialities of our bodies.

The 'Grammar' of Bharatanatyam

After revealing the process by which martial principles are concretised through animal walks, *Angika* introduces the most basic units of dance as explored in Bharatanatyam. This section of the choreography has been dismissed by many professional dancers who could never imagine performing such seeming 'simplicities' on stage. In response, Chandra emphasises that most dancers today have moved away, if not camouflaged the 'fundamentals' of dance in their search for virtuosity. A confrontation of the 'grammar' of dance is both necessary and difficult because it exposes those very traps and deceptions that one acquires through performance. Besides, the 'fundamentals' of dance reveal the richest sources of poetry in the language of the body. 'What they call grammar,' as Chandra says of her detractors, 'is poetry to me.'

Tellingly, the dance sequences of *Angika* are interspersed with lyrical expositions of the basic units in the 'grammar' of Bharatanatyam. Beginning with a series of *mandalas*, Chandra exposes the martial origins of these primary dance positions, particularly the *ardhmandala* or *aramandi* (as it is more popularly called), which conjures up in its half-squatting position the image of a warrior sitting astride a horse.[4] To her dancers, Chandra constantly emphasises that the *mandalas* are not poses. They are 'circuits of energy' which contain the entire body within a circular form. *Mandala* literally means 'orb' or 'circle.' The challenge for the dancers is to maintain the circularity of this form incorporating the numerous deflections and angularities of movement that function within it. It is in this strongly 'rooted' position that the dancers are most likely to find their 'centres', which are enhanced through the shifts in the balance and weight of the body.

With pristine simplicity, the *mandalas* in *Angika* are performed with the dancers standing in one vertical line centre-stage, the superimposition of the bodies contributing to the density of the image. Minimising the use of *nrtta hastas*, which are used not as decorative gestures but as 'accents' highlighting the physicality of the body-structures, Chandra urges her dancers to 'hold the earth' with each of the *mandalas*. One after the other, these conglomerates of energy dissolve into one another, radiating the martial power of dance.

Following the *mandala* sequence is the first *nrtta* or 'pure dance' sequence in *Angika* in which we are introduced to the basic *adavus* of Bharatanatyam. *Adavu* is a Telugu word deriving from *adu* or *atu* which refers to 'the foot striking the ground.' As it has evolved in the world of dance, *adavus* are generally described as hand-and-foot units of dance which are woven into patterns and larger sequences of movement.[5] Already in the most familiar *Natu adavu*, we are introduced to an entire gamut of movements including the stretching of the leg with the heel placed on the ground, the bending of the waist, the turning of the head at a three-quarters angle, the eyes following the hand, among a composite of minute details in which the texture of Bharatanatyam is grounded.

All these elements become multidimensional through Chandra's inspired choice of making the dancers perform the same *adavu* but at different points in its sequence of movements. In this way, the multiple directions of the movements are enhanced through the different angles in the dancers' bodies. The effect is heightened through the use of *vilambit kaal*, the slow speed that is almost never used in performances today but which enables one to see the interstices of the Bharatanatyam form. Slowly, the entire space is transformed through a kaleidoscope of perspectives, the dancers 'throwing' their energies simultaneously in multiple directions, which are contained within the tensile framework of Chandra's choreography.

In this manner, Chandra intersperses more *adavu* sequences with minimally choreographed vignettes focusing on specific elements in the 'grammar' of Bharatanatyam like *utplavanas, bhramaris, hastas, gatis* and *caris*.[6] Now we are able to see the elaboration of those very martial principles embodied in the animal walks and the *ashtavadivu* depicted earlier. In the sensuality of dance, there is a more joyous sense of play and flow which Chandra accentuates through the element of surprise in her choreography. The dancers meet, scatter, appear, and disappear to create a chimera of movement on stage.

Therein lies the beauty of the 'grammar' in *Angika*: it breathes with life. Having explored the crystallisation of dance from primary movements and energies, Chandra now shifts her focus in the production yet again to reflect on the socialisation of dance. From the kinesics of movement,

Angika now enters the more problematic area of interpreting dance within the mutations of its history.

The Socialisation of Dance

> Bharata gave us the concept of *Sharira-mandala* — Our body as the centre of the universe.
>
> What happened to this inspired body-language?
>
> Across time, the essence and content of the body got diverted, fragmented and negated.
>
> First, body became a vehicle to serve gods, priests, religion,... Then the body became a vehicle to serve kings, courtiers, men. *Devadasi* becomes *Rajadasi*... And then the body became a victim of moralistic society, and the dancer an object of social contempt.[7]

Briefly, this is how Chandra has conceptualised the socialisation of dance which becomes the primary subject matter in the second half of *Angika*. After showing us the cosmic, material, and martial origins of dance, she proceeds to trace the denuding of its energies in a larger historical process. To demonstrate the appropriation of dance (and more specifically, female dancers) by 'gods, priests, religion', she opens the second half of the production with a *pushpanjali*, literally an 'offering of flowers', a traditional dance that was originally performed by the *devadasis* during their initiation ceremony in the presence of the deity.

Over the years the *pushpanjali* has lost its ritualistic content as it has been secularised through contemporary dance practice.[8] In *Angika*, it is presented as a formal dance piece without the trappings of religiosity. There is no visual image of any god or divinity to which the dance is addressed, no obligatory garlanding of a deity on stage. Interestingly, Chandra has two dancers perform the *push-panjali* at the same time, one standing directly behind the other, to create a sense of a shadow or a double. It is an extremely intuitive choice that has yet to be fully conceptualised. Indeed, what is missing in the insertion of the *pushpanjali* in *Angika* is a critical intervention *in dance language* that could substantiate the appropriation of the dancer by the temple order. The dance is performed sensuously, even joyously, but with a total absence of any critical attitude to the context being addressed. Consequently, though one enjoys the *pushpanjali*, one cannot readily associate it with the larger critique of religiosity that Chandra assumes in her concept of the production.

Set to *Aarabi Raga* in *adi tala*, the musical score of the *pushpanjali* is a rich combination of *swara*-patterns, *sollukattus* that are rarely heard on the stage today, and an invocatory verse: '*Arithiru marugane/Vigna Vinayaka/Vinaikeda Varuzhiya/Croya Mukha/Jaya Jaya/Ganapathy Kavuthuvam Katravar Vinai Ara*' (Praise be to you, Vishnu's nephew, Remover of obstacles, remover of universal sorrow, O Elephant-faced one, No more sorrow for those reciting these verses).[9] The composition of the *pushpanjali* was created by Guru Ellappa Pillai, who had taught the piece to Chandra, who in turn had performed it in her production of *Devadasi* in 1960.

What is needed today in the larger context of *Angika* is a subtle subversion of the ritualistic context of the *pushpanjali* by which its sensuousness can be juxtaposed with the system that validates 'feminity' for its own purpose. Indeed, what are the implications of 'dancing for God' in our times? How do we represent a *devadasi* on the very stage where she has been appropriated? While the *pushpanjali* in *Angika* does not confront these questions, it does provides us with a glimpse of a dancer who seems to be dancing as much for herself as to attract the attention of the audience. In the meantime, the woman behind her remains a shadow, complementing her movements, yet retaining her own 'invisible' identity. Perhaps, it is through this 'invisible presence' that Chandra can begin to problematise the context of the *pushpanjali* sequence in *Angika* more provocatively and meaningfully.

The 'Male Gaze' of the Varnam

In sharp contrast to the *pushpanjali*, the subsequent *varnam* of *Angika* is, perhaps, one of the first pieces of choreography in Indian dance that could be termed 'feminist.' While the music and dance-steps of the *varnam* are 'traditional', Chandra's critical intervention in the structuring of the piece offers one of the clearest examples that I have seen in performance of the 'male gaze.' This is one of the major issues in feminist theory which attempts to examine how a work of art (and more precisely, the body of woman) gets 'constructed' through the scrutiny and surveillance of men as producers, directors, spectators, consumers, and critics.

The *varnam*, as is well known, is one of the most elaborate items in any Bharatanatyam dance recital, offering a dancer the greatest scope to reveal the possibilities of her art, both at the levels of *nrtta* and *abhinaya*. Significantly, the song chosen for the *varnam* in *Angika* is addressed to the Chola King, Datta Rajendra, who has been transformed into Krishna in the bowdlerisation of the same *varnam* taught in Kalakshetra. It is obvious that the song is openly erotic, sung by a woman ostensibly complaining to the king about his attraction for another woman. Not only does the Kalakshetra attempt to 'refine' the erotic content of the *sahitya* reveal a false puritanism, it totally contradicts the secular norms and values of our own society in which sexual betrayal is a widely accepted social reality. More significantly, the bowdlerisation negates the possibility of a critical reading of the *sahitya* itself.

For Chandra, the purpose in retaining the 'erotic' text of the song was directly related to what she believed was its 'anti-woman' content. Therefore, instead of 'divinising' Datta Rajendra in the tradition of Kalashetra and thereby endowing him with a superhuman grace, she strategised a way of representing her own dissatisfaction as a woman with the values expressed in the song.

First of all, it was sheer brilliance on her part to get two dancers to perform the *varnam* simultaneously, both of whom are equally important and visible (unlike the use of the second dancer in the *pushpanjali*). Not only was Chandra challenging the normal practice in which a solo dancer is expected to interpret a *varnam,* she found the clearest way of representing the 'other woman', whose presence was visibly problematised. In addition, Chandra did something even more unprecedented by getting the two dancers to perform not only for the audience in the auditorium but for two groups of men who sit informally on either side of the stage. Therefore, the 'real' audience has no choice but to see itself mirrored on stage.

At one point in the *varnam*, the situation becomes even more ironic as the dancers simply switch sides and perform for the 'other' group of men. It does not seem to make any difference to them. Nor are they viewed differently. Whether it is Datta Rajendra or another king or another courtier, the dancers continue to be objectified through the same 'male gaze.'

Perhaps, the most daring intervention in the choreography occurs when, quite suddenly, one of the men who has been watching the dancers with detachment, turns his head and looks directly at the audience with piercing eyes. Another man, on the other side, does the same, perhaps a little more quizzically. These two turns of the head automatically direct the 'male gaze' outwards. And the audience has no choice, I think, but to confront what it means to be constructed in someone else's 'gaze.'

Set to *Husseini Raga* in *rupaka tala*, the text of the song (`Ye maayala adira ...) reads as follows:

> Why are you toying with me, Swami?
> What did she whisper in your ear?
> You, Datta Rajendra, who suffuses the earth with light
> Son of Shri Mallaji Chandra
> Swami, listen to me and show your love
> Why have you forgotten me?[10]

At a very obvious level, it can be read as part of a rhetorical convention that flatters the male ego. It implies that Datta Rajendra is desirable as women vie for his 'love.' He can afford to choose among them, reject them, or play with one against the other. While the dancers seem to play the surface of the song with some irony, they do not reveal, to my mind, any sense of hurt that this 'game' is actually painful to them as individual women. Nonetheless, through their juxtaposition of gestures, they convey the larger reality of being trapped in a system where the 'other woman' could be the woman herself.

Following the first verse, there are *swara* patterns in which time the women exchange places and thereby convey with a certain nonchalance that men are 'interchangeable' within the purview of their gaze. Once again there is an excerpt from the song, which describes the 'other woman' attributing all the Mohini-like wiles of seduction that are inextricably linked to such a woman:

> You have been touched by the lotus-eyed glance
> of that woman which makes you forget me.

Then, following the rendition of *swara* patterns, the dance ends with the concluding verse of the song:

> Apart from you, I have not seen anyone else
> (That's what you said)
> I trusted you and gave you my heart,
> and I am suffering for it.

By this time the two men have turned their 'gaze' outwards to make the audience question what they are seeing.

While the song attempts to objectify the 'other woman', Chandra's choreography reverses the process by objectifying the 'male gaze.' What should be stressed, however, is that Chandra's intervention does not come about through a self-conscious attempt to embody feminist theory in dance. Her choices are invariably intuitive or 'visual' as she likes to describe it. What is special about her visual perception, however, as can be seen from the interplay of two women in the *varnam*, is its close relationship to a critical consciousness about social realities that extend beyond the world of dance. In this case, her consciousness cannot be separated from the visual play of the *varnam*, they are so finely integrated.

Significantly, while making a critical intervention in her choreography, Chandra gives considerable freedom to her dancers to explore it for themselves. In fact, that is what they enjoy most about performing the *varnam*, because it is refreshingly free of the expectations attached to it in the larger context of a traditional *margam*. Here one is invariably judged, assessed, and compared to other dancers. The dancer's expertise is scrutinised at the expense of examining her relationship to the content of what she is dancing.

In *Angika*, the technical execution of the *varnam* is emphasised but in relation to the larger social dynamics of the situation. No wonder the dancers are integrally involved in the performance. As Tripura puts it: 'I enjoyed the *varnam* because Chandra encouraged us to shape it according to our feelings. The *hastas* are extremely flexible, natural. For me, it is a new experience each time. I found that there were a lot of things that I could do, teasing the men, for instance. But the strongest moment for me was when I did nothing ... when I just looked into Nandakumar's eyes without moving.'

Clearly, this is the kind of moment that approaches 'acting' in which the performer is free to explore a particular emotion without the mediation of a particular code. One is free to 'see' without succumbing to the norms determined by a dance tradition in which the 'male gaze' is inscribed.

On a less ironic note, the *varnam* ends with the two women standing one behind the other in postures of humiliation. It is a very brief 30-second image of degradation in which we are made to see the transition of the female dancer from her role as courtesan/entertainer to that of a mere *dasi*, or slave of men. Once again, Chandra has not 'fixed' the choreography of this brief, yet powerful visual motif giving her dancers the freedom to express this intense moment of humiliation in their own way.

In most performances, one of the dancers invariably bends her back from the waist downwards, while the other covers her face. This degradation is merely glimpsed, not elaborated, with a minimum of melodrama. Thus, the sheer brevity of the scene prevents it from overpowering the larger statement about the 'male gaze' in the *varnam* which precedes it. Nonetheless, it leaves the audience thinking about the dehumanisation of women that has emerged through our cultural history in the name of 'art.'

Naravahana

After the devastating image on which the *varnam* concludes, it seemed contrived to move directly on to the *tillana* with which Chandra wanted to end *Angika* and thereby, assert the 'renewal of energy' in dance. Some transition was needed to bridge the gap, both conceptually and experientially, between the critique of patriarchy in the *varnam* and the ebullience of the *tillana*. Late in the rehearsal process, Chandra had one of her flashes of inspiration in which she was compelled to include herself in the production in what might be regarded as one of the most memorable images from her choreography.

Naravahana: a warrior-like woman sitting astride a man. This is the iconic image that emerges from the blackout following the closing image of the *varnam*. In what would seem like an illumination of *shakti* from another time, Chandra breaks the linearity of her narrative for the first time in *Angika*. In this context, there is no attempt to create a false causality between the *varnam* and the *tillana*. The *naravahana* sequence defies such logic through the sheer immediacy of its evocation.

Sitting like a martial goddess with her white hair gleaming under the glare of the spotlight, Chandra embodies sheer power in her presence. Using clearly defined *hastas*, she wields weapons like a spear, bow and arrow, sword, chopper, claws, and a *trishul* (though no *chakra*), choosing her victims in the audience with precise calculation. The configuration of her gestures conjures up images of Durga and her origins in the cult of mother goddesses. Here we see woman as warrior, triumphant, but not vindictive. She is sure of her force, and therefore, can afford to be awesome in a state of resplendent grace.

Chandra's particular signature to the composite of traditional gestures is a very slight smile of victory, a mere slit in her mouth, which is accompanied by minute jerks of the head from side to side. It is a witty moment, carefully timed to counterpoint the slow raise of the man's head from the ground. Till this point he remains a vehicle, literally the 'seat' on which the goddess sits. As played by Ashok Kumar, it is difficult to gauge what the expression of his face could possibly connote. Baleful sufferance? Resignation? The *nara* (man) remains mutinously silent.

A predictable critique of this assertive projection of female power could relate to the fundamentalist appropriation of militant images of goddesses. One can only reiterate that there is also a need, at once strategic and aesthetic, for secular artists to appropriate these images for their own creative purposes and idioms of resistance. What should be kept in mind is that the image cannot be separated from the particular way in which it is embodied in performance. The *Naravahana* sequence in *Angika* is not a replica of a religious icon but a personally investigated representation of particular aspects of this icon which are defined through the immediacy of Chandra's personality and consciousness.

Ultimately, the power of the performance lies in the fact that Chandra is capable of making the image her own. As Sadanand puts it so vividly: 'The Naravahana is like a bolt of lightning that illuminates a living icon, something that is terrifyingly alive and vibrant.' One should also keep in mind that the image cannot be decontextualised from the larger framework in which it is placed, from what has preceded and follows it. The thrust of *Angika* is decisively 'secular' in its focus on the material and martial origins of dance and its critique of patriarchy in the *varnam*. If one chooses to read the *Naravahana* as a predominantly 'religious' image then one is failing to grasp the significance of its martial energies within the larger context of the production.

However, it should be acknowledged that the image could have 'misfired' badly in performance if it had not been played by Chandra herself. I cannot see any of her dancers doing the same role without failing to convince. It is not entirely a technical matter — the gestures of the *Naravahana* can be easily learned — but it is the entire consciousness that goes into the performance of these iconic gestures that makes all the difference. Chandra has lived with images like *Naravahana* for a long time; she has questioned them, drawn her inspiration from them, occasionally rejecting them only to return to them with a different sense of belonging. She has made these images part of her own creative chemistry as a dancer and choreographer. And therefore, one has no choice but to view her use of these images as an appropriation in its own right celebrating the life-sustaining and martial aspects of our so-called 'religious' cultural resources which are increasingly marginalised in secular discourses and idioms of creative expression.

Tillana

After the *Naravahana* image fades into darkness from which it initially appeared, the stage brightens for the final *tillana* which is a joyous celebration of multiple energies from different physical traditions. The idioms of dance, martial arts and Yoga come together in a vibrant series of movements which build to a thrilling climax in which the entire company performs a martial *namaskar* in unison.

Intercepting rather than interrupting the *tillana* are a series of martial walks and kicks — the *nerkal* in which the leg is kicked with such flexibility that the knee touches the shoulder, and the *iruttikal* in which the forward kick is complemented by a sitting posture and later by a *bhramari* movement around the hip in which the chest is swivelled around the waist, first clockwise, then anti-clockwise. There is also a *meippayatt* in which one witnesses a maelstrom of movements incorporating leaps, jumps, kicks, stretches, rotations of the body in an almost ceaseless flow of movement. Complementing these martial sequences is a mock-fight followed by a display of *silambam* or staff-fighting in which the staff is wielded with lightning speed to create whirlwinds of energy on stage. In the most recent version of *Angika,* the *silambam* has been replaced by one of the dancers performing cartwheels and somersaults with youthful abandon. The female presence is also inserted in the mock-fight with Chandra consciously pitting woman against man in an equally contested display of strength.

More silently, there is a series of *asanas* in one particular section in which the performers seem to mirror each other, while the dancers continue to hold the *tala.* In the last version of *Angika,* Chandra has introduced an element of 'theatre' by making the dancers observe the martial and yogic actions on stage. As they become spectators on stage, the stylisation of the choreography is broken through a different level of energy and involvement. This is just one indication of how *Angika* has continued to grow, responding to the particular sensibilities of the performers.

In the final image of the production, the entire ensemble of dancers and martial performers thrust their bodies forward in a vibrant *namaskar.* In this moment, there is a tumultuous meeting of all the heterogeneous elements that have been seen at different points in the production. What needs to be stressed is the specificity of these inputs, which have been juxtaposed rather than 'mixed.' At no point are the martial movements, dance, Yoga, or *silambam* performed simultaneously. The closest we get to 'simultaneity' is when the dancers are present on stage while the Yoga and martial sequences continue. But the dancer's presence is registered through *standing,* not dancing.

It is through this rejection of simultaneity in performing different physical idioms that Chandra avoids making a cultural *khichri* in the name of 'fusion.' Thereby she also keeps her distance from making any kind of pan-Indian statement about the overall interrelatedness of our physical and philosophical traditions. While she believes in the commonalities of our physical traditions, she refuses to succumb to any homogenising tendency by grouping them together.

If the 'unity' of the ensemble comes through in the final moment of the production it is because it follows a celebration of *difference* that has been experienced through the juxtaposition of multiple physical traditions.

The Impact of 'Angika'

The rousing climax of *tillana* follows a most rigorously sustained energy that can be felt from the concentrated silence of 'Cosmic Energy' in the opening sequence of the production. At no point is this energy diluted or diffused. Even those performers who are not on stage 'feed' the performance with their silent energies from the wings. No wonder the closing image of the production serves to 'release' this energy with an almost explosive effect. In my experience of *Angika,* which I have seen many times in different forums, the audience has never failed to respond with heartfelt emotion and gusto. They are perceptibly moved and energised by the production. One such response to the production in London is worth noting for the sheer exuberance of its idiom:

> STANDING OVATION — SHOUTING — STUDENTS IN SHOCK — ME IN TEARS. We experienced Indian dance. I was proud to be a woman. The Asian women around us squealed with delight as female dancers exploded in controlled bursts of directness everywhere — rolling, punching, balancing. These are the models all women need — new icons based on all tradition but reformed for now. I FELL IN LOVE AGAIN. (Correspondence conveyed to Abha Adam Sood, ADITI, forum for Asian dancers in England).

In Germany, where the applause continued for close to twenty minutes in some towns, notably Wuppertal (the hometown of the internationally renowned choreographer, Pina Bausch, who was also cheering in the audience), the group had to learn how to deal with curtain-calls. This is not part of our performance culture in India. While we have the freedom to show our appreciation for a dance during the performance, western spectators are obliged to express their appreciation after the performance in the form of a 'curtain call' which frequently becomes a performance in its own right. In Germany, the curtain-calls for *Angika* invariably disintegrated into utter confusion with dancers sauntering off-stage, some waving to particular members in the audience, others getting very 'traditional' all of a sudden by lining up to touch Lakshminarayan's feet. In short, a disaster. But I think the very informality of the group endeared the audience to the dancers even more, and the applause continued with a very genuine warmth of feeling.

In India, the opening performances of *Angika* at Skills and the National Centre for the Performing Arts received an unprecedented reception. Some excerpts from the reviews will convey the general excitement with which the production was received:

> Nothing has happened in the sphere of traditional dance in India like *Angika* ... It is likely to go down as a major landmark in contemporary dance history.
> Sunil Kothari in *The Times of India*.

> The total effect is electrifying. Just as a single shaft of lightning on a very dark and troubled night can suddenly illuminate the way, thus does Chandralekha's intellectual insight provide a direction for dance...
> Shanta Serbjeet Singh in *The Economic Times*.

> In *Angika*, Chandralekha has materialised a gift. She has presented the pristine truth of dance... *Angika* is not innovation but a proclamation of the necessity for innovation.
> Arudra in *Sruti*.

> Angika sets the body free ... after this, Bharatanatyam need never be the same again.
> Sumitra Srinivasan in *Mid-Day*.

Undeniably, this is a series of 'raves' (we will get to the 'brickbats' in the next chapter). But as I stated at the very start of this chapter, *Angika* can be viewed more meaningfully as a process rather than a finished product. Though the last group of *Angika* has been dissolved with many of the individual performers going their own ways, the concept of the production will surely continue to stimulate new forms and interactions. Instead of becoming 'bigger' and more spectacular, *Angika* could well become a chamber work with an even deeper concentration on the inner energies of dance.

Today, it is my own dream that *Angika* should tour extensively throughout India and not just in cities but in rural and mofussil areas as well. The purpose would be not just to perform the production but to interact with different communities, primarily young people who need to be exposed to the multiple resources of our physical traditions. In the best sense of the word, *Angika* could be an 'education.' As the critic Arudra has put it so perceptively: 'It should be shown to children as a means of encouraging them to understand the evolution of our dance traditions — to understand it without tears.'[11] *Angika* could also be a most meaningful counter to the stereotypes of physicality represented in the mass media. It could also oppose the reactionary assumptions of 'tradition' propagated by our more 'classical' artists in whose performances our cultural heritage is reduced to some kind of monolith that is 'ancient', 'religious' 'sacrosanct' and definitely beyond questioning. *Angika* teaches us to question and celebrate some resources of our tradition in a spirit of sensuousness and fun. Its very directness embodies its transformative potential.

At a show in Khajuraho some years ago, where *Angika* was invited to participate in the annual festival set against the backdrop of temples, the power system failed while Chandra was introducing the show. Sensing the restlessness in the audience, she realised the need to be brief about what the show was about. So, at the top of her lungs, without the aid of a microphone, she found herself saying: '*Angika* has nothing to do with gods. It has nothing to do with

temples. It has everything to do with US. With out BODIES.'
One cannot be sure how much her voice carried, but the audience settled down to watch the production with a different sense of involvement.

Angika has to do with our bodies. And in these bodies — if we could only begin to understand what they mean and how they work — we could find energies that could help us to establish a more joyous and significant relationship to ourselves and the world around us.

16

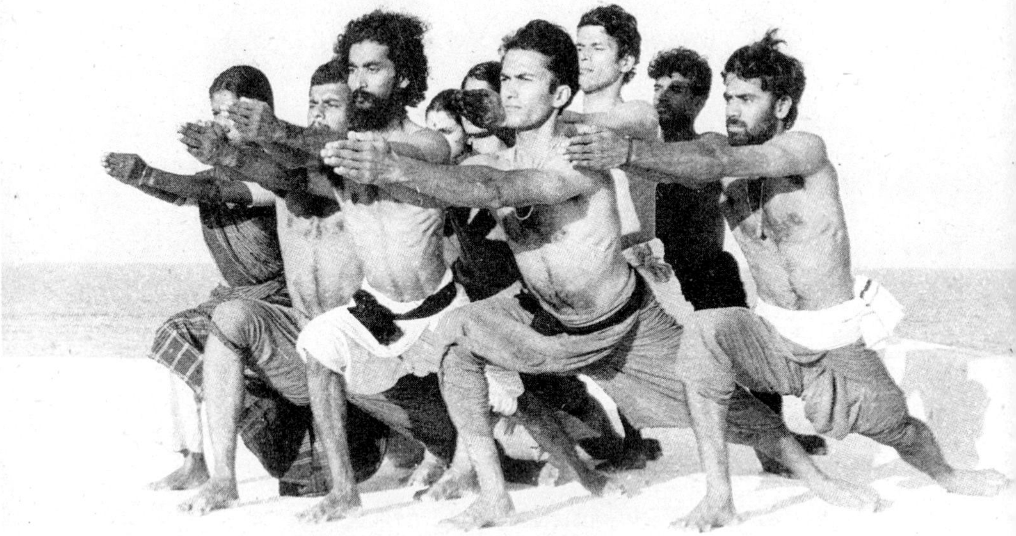

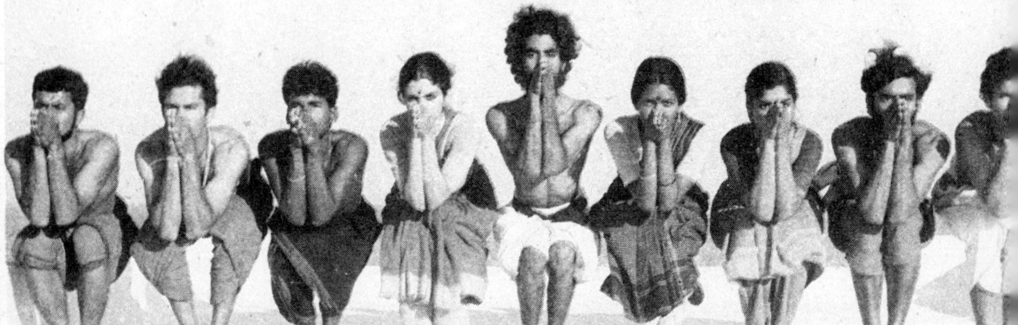

19

20

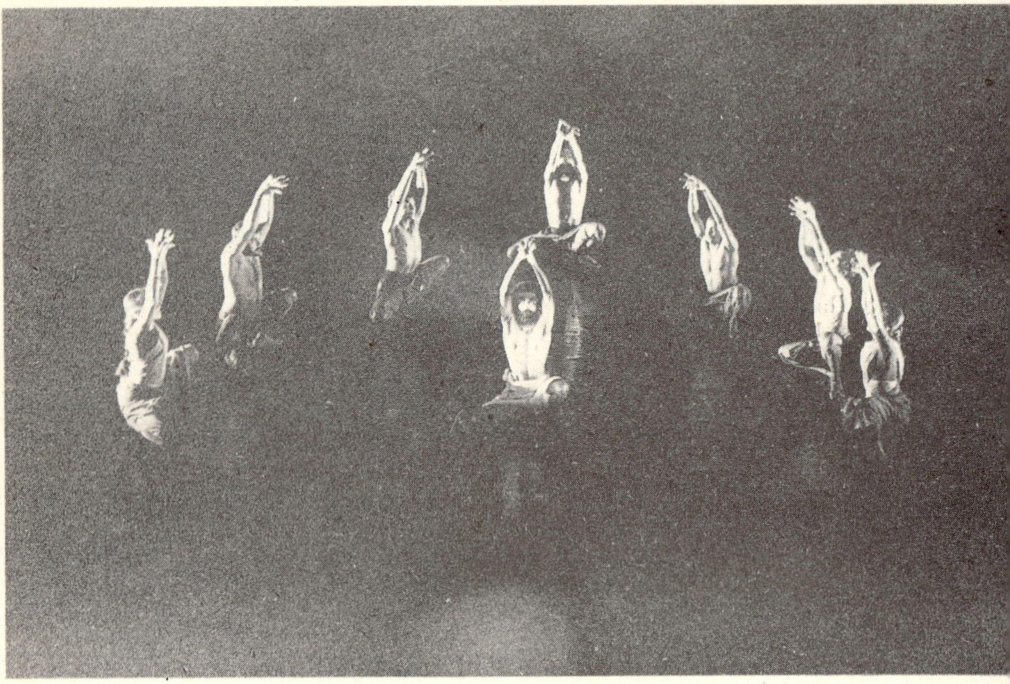

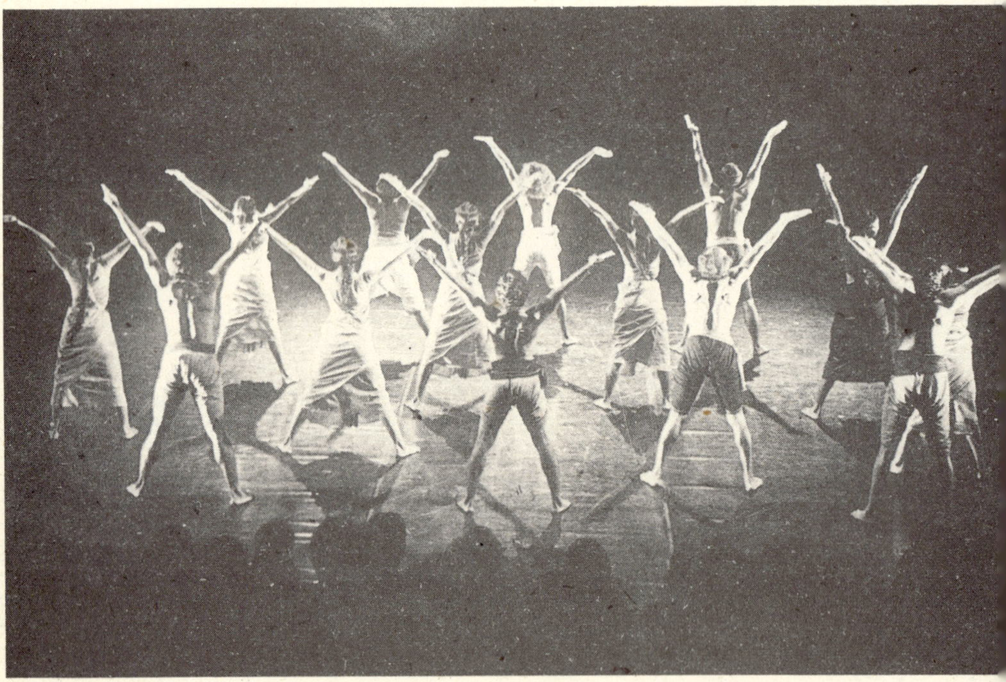

23

24

7

After 'Angika'

It is widely acknowledged in the world of performance that bouquets are generally accompanied or followed by brickbats. *Angika* was no exception. After being hailed as a major intervention in the recent history of Indian dance, if not a cultural landmark in its own right, there was a reaction to the production which manifested itself through dissensions, hostilities and petty politicking with a polemical focus on Chandra herself.

At one level, the dance world in India was compelled to confront a new reality which was promptly appropriated by official culture: *innovation*. 'You are to be blamed,' as Chandra has often been told, 'for letting loose innovation on to the stage.' Indeed, there is much to be regretted about the choreographic innovations that have emerged in recent years which amount, more often than not, to a pastiche of traditional forms, a mere padding of effects and tableaux on to the solo dance tradition. Along with this new fascination for 'innovation', supplemented by a renewed interest in marginalised disciplines like martial arts, there was also an upsurge in the aftermath of *Angika* of what could be termed neo-traditionalism: an affirmation of so-called 'traditional' aesthetics based on a pedantic paraphrase of its alleged rules and norms of taste. It was around the dictates of this neo-traditionalism orchestrated by a coterie of critics in the dance media that the campaign against *Angika* was consolidated.

Indeed, it could be argued (as many dancers themselves have expressed) that what passes off as 'criticism' in the dance world is, in actuality, an opinionated review which reveals very little perception (indeed, preparation) on the part of the reviewer for judging the subtleties of performance in an appropriate way. The only widespread reportage of the arts is available in newspapers through reviews and occasional features in which perceptions of 'culture' are generated and established. There is almost no counter to this generally irresponsible, if not flippant discourse, which could be better described as an extension of public relations rather than a critical illumination of art practice.

In this chapter, it would be useful to evaluate the 'critical' reception to Chandra's work within the larger politics of the media. It is also one way of studying how her choreography has been viewed 'from outside.' On the one hand, she has been damned in the press, and on the other hand, set up as some kind of avatar of modern dance. Both views are inherently flawed, implicated within a system in which the denunciation and 'gurufication' of artists feed almost parasitically on each other's priorities.

In retrospect, one can speculate that the very hype of the coverage for *Angika* was itself responsible for the backlash. An eight-page feature on the production in *India Today* (May 15, 1985) co-authored by Coomi Kapoor and Sunil Kothari, accompanied by some strikings stills from the production by the renowned photographer Raghu Rai, was particularly conspicuous in its unqualified praise of the show. Not even celebrities like Ravi Shankar or M.F. Hussain had received this kind of media attention before. In addition, the production was featured prominently in almost all the important national newspapers and magazines.

At this point, one should acknowledge Chandra's connection with close friends who happen to hold key positions in the media. Sadanand, of course, who has lived and worked with her for more than fifteen years, is a journalist by profession and commitment. In the dance world, Chandra has also been greatly supported by veteran critics like Shanta Serbjeet Singh and Sunil Kothari. For the most part, however, Chandra keeps her distance from the critics preferring to discuss her work with other writers, historians, thinkers, with whom she has been connected over the years through her numerous projects in design, graphics, feminism, film, publishing. One needs to keep this wide background of associates in mind to counter the totally unjustified criticism that Chandra manipulates her contacts in the media.

The fact is that whether she or her critics care to admit

it, Chandra has all the qualities of an artist that the media loves — a strong and vibrant personality, strikingly unusual looks, outspokenness, and above all, the courage of her conviction. Let us face it: if Chandra attends any forum or seminar, the camera is ultimately going to focus on her. There can be very well-known celebrities in her company, but there is something that individuates her as an artist. At a very obvious level, one could say that it is simply her white hair that inspires journalists to conjure up images of 'the silver-haired danseuse-feminist', or in more sensational terms, 'a living Shakti.' Chandra cannot be entirely blamed to my mind, for this kind of representation even though she inspires it by being so strikingly individual.

Apart from the hype around *Angika*, the really negative reaction to the production was orchestrated primarily by a coterie of critics based in New Delhi, which has become the centre for all major decisions relating to the propagation of 'Indian culture.' *Angika* itself was staged as part of a *Nritya-Natika* festival organised by the Sangeet Natak Akademi. Initially, the critiques were neither vituperative nor overly polemical. One could disagree with their premises in a spirit of professional dissent. For instance, one critic complained that *Angika* was not 'dramatic' enough: 'There has to be a core theme for the dance to bring out the drama — not merely an elaboration of body dynamics.' (*The Statesman*, New Delhi, Nov. 21, 1985) The fact that these 'dynamics' are integrally related to the overall concept of the production relating to the history of the body and its socialisation, was obviously lost on the reviewer.

Then there were snide remarks that the movements created a sense of watching a 'pretentious demonstration class, where the process is revealed rather than what it is used for.' (*Patriot*, Nov.21, 1985) Here again, as I have pointed out earlier, the 'process' has its own significance within the overall 'evolution' of the production, and it is subtly 'choreographed' in accordance to principles of energy rather than to details in a clearly worked-out story.

More bluntly, the *Evening News* (Nov. 21, 1985) regretted that the production lacked 'spirited entertainment' which

Angika clearly questions in its rejection of popular norms of 'entertainment,' though I would certainly claim that it is 'entertaining' in its own right. At a more ludicrous level, Chandra was reprimanded informally by cultural officials closely connected to the Music Academy in Madras for 'bringing too many beards on to the stage.' (For 'beards', read 'men', not dancers but martial performers.) In fact, one of the captions to a photograph of *Angika* showing the martial performers reads as follows: 'Back to the body beautiful as the centre of the universe...' (*Patriot*, Nov. 21, 1985).

All these reviews could be dismissed were it not for the fact that they represent the mere glimmers of a growing resentment that ultimately surfaced a year later when Chandra returned to Delhi in December 1986 with her new production of *Angamandala* and a revival of *Primal Energy* (with Ashok Kumar). Some background to these productions is needed.

After *Angika*, Chandra once again found herself unable to support a group on a permanent basis. Some of her dancers would drop in to the Mandala theatre once a week to rehearse some basic movements. In the absence of a professional infrastructure, Chandra was, perhaps, more vulnerable than she had been earlier in her career. For now, having established herself through *Angika*, there was no way that she could turn away from dance. Her friends and supporters were eagerly awaiting her new production, which her critics were only too keen to 'pan' and thereby demolish the growing mystique around her.

In this situation, Chandra should have been extremely careful about her next step as a choreographer. Continuing to function however, within her essentially 'amateur' response to creativity — and by 'amateur' I mean inspired within a non-professional set of working conditions — she just walked into a trap. At least, this is how I view the situation in retrospect.

By December 1986, when *Angamandala* was performed in New Delhi, most dancers and artists in India were alerted to the fact that India was going to hold one of its major 'festivals' in the Soviet Union. This was at the height of the close understanding between the two countries that was strengthened through the particularly warm relationship that existed between President Gorbachov and Prime Minister Rajiv Gandhi. The Festival of India in the Soviet Union was being advertised on the grapevine as one of the 'biggest' endeavours of its kind yet undertaken. Needless to say, the earlier festivals in France, America, and the UK had already provided the foundations for 'festival culture', creating all kinds of tensions among artists, while strengthening the role of bureaucrats and cultural *dalals* or middlemen. Despite these obvious tensions, it would be difficult to think of a single artist who did not, at some level, want to be included in the Festival of India in the Soviet Union. Even for those opposed to 'festivals' in general, the opportunity of visiting and performing in the Soviet Union, the erstwhile centre of socialism, could not be denied.

Chandra, too, was tempted by the possibility of performing in a country that she had visited in the early 50s as part of the first official cultural delegation to the Soviet Union from India. She also had warm memories of sharing a dance programme with Maya Plisetskaya in her youth. Now the 'real' reason to revisit the Soviet Union was tied up with a 'dream' that she had nurtured for a long time: to choreograph a massive Bharatanatyam work with pure elemental movements using thirty to fifty performers, preferably trained in the Kalakshetra school of dance. The fact that the Bolshoi stage could be made available for such a venture further 'sparked' Chandra's thoughts on the possibilities of the venture.

This was the 'dream.' The reality was that Chandra did not have thirty or fifty dancers to work with. Therefore, she had no choice but to work with a few new dancers and create a small production which she hoped would serve as a 'model', a mere suggestion of what the bigger production could be. *Angamandala*, thus, was not meant to be viewed as a completely realised production but as the 'germ' of a larger work-in-progress. This, alas, was not adequately conveyed to the organisers who made no attempt to publicise it in an appropriate way. Thus, the audience came to see another *Angika* only to confront a work that belied their expectations.

In essence, *Angamandala* attempted to abstract the basic principles of movement animating the grammar and constituents of Bharatanatyam, including the *alarippu*, and a *tillana*. Since the work itself was not fully realised, Chandra was compelled to revive *Primal Energy* to lengthen the duration of the programme. This, too, was another fatal mistake because, as I have discussed earlier, the tuning of the two performers in *Primal Energy* is essential for the realisation of the *purusha-prakriti* principle. Not being a dancer, Ashok Kumar radiated power in his martial movement but was unable to 'tune' into Chandra's energies or to the larger erotics of the piece. What had worked so sensuously with Kamadev was simply not possible in the new partnership of performers. Martial artists, however disciplined, have their own limits of expressivity unlike dancers whose *sattvika* is an essential constituent of their overall preparation.

Predictably, those who had been cautiously critical of *Angika* now seized the opportunity to attack the production with some of the most negative, if not vicious reviewing that any Indian dance company has received in recent years. One would have respected an analysis of the limits of Chandra's conception and its realisation. Instead, one was compelled to confront 'brickbats' in print disguised through witticisms and categorical judgements that attempted to pass off as 'criticism.'

The 'Critical' Reception

By far the most vitriolic review was penned by the veteran critic, Subbudu, who is frequently described as a 'terror' by most dancers. His word goes a long way in promoting a dancer's career. Beginning his review of Chandra's performance in the Delhi edition of *The Statesman* by invoking the tale of the Emperor's New Clothes, he concluded by echoing the child's words: 'Mummy, the Sultan is stark naked.' Continuing in this 'acerbic' mode, the review accused Chandralekha for 'assiduously trying to go back to the Stone Age on the pretext of harnessing primordial energy through dance forms', which was followed by the punch line: 'One hopes she would not revert to raw meat.' Dismissing Chandra's attempt in exploring 'totemic forms' as 'tortuous poses' reminiscent of a 'physio-therapic wing', Subbudu proceeded to mock the *gatis* performed on stage by saying that 'he would have preferred the originals in their natural habitat, or as an alternative a visit to the zoo.' Similarly caustic about *Primal Energy*, he nonetheless acknowledged the 'highly spiritual content of Adi Shankara's poetic concept of creation' in the *lingashtakam*.

Amusingly, Chandra was taken to task by K.S. Srinivasan in yet another tetchy review (*The Times of India*, December 8, 1986) for 'misusing' the name of 'venerable personalities' like Adi Shankaracharya 'for it is NOT the handiwork of the great philosopher of monism.' It never fails to amaze me how reviewers exhibit their 'scholarship' through such passionately held views that are invariably expressed in one line. Instead of acknowledging that the authorship of compositions like *lingashtakam* is, indeed, a complex matter open to many interpretations, the reviewers pose as pundits whose word is unquestionable.

Even more judgemental was V.V. Prasad's review in *The Hindustan Times* (December 8, 1986) which categorically stated: 'Chadralekha is a bad dancer, but a worse choreographer.' It is the last line of this review, however, that reveals its essential purpose:

> These awful choreographic monstrosities are said to have been already selected to be sent to the Festival of India in the USSR. That would be a grave error.

In this very specific statement, Prasad was merely echoing what Subbudu had expressed in a more convoluted way:

> ... the exhibition of this pot-pourri might make our reputation go on deputation. At this moment, our

> Government has entered into a historic treaty with Russia and nothing should be done to change our relations.

The sheer effrontery, if not absurdity, of this statement had its own repercussions among saner critics than Subbudu, who exposed the cultural politics of the situation. Thus, in the Delhi Diary published in *The Times of India,* the premises underlying Subbudu's 'peevish' criticism were clearly exposed:

> What gives this carping a rather nasty edge is that it seems to be part of a campaign, itself connected to the Capital's cultural politics, to deprive *Angamandala* of state or institutional support and keep it out of cultural festivals.

Reflecting on this 'cultural' phenomenon some months later in one of the most balanced assessments of the production, Krishna Chaitanya wrote:

> How fanatically orthodox our classicists can be came out in the critiques of the presentation of the choreographic creations of Chandralekha in Delhi last December. One critic said that if she and her team were sent to Russia, Indo-Russian relations would be damaged; another critic echoed him. Chandralekha was partly to blame for such overreactions because of her programme notes which were insufferably wordy and alienatingly pretentious. But it was totally unfair to dismiss her creations as nothing but the routine *Adavus* or etudes of Bharatanatyam. For the first time serious attention was paid to floor pattern, the movements and postures in quartets and bigger groups were designed sensitively for visual counterpoint — fluid transitions of symmetric and asymmetric groupings. It can of course be said that from the point of view of Western dance this was elementary. But such a criticism would hit the classicists more

hard than it would hit Chandralekha. For it would only reveal that we have abstained too long from experimenting with desirable even if elementary innovations in pure movement.
(*Sangeet Natak*, No.83: Jan-March 1987, p.6)

Even though one need not accept Chaitanya's description of Chandra's innovation as 'elementary', he has the grace to acknowledge the 'seriousness' of her intervention.

An even more perceptive view on the inner dynamics of *Angamandala* was articulated by Shanta Serbjeet Singh, who was the only reviewer to contextualise the choreography within the 'aesthetics of *mandala.*' In an illuminating review (*The Economic Times,* Dec. 7, 1986), she connected the primary principles of Chandra's choreography to the concepts of creation (both creative and cosmogenic) upheld by the art historian John Irwin, who happened to be visiting India at the time.

Drawing on the etymology of 'evolution', which literally means 'rolling out' or 'unfolding' of what previously existed, Shanta Singh traced a similar process in Chandra's work: 'a rolling off first of the false layers of sentimentality and religiosity, then a slow and measured "unfolding" of the strength, beauty, and sheer magic of the Bharatanatyam form underneath it all.' More acutely, Shanta Singh dispelled the assumption that Chandra's emphasis on 'grammar' amounted to a mere 'display of exercises.' What she emphasised instead was Chandra's 'conscious observation of the principles of control, balance, coordination, and in essence the twin principles of contraction and relaxation.' In addition, these movements were 'choreographed' in such a way that 'each of the seven dancers move as one *Mandala* of energy.' Clearly, the critic in this case has grasped one of Chandra's most basic principles, whereby the human body itself is viewed as a *mandala* in its own right, functioning within a tensile framework of multiple energies moving in and out, from centre to periphery, and by analogy from individual to community to cosmos.

Sadly, critics like Subbudu did not care to confront the

conceptual foundations of the production if only to state that they were not realised in the production. The work was summarily dismissed as juvenile. But even this could be excused were it not for the offensive sexism underlying much of Subbudu's review, which was exemplified in the postscript: 'P.S. Good tidings for ICCR invitees. Frisking is now by women cops. No more of the Haryana variety.' This kind of 'wit' is simply a brazen example of the anti-woman biases determining much dance criticism, which reflects the larger patriarchal stranglehold of dance in India today.

Power Play

Despite the sheer inanity of much dance reviewing in India, the reality is that some of the leading reviewers have become increasingly powerful in determining official cultural choices. Such was the impact of the negative press received by *Angamandala* in New Delhi, despite rejoinders and a few perceptive reviews, that Chandra's project for the festival was rejected. Alluding to the power assumed by reviewers, Chandra made a statement on the matter a few years after the Festival in the Soviet Union was over:

> You can count the critics who are scared of (new) work on your fingertips. Two-three-four. I can almost see this clique operating in sheer panic. They don't have the necessary refinement. Their criticism operates in a total vacuum. I can have no respect for these commercial columnists who have the power of their column and nothing else. They write for bylines. And they get drunk on those bylines. And they come with their measuring tapes wanting to measure everything and collect vital statistics.
> (*The Times of India*, 'Culture', October 1988)

After stating her opposition to 'commercial columnists', Chandra then went on to make an important qualification about her work:

> My work is small. It reaches out to a few people to whom it makes a crucial difference and with them one has the possibility of a creative dialogue.
>
> (Ibid.)

One only wishes that Chandra could have heeded her own words after *Angamandala*. Instead of returning to her work with greater intensity, nurturing the integrity of its 'smallness', she entered the 'power play' of cultural politics.

First of all, she was angry about the fact that her work was not being respected. What was even worse was to see it being 'politicised' in so distasteful a manner. Her instinct was to 'fight it out', but what she seems to have ignored were the stakes and tensions involved in the fight. In addition, Chandra responded somewhat too easily to the new opportunities that were presented to her after *Angamandala*, which she had wanted to use 'strategically.'

Though her production had been rejected by the Festival Committee, Chandra found a ready ally in Dashrath who had been appointed as the designer for the entire festival. This penchant of Dashrath's to work on a large scale is at once part of his great talent to create 'environments', but it has also been largely responsible, to my mind, for feeding his child-like ego apart from numbing his political consciousness. Nonetheless, one cannot deny that he enjoys the sheer scale of the operation in which he fully participates with a tremendous spirit of fun and creativity.

Earlier, as we had mentioned, he had collaborated with Chandra on an exhibition on Gandhi entitled 'The World is my Family.' But apart from this experience which had motivated Chandra to read at least 33,000 letters of Gandhi, she had consciously stayed away from his other design projects in various World Fairs and Festivals of India. Her work, as she herself has described it, was 'small.' And therefore, working on 'spectacles' was at best a kind of flirtation with concepts of space and environment, at worst an indulgence, if not a total waste of time and energy.

Despite these reservations, Chandra's own desire to explore a new sense of scale in dance by choreographing a Bharatanatyam piece with fifty dancers on the Bolshoi stage, ultimately compelled her to seek participation in the Festival of India in the Soviet Union. Despite the negative reception received by *Angamandala*, an opportunity presented itself in the form of an invitation to choreograph the opening ceremony of the festival which was being designed by Dashrath. He needed a choreographer and Chandra was an obvious choice. It is at this point, I believe, that Chandra needed to question the validity of 'choreographing' an official ceremony in the larger context of her own resistance to 'big' events and the politics associated with it. She discussed the matter with Sadanand who made it clear that he would not participate in the Festival in any way. The opportunity to work with diverse groups from all over India ultimately stimulated Chandra to accept the role of the choreographer.

In retrospect, the experience lingers like a bureaucratic nightmare that Chandra never fails to regret. Yet, she does not readily admit that she made a mistake by taking it on. This could be that Chandra constantly works with the assumption that there can be 'no regrets in life.' And while this is certainly true for most of her major choices relating to her search for freedom, discovery of space, exploration of relationships, rejection of marriage and child-bearing, it would seem to me that in this much smaller matter of working on a festival sponsored by the government, Chandra did make a mistake. She blundered by imagining that she could 'energise' an official spectacle with her own creativity. However, once she had accepted being part of the official scenario, she had no option but to function within its constraints, while attempting to subvert its premises.

Chandra's entire sojourn in the Soviet Union was divided into two parts relating to two very different kinds of activity — one related to the choreography of the inaugural ceremony, in which Chandra had to mastermind the coordination of hundreds of folk, traditional and tribal performers in the Lenin Stadium. This public ceremony in turn was preceded by a more formal closed-doors inauguration ceremony in the Kremlin for which Chandra choreographed a special piece entitled *Namaskar* using most of the members in her *Angika* group.

The second activity for which she returned to the Soviet Union for a longer stretch of time, concerned the mounting of one of the most comprehensive and creative exhibitions on Indian women entitled *Stree* which was conceptualised and directed by Chandra. I will provide a description of this exhibition and the problems Chandra confronted with particular reference to the Indian government's censorship of Aravindan's film *Sahaja* focusing on the concept of *ardhanarishwara*. Here, too, Chandra faced any number of bureaucratic obstacles, but the exhibition itself was so important and charged with the commitment of its participants that Chandra did not feel isolated. Ultimately, she came through the rigours of the exhibition with a sense of having achieved something, most of all, a tremendous sense of solidarity with any number of women, both in the Soviet Union and India with whom she was able to share her thoughts and images about women's liberation.

The opening ceremony, however, was an entirely different matter. Here Chandra found herself at loggerheads with two of her chief 'collaborators', K.N. Panikkar and Ratan Thiyam, both renowned theatre directors, whose work Chandra had never seen. Nonetheless, through the glowing reports she had received of their productions, she herself had suggested their names as collaborators on the project. Since both Thiyam and Panikkar are closely connected with the cultural resources of their home states, Manipur and Kerala respectively, which are among the richest storehouses of traditional performances and rituals in India, it was only appropriate that they should be approached for contributing to the wide spectrum of cultural resources to be used in the opening ceremony.

Unfortunately, even during the initial rehearsals of the ceremony in New Delhi, it became obvious that Thiyam and Panikkar were on one side, while Chandra turned to Guru Kedar Nath Sahoo and the veteran director, Habib Tanvir, to support her in particular moments of crisis when her leadership was questioned. While Thiyam and Panikkar did their best to highlight her 'domineering' ways, it is also likely that they were suffering, in Sadanand's pithy diagnosis, from a 'castration complex.' This was undoubtedly the first time that either of them had to accept the decisions of a woman in professional matters. And she was not going to play second fiddle to their assumptions of power. She was going to articulate and realise her own *concepts* for which she demanded neither deference nor blind acceptance but due respect.

The tensions generated through this power play are symptomatic of the cultural politics of our times. What is it about official cultural forums in particular that brings out the worst in people? Is it simply a desperate need to compete or to seize power under the aegis of the State? Or is it a kind of massive insecurity that gets manifest in any number of ways, at times repressed, or else unleashed through bursts of aggression?

Reflecting more generally about 'festivals', one would have to acknowledge that nobody seems to 'enjoy' them. There is so much talk about 'participation' and 'celebration' and 'interrelating',but ultimately, what emerges is a mechanised spectacle in which performers are 'slotted', their 'spontaneity' subtly regimented. More painfully, 'festivals' serve to homogenise different communities of people who are made to share a 'common space' and affirm a 'unified' message. It would be different if the participants had some say in the creation of this 'space' and 'message', but the point is that the spectacle is so vast and mechanised that there is no possibility of an organic process of decision-making 'from below.' Even 'from above', the decisions are ultimately controlled not by the coordinators of the festival but by the State in whose name the festival is sponsored and sold.

Today, when Chandra chooses to recall this period in her life, she acknowledge a deep feeling of 'sadness.' 'I think we all missed a great opportunity to work together and *create* something.' And then, with her characteristic candour, which is sometimes mistaken for arrogance, she adds: 'I would say that they (Panikkar and Thiyam) missed a great opportunity to work with me.'

What sustained Chandra during the preparations for the inaugural ceremony was her meeting with diverse cultural groups from different parts of India. There were approximately 800 folk artists and tribal performers affirming a rich variety of cultural idioms. At least sixty traditional and folk forms were represented in the festival which was inaugurated in a special half-hour programme conducted within the Kremlin. This closed-doors ceremony was conducted with due solemnity with the presentation of two *kumbhas* of *gangajal* to the two heads of State, which in turn was followed by a benedictory hymn sung by the legendary Carnatic vocalist, Smt. M.S. Subbulakshmi. Thereafter Chandra's *Namaskar*, a specially choreographed piece for the inauguration, was performed by her contingent of dancers and martial artists.

Namaskar

Since the purpose of *Namaskar* was to provide an auspicious note to the inauguration ceremony, Chandra focused on one of the most familiar of traditional gestures — the *namaskar* — which can be seen throughout India performed in so many different ways. More than a gesture that symbolises 'meeting' and 'greeting', the *namaskar* is also integral to the gestural languages of various martial arts traditions. These traditions were Chandra's points of departure for the choreography of the work, which was not naturalistic but iconic in its 'salutation to land, salutation to people, salutation to elements, cosmos.' Thus, once again we see how Chandra begins with a seemingly 'small' concept and then enlarges on it, moving from the locus of the body to larger, more elemental considerations of space and time.

In terms of its actual structure, *Namaskar* is a most concentrated, non-virtuosic 'salutation' with clusters of dancers moving like one coordinated mass of bodies. Working on the yogic and martial premise that the *namaskar* is performed with all eight limbs of the body — the *sashtanga*

— Chandra has her dancers explore the full stretch of their movements. Through a combination of lunges, chops, thrusts, kicks, the dynamic thrust of the choreography is greatly accentuated through its orchestration of movements on the diagonal. Moreover, since the entire piece is performed in *vilambit*, we get to see every tension and flexion in the mass movement, which becomes particularly evident during the moments when the dancers 'hold' their positions radiating a dynamic stillness.

At particularly heightened moments, the bodies of the dancers almost seem to be interlocked, their backs arched, heads thrown back, with the hands folded upwards in a *namaskar*. Then, there is an abrupt break as the dancers separate into two groups, directing their energies in opposite directions. With the diagonal thrusts of their bodies, they almost seem to 'stretch' the entire space almost to breaking point. Ultimately, it is the tautness of the choreography which one remembers, consolidated by the total discipline of the performers both individually and collectively.

Sadly, the *Namaskar* item came in for a lot of snide criticism from many dancers and artists who thought (once again) that it was too 'simple.' What they failed to realise is that this very 'simplicity' contributed to its power. Moreover, in its assertion of the martial temperament, the piece was celebratory without being effusive, dignified rather than virtuosic. It also radiated a spirit of boldness and self-respect which is normally absent in most official forums where artists tend to wallow in false deference. Avoiding an overstatement, *Namaskar* affirmed the dignity of the human body within the specific physical resources of the martial tradition. If Chandra's critics were expecting to see a dance number with a lot of garlanding of dignitaries and gods, they were mistaken.

And yet, it is amazing how 'criticism' is generated around official forums. One absurd accusation was that Chandra had attempted to flatter Rajiv Gandhi by surreptitiously including the word '*rajiv*' in a *sloka*. A more 'scholarly' objection was that a *mangalam* should not be performed at the start of an inauguration ceremony to which Chandra and Udupi

Lakshminarayan had to clarify that there were different kinds of *mangalam*. Besides, if one wanted to be somewhat literal in Chandra's defence, it could be said that the *mangalam* used in *Namaskar* concluded the inauguration ceremony after which the festival technically began.

Returning to India, Chandra found herself maligned in many newspaper reports in which there was a systematic attempt to blame her for the 'lapses' in the ceremony. More objectionably, there were also attempts to play on chauvinist sentiments through 'critiques' that accused her of marginalising particular 'regional' cultures. In response, Chandra defended herself in as dignified a manner as possible; she also immersed herself in preparing for the exhibition on *Stree*. This was her way of confronting her critics through an exploration of wide-ranging concepts on the empowerment and enslavement of Indian women through which she was determined to make her own statement about resistance as an artist. It was also her way of confronting the bureaucracy in a forum controlled by the State.

I will contextualise the problems and strategies confronted in *Stree* in a longer chapter in which I will also relate Chandra's various 'languages' of resistance as a writer, thinker, choreographer, and designer within a larger feminist context. Also in this chapter I will describe my own theatrical collaboration with Chandra on *Request Concert* in which she adapted (and subverted) Franz Xaver Kroetz's one-woman, wordless text about a woman's mechanisation and suicide in an altogether radical treatment of the subject through Bharatanatyam. It was only after the *Stree* exhibition and *Request Concert* were produced that Chandra found time to return to dance in her second major production, *Lilavati*, which we will examine in the next chapter.

8

26

Background on 'Lilavati'

If the impulse to get involved in the Festival of India in the Soviet Union was not a particularly wise choice on the part of Chandra, the same cannot be said about her decision to do *Lilavati*. It was the right choice at the right time, the most strategic and creative way of disarming her critics. After *Angika*, Chandra still needed to confront those traditionalists who imagined that her understanding of Bharatanatyam was inadequate. The more condescending among them were beginning to acknowledge that she was an 'innovator' but without a real grasp of 'tradition.' *Lilavati* was Chandra's way of countering this criticism with a production that is a positive joy, a tribute to the choreographic possibilities of Bharatanatyam. Witty and almost effortlessly creative, *Lilavati* is also an affirmation of the poetic possibilities of what Chandra has described as 'the non-sublimated content' of dance.

Based on Bhaskaracharya's visionary mathematical treatise written in the tenth century in which he poses the most intricate questions of algebra, geometry, arithmetic, and calculus to his daughter Lilavati, the production provides an altogether different *sahitya* (text) for Bharatanatyam. In fact, the choice of the text is a *coup de théâtre* in its own right, and therefore, risky for that very reason. So many brilliant concepts in the world of performance remain at the level of concepts; they are rarely actualised in performance. What makes *Lilavati* so special is that the choreography meets the challenge of the concept with an interplay of creative energies and wit.

Needless to say, this 'play' would not have been possible if *Lilavati* had not hibernated in Chandra's mind for a long time. First performed at the Sachin Shankar Festival in Bombay in February 1989, the production is her response to a text which she had read almost ten years earlier when she was exploring the connections between 'Science and Art' while working on the concept of the Nehru Science Museum in Bombay. Her 'homework' on the production began from that initial encounter with the text, which she had read, dreamed, memorised, and fantasised over the years so that Lilavati became a real woman with whom she could empathise. She was also a model among women in so far as she became a great mathematician in her own right. This combination of wisdom and lightness of spirit, which is how Lilavati can be evoked, is something I have come to associate with Chandra herself. And therefore, it is only appropriate that in the production she presents the questions posed to Lilavati rather like Lilavati herself. Though the text is Bhaskaracharya's, the actual wording and rendition of the text is Chandra's, so that through her *vacika,* she makes it very clear to the audience that the questions have already been answered.

Principles of Selection

While the selective process of the various questions posed to Lilavati were based primarily on Chandra's instinctive preferences, there were a few determining factors that helped her to crystallise the choices for the *sahitya* of the production. One important consideration related to the specific visual possibilities contained in particular questions. Those problems, focusing on more mundane realities like the prices and measures of grain, were obviously harder to embody in the language of classical dance than the images of swans, bees, cranes, lotus, water, wind, and trees incorporated in the particular problems posed by Bhaskaracharya.

Inevitably Chandra was drawn to those questions in which nature becomes the locus for the exploration of mathematics, which in turn becomes a metaphor for the exploration of space and time in dance. The only question not specifically related to 'nature' in Chandra's production deals more erotically with a man-woman relationship in which a scattering of pearls on a necklace in 'an intense moment of love-making' provides the stimulus not just for another mathematical problem but for an examination of *eros* in the world of numbers.

A more practical consideration for the choice of questions in the production related to the knowledge of mathematics available to most spectators. Consciously, Chandra decided to focus on the problems of arithmetic, algebra and geometry avoiding the more abstract intricacies of calculus and trigonometry. This was because she wanted to involve the spectators at a mental level apart from engaging them in the exploration of the 'poetry of numbers' in dance. At some level, this choice has somewhat confused the more 'mathematically-oriented' spectators because they feel obliged to answer the questions rather than submit to the work imaginatively. The calculation of numbers takes precedence over the poetry of its interactions, and in the process, the dance itself is scrutinised rather than enjoyed. Chandra herself is somewhat responsible for this development because her commentary occasionally assumes the nature of a quiz rather than a playful query on the 'constant of pure numbers.'

Though Chandra has made no attempt to seek literal equivalences between the movements of the dancers and the numbers posed in the questions, it so happened that the very specificity of the problems inspired her choreography in particular ways. For instance, she found connections between particular combinations of numbers and the use of specific *talas* and *jatis,* which constitute the 'mathematics' of Bharatanatyam. At times the numbers in Bhaskaracharya's questions inspired the choice of the number of dancers on stage.

In fact, one of the great achievements of *Lilavati* is the way in which the *sahitya* is used in the production, at times for its pure musical value, its poetry, at other times for fluid *abhinaya* which is rendered primarily by Sujata but also shared with the other dancers. Consequently, the narrative of the production is constantly being 'broken' through combinations of pure dance, solo *abhinaya,* group *abhinaya,* music, and most magically, the use of *nrtta* as *abhinaya* where the so-called 'grammar' of Bharatanatyam assumes an expressivity rarely seen in dance performances today.

It would be difficult to think of another dance production like *Lilavati* that has managed to use the very formality of the idiom to deepen the clarity of the narrative. And the beauty is that every single movement in *Lilavati* is based on the 'traditional' language of Bharatanatyam that Chandra has learned from Guru Ellappa Pillai. At a conference in New Delhi, Chandra had to emphasise this fact when it was suggested that most of the movements were 'innovative.' She was compelled to clarify that, '*Lilavati* is pure Bharatanatyam, only it has never been seen this way before.' The one movement *not* from Bharatanatyam in the production is the *chakravaka asana* used in the *chakravaka* sequence, and that was, as Chandra claimed with due pride, her 'signature' as the choreographer of the work.

'Amala-kamala-rashe . . .'

The opening sequence, which is the most sedate and measured in the entire production, gently weaves patterns of movement around the central question: 'Lotus flowers, offerings for the gods. One-third for Siva, one fifth for Vishnu, one-sixth for Surya, one-fourth for Devi. Balance of six placed at Guru's feet. Lilavati, quickly tell the total number of lotus flowers.'[1]

At a particularly lyrical moment in the choreography, the dancers cluster on the floor, their fingers splayed in *hastas* suggesting the profusion of lotuses. Later, they represent the four deities — Shiva, Vishnu, Surya and Devi — with four specific *mudras,* raising their hands outwards at specific intervals, one movement following the other to create an overall sense of continuity. In these positions, the dancers 'hold' the *sahitya* with the stillness of their bodies. The treatment is predominantly iconographic with minimal elaboration. Through slow, hieratic movements, the deities are evoked without being sentimentalised.

Breaking the iconic structure with a dramatic gesture,

Sujata snaps her fingers as she poses the first question as Lilavati. At this point, the *nrtta* intervenes with the dancers positioning themselves at the far end of the stage. Then, with a slight angling of their bodies, they proceed to 'walk' briskly towards the front of the stage exploring the *nadai* or stylised walks of Bharatanatyam. The point is not just to display the precision of the walk, but to 'challenge' the audience with the full thrust of the forward movement. This becomes a recurring motif through the production with the final 'exit' of the dancers in one curved line connoting the confidence with which the question is answered. This attitude is conveyed through the energy of the movement itself, embodied in the tilt of the head, the hands on the waist, and the slightest smile of having accomplished something but in a spirit of fun rather than victory.

If one is searching for any 'feminism' in *Lilavati*, then one has to turn not to any heavy-handed, self-conscious interpretation of a woman's wisdom trapped in a patriarchal structure, but to the way in which Chandra's dancers question the audience with their bodies. They are not so much performing *to* the audience as they are playing *against* their expectations. Once again, it is through the stretch of their spines that Chandra's dancers seem to radiate their own assertion of a particular personality. In their final exit, they almost challenge the audience to question their right to answer the 'problem' posed to them.

'Panchamsho-Alikulat....'

The second question concerns a swarm of bees. The *sloka* specifies that 'one-fifth of the bees are on *kadamba* flowers, one-third on *shilindhra*. The difference multiplied by three on *kutaja*. One bee alone wanders from flower to flower.' Once again, through the question posed to Lilavati, we are asked to count the total number of bees.

The visual definition of this sequence lies in its elaboration on a single *hasta* — the *bhramara* (literally 'the bee') in which 'the thumb and middle finger touch in a curve with the forefinger curved in, with the other fingers separated and stretched out.'[2] In a shaft of light at the back of the darkened stage, we see this *hasta* in different combinations as the dancers enter in particular groups and configurations holding their hands aloft. As their fingers flutter like 'bees', the effect in almost surreal as we are compelled to look upwards at a flurry of seemingly disembodied gestures.

After this initial visual motif, the question is elaborated through *abhinaya* on a fully lit stage with Sujata creating the interplay of bees, flowers, Lilavati, and herself. At precise moments, the solo *abhinaya* is interspersed with sharp and occasionally skittish entries and exits of dancers corresponding to specific details in the question. Thus when the *sloka* says *'panchamshaho'* or one-fifth, three dancers enter to the *tala* beat of three; at *'trayamshaha'* or one-third, five dancers enter to the beat of five; at *'vishleshatriguno'*, six dancers enter to the beat of six.'[3]

The flight of the solitary bumble bee is danced to *ektala*. What we see in this breathtaking interlude is a totally free abandon of movement on stage, the flower and the bee almost chasing each other in a myriad of playful patterns. As they exit, Sujata who has been watching the sequence enters the abandon of the 'bee' herself, covering the entire width and depth of the stage with a series of sparkling movements. In the process, her use of the *hasta* acquires a life of its own, at once defined in itself, yet kinetically connected to the full flow of energy in her body.

The way in which Sujata plays multiple roles in *Lilavati* adds considerably to the fluidity of the narrative. By moving in and out of multiple states of being, she is at once identified with Lilavati herself through the vitality of her solo movements, but she is also intrinsically a part of the entire group. The *abhinaya* therefore is a *shared experience* among the dancers, which is quite different from most dance productions where the solo performer monopolises the attention. Here the choreography is always breaking and dissolving, dilating and contracting, so that the production seems to be structured on the principle of surprise. There is a 'spill of energies' as it were from Sujata to the other dancers and then back to Sujata, so that Lilavati (one could say) is 'here, there, and everywhere.' She becomes a pervasive presence, a composite of multiple energies rather than a single character.

Significantly, the sequence ends as in the first part with the entire company lining up at the back of the stage, moving forward, and then exiting with the 'Lilavati signature' — heads tilted, hands on waist, shoulders arched, the spine stretched. In this movement, each of the dancers is Lilavati in her own right while contributing to a larger statement on *Lilavati* itself.

'Yatam-Hamsakulasya...'

With the third question we enter the world of swans. Tantalisingly, we are told that 'ten times the square root of an x number of swans fly away to Manasarovar as the rainclouds gather. One-eighth retreat to a lake of lotuses. Left behind are three pairs of swans lost in love-play. Quickly tell, Lilavati, the number of swans.'

Around one movement only — the *hamsa gati* — Chandra choreographs the intricate details of the entire question. This is a slow, undulating movement where the body is bent from the waist below with the hands in *hamsasya hasta*. In *Lilavati* this one movement takes on a hypnotic quality as it is repeated over and over again in many combinations, directions, groupings, assemblings, separations, at different body levels with occasional punctuations of neck movement. Through the sheer depth of exploring one movement, Chandra makes us respect the multiple possibilities of the classical dance idiom.

Apart from using the conventional *hastas* and facial expressions to convey the details in the *sloka*, the *bhava* is conveyed through the abstractions of the body, so that the feeling of swans flying through rain-drenched clouds in the direction of Manasarovar is represented in the *yearning* of the entire body for Manasarovar. The body is thrust upwards with the *hamsasya hasta* held aloft. If such movements are steeped in sensuousness, it is because they are contextualised (if that is not too heavy a word) in a specific environment. As Chandra remarked in an interview: 'The movements of the swan that I have designed in *Lilavati* are the movements of a very Indian swan. When it raises its long neck to gaze at a rain cloud, there is a specific environment which is evoked.'[4]

It is through this questioning of the fundamental relationship between the forces of nature and their abstraction in dance-language that has contributed deeply to what one might describe as Chandra's perception of the *ecology of dance*. Here the body is not viewed as an anatomy or a vehicle or a composite of techniques, still less a machine that can be controlled. It is an organism that is part of a much larger spectrum of life-sustaining forces, which are capable of renewing themselves through a ceaseless cycle of energies. This is what underlies the strong emotional impact of *Lilavati* because at a time when the 'environment' has been denuded of its energies by so many malevolent forces, Chandra's world of dance reminds us that there are ways of transforming the invisible energies which lie within our bodies.

Needless to say, one cannot take these energies for granted because they, too, are under attack through all kinds of assaults — political, social, environmental. Through the rigour of a particular discipline, and most of all through the discovery and stretching of the spine, which holds the body together, there are ways in which the ecology of the body can be preserved and made to resonate in the language of dance. Once again, Chandra would not be falsely euphoric: 'You have to be truthful to the spine. It provides the energy circuit for dance. This energy, if truthful (i.e. divested of sentimentalism, false virtuosity, and decorative embellishments) will reach out to the audience as well.' Therefore, whether one is dancing swans or bees, the core of the energy in these diverse movements is centred in a knowledge of spine as related to a particular *hasta* and its extensions in space.

'Chakrakrauncha-Akulita Salile...'

In the most evanescent of episodes, we are introduced through the opening *sloka* to 'a lake rippling with waterbirds: *chakravaka* and *krauncha*. In the middle of the lake, a lotus blooms half a foot above the water's surface. A gentle breeze sways and dips the blossom in the water two feet away.' Using the primary lessons of geometry, Lilavati is expected to calculate the depth of the water.

If in the earlier sequence with the swans the focus was on details of individual movement, the opening images of the water-bird sequence evoke the magic of flight. Thus, the dancers enter in pairs with circling movements which culminate in *garuda bhramaris* in which they appear to be suspended in the air, as they support themselves on one leg, the other raised backwards above the level of the waist with the two hands stretched outwards. As the dancers 'fly' into this position in successive pairs, those who have already arrived rotate their bodies slowly holding the *garuda bhramari*. Then, in a flurry of movements, they all disappear and the stage is empty like an open sky.

Once again the dancers enter with a rotating movement which culminates in the *ekapada bhramari*, another variation on a one-legged standing position. Once the dancers have all assembled together, they hold the *bhramari en masse* for a split second, and then disperse yet again to reveal the empty stage. Through such seemingly small, yet powerful choreographic choices, Chandra makes one realise that the 'empty space' of theatre only begins to resonate when it has been previously filled with energy. Without this energy, the 'empty' space would be quite 'dead.'

In an even more magical evocation of flight, or more precisely, levitation, Chandra has her entire company lie on the floor and suspend a leg in the air with their bodies pressed against the ground. This is the only conscious departure from the Bharatanatyam idiom which is used in the rest of the production, inspired by the *chakravaka asana* from Yoga. More visibly than in the other movements in *Lilavati*, we get to see how the entire body has to be 'stretched' in order to evoke the sense of flight.

Following the representation of the water-birds, the dancers then proceed to evoke the movement of water and wind, swaying their bodies from side to side with a gentle flow of their hands. Later, they create the sense of undulating waves, each dancer alternately moving up and down in a vertical line to create the illusion of water. Once again, we are compelled to note how the entire body is used to create an empathy with water. In this regard, Chandra is constantly challenging her dancers to 'become' the water, 'become' the breeze, and not just represent it through codified gestures.

Out of the flow of movement in a vertical line, a *kamala-kalika* emerges held aloft in the air by Meera, who creates a most vivid image of a lotus with an intricate *hasta*. This insertion of a formal gesture within the free flow of movement enhances its immediacy. Thereafter, Meera glides on her toes to the far end of the stage, continuing to hold the *kamala-kalika* which almost seems to float over the surface of the water. The edge of the lake is now suggested through the dancers standing in a straight line, while Sujata (in a most brilliant visualisation of the geometrical problem) proceeds to move towards Meera on a diagonal with a brisk 'walk', after which she cuts across on a horizontal to the straight line of the dancers and then proceeds vertically to her original position. Thus, through her movements, she literally shapes a right-angled triangle on the stage which provides us with a vivid clue as to how the depth of the water can be calculated.

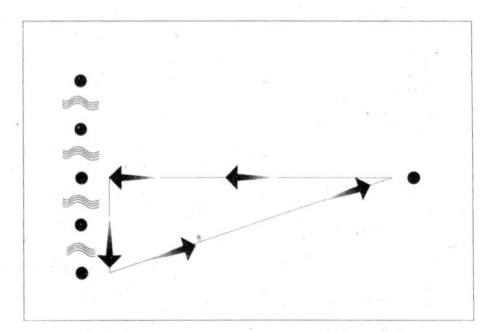

Once again, one should emphasise that it is not the calculation that is imperative but the poetics evolving through it which inspires the choreography. Breaking the pattern of the usual exit, Chandra has her dancers cluster in a group on the ground, their heads slightly thrust forwards, their hands stretched backwards like wings, as their bodies are gently lowered to create an illusion of water-birds roosting in their sleep. On this lyrical movement, the lights fade into darkness.

'Haras-Taras-Tarunya...'

Breaking the continuity provided through the abundance of images relating to nature, the last question posed in *Lilavati* concerns a man and a woman. 'In an intense moment of love-making, the woman's necklace snaps. Pearls scatter — one-third on the floor, one-fifth on the bed, one-sixth picked up by the *sakhi*, Sukeshi, one-tenth collected cautiously by the lover, with six pearls continuing to cling to the body of the woman on a thread.' After such an intimate evocation of the situation, the question is almost anticlimactic: 'What is the total number of pearls in the necklace?'

In this elaborate episode, Chandra uses the human dimensions of the problem to focus on one of her recurring concerns — the male-female interplay of energies. Beginning on an exceptionally brisk note, Chandra has the man and woman enter at lightning speed from either end of the stage. They dash past one another over and over again as they cross the stage in horizontal slashes of energy.

This is followed by the formation of the dominant vertical line used in the dance, with the woman standing in front with her back to the audience almost covering the man who faces her. Almost the entire choreography is structured on this line centre-stage with 'the woman pushing the man against the wall', which is Chandra's pithy description of the entire scene. Back and forth, the movement continues relentlessly, at times with the man approaching the woman with a forward movement while the woman counters his momentum with her own energy which is concentrated in the back.

Needless to say, the proximity of the dancers and their varying intensities of speed used in approaching and retreating from each other, contribute to the sensuousness of the encounter. There are no embellishments beyond this repetition of movement. The first variation occurs when the dancers suddenly separate to face each other on a horizontal axis on either side of the stage. Now they come together with the first gesture of 'endearment', which is nothing less than a martial slash of the hand raised upwards almost like a sword. When Udupi Lakshminarayan saw this movement for the first time, he was compelled to acknowledge that this love-making was more like war to him. But it is precisely this confrontational element in the love-play that makes it so startlingly different from the usual syrupy encounters that pass off as 'love' in the dance world.

Following this 'foreplay' between the man and the woman, the actual act of love-making is dramatised through a series of 'stills' in which the intimacy is at once cut and heightened through the use of a half-curtain. Needless to say, the curtain automatically enhances the theatricality of the situation by creating the sense of an interior space in which the two lovers are lost in a world of their own. Screening their intimacy judiciously, yet gracefully, the attendants manoeuver the curtain so that the lovers' bodies are fragmented. At times we only see the slow drift of an arm which is cut by the curtain which is then removed to reveal the man and woman 'held together with the eyes', their hands clasped around each other's necks.

Till this point in the sequence, Chandra has simply prepared the ground for a question (*'Haras-Taras-tarunya...'*) which is now vocalised for the first time and expressed by Sujata through a predominantly facial *abhinaya*. The spirit of fun continues as Chandra 'takes off' on the central image of the question, which is a *necklace*. In what would seem like an almost giddy improvisation, the dancers whirl on to the stage like pearls, and then whirl away, only to return to the back of the stage to create the visual of a necklace through a semi-circular formation. As the 'pendant', Sujata leads the dancers through a series of joyous walks, which accentuate the visual dimensions of the necklace. At times it seems to dilate, then contract, then shimmer, then sway in relation to the 'purest' of Bharatanatyam walks. The choreography could be described as sheer visual animism that brings to life the seemingly decorative image of a necklace.

In addition, a dramatic interlude is provided through the introduction of the *sakhi*, Sukeshi, who 'indicates' her character by holding on to the end of her plait. This is, perhaps, the only example of 'characterisation' in Chandra's work to date, but predictably, it is rendered through a formal interplay of rhythm, gesture, and movement. The five pearls picked up by Sukeshi are represented by five *jatis* which necessarily stimulate variations in *tala*. Following Sukeshi's exit, the man and woman return for a brief sequence where, in the seemingly domesticated mode of 'conjugal bliss', the man picks up the pearls from the ground and hands them over to the woman. The pearls sticking to her body are passed over lightly, and the couple saunters off-stage, hand-in-hand, more like friends than lovers.

Then follows the coda when the entire company of dancers enters and exits from side to side in opposite directions in varying combinations. This is a dance variation on the *sarukku* of *Angika* which serves both to punctuate and clear the performance space. In *Lilavati*, the sudden upsurge of energy and the sheer speed of the movement brings the work to a very energetically defined end.

As in the previous sequences, the dancers line up at the back of the stage punctuating the overall rhythm of the music with strong stamps of their feet. Then, in the 'signature' for which *Lilavati* will surely be most remembered, they move forward and with a swerve of their bodies exit in a curved line with their heads tilted and shoulders arched. And as they walk out briskly, having answered yet another question which leaves the audience guessing, there is a renewed sense of joy in celebrating the playful wisdom of Lilavati.

Touring 'Lilavati'

Of all the works in Chandra's repertoire, *Lilavati* is, perhaps, the most popular. Professional dancers like it because of its unprecedented use of the Bharatanatyam idiom as part of an overall choreography. Theatre people, on the other hand, respond to its wit and exploration of dramatic situations in the language of dance. Scholars appreciate its acknowledgement of Bhaskaracharya's genius. And so, this is one work in which Chandra has been able to 'reach out' to wide audiences cutting across aesthetic priorities and prejudice. It is not surprising that *Lilavati* is her only production to date that has been shown on television in a programme that set new standards for the design of dance in the mass media. Dashrath's inspired use of a painted back-drop incorporating earth colours and running lines contributed so considerably to the visual dynamics of the programme, that his paintings are now used as back-drops in the live productions of *Lilavati* as well.

Most recently, *Lilavati* toured Karnataka where it was seen in Mysore, Udupi, and smaller rural centres like Heggodu (where the production was sponsored by the grass-root cultural organisation Ninasam) and Manchikere. In these last two places in particular, it was heartening to see how the seeming 'sophistication' of the production did not impede the very warm rapport between the dancers and the predominantly rural-based spectators. Despite intense technical problems faced in Manchikere in particular, ranging from breakdowns in power supply, voltage fluctuations, an improvised performance space, it was also reassuring to see how the dancers responded to the specific challenges without compromising on their own emerging professional standards. The show at Manchikere was taken as seriously as it would have been performed in more seemingly prestigious dance forums.

One particular forum that revealed the conceptual vitality of the work was sponsored by the organisation Premio Gaia, which is known internationally for its groundbreaking interventions in preserving the ecological balance of the earth. Inspired by the environmentalist James Lovelock's affirmation of 'Gaia' as 'Living Earth', this organisation honoured Chandra among many other distinguished ecologists, ethnobotanists, and artists at a refreshingly informal ceremony held in Palermo, Sicily in September 1991. Here there was a concern not only for the 'ecology of nature' but an openness to various creative idioms celebrating the 'ecology of the mind.' Thus, one had an opportunity to see and discuss Godfrey Reggio's inspired film on the animal world, *Anima Mundi* (set to Philip Glass's music), and relate its abstractions of movement to the poetry of nature in dance celebrated in *Lilavati*, which was staged as part of the forum.

Though the Sicilian audience did not succeed in answering any of Bhaskaracharya's questions, which were translated into Italian, they responded to the sensuality of the dance with a very perceptible *joie de vivre*. The more questioning among the environmentalists were more fascinated by the aesthetics of ecology embodied in the rarefied idiom of Bharatanatyam, which was a new 'language' for most of them. Thus, along with intense discussion about the very real problems of deforestation and monoculture, the participants in the Palermo forum also had a unique opportunity to relate their 'politics' to 'art.' More specifically, through Chandra's intervention, they were able to begin an understanding of how the energies of nature get crystallised through abstractions in dance which are themselves based on the principles of body as *mandala*.

These exchanges of notes on ecology and art were at once useful and suggestive, reminding its participants of the creative possibilities of the 'living earth' of which we are all a part. One left Palermo with a renewed respect for *Lilavati's* hidden powers. The 'ecology of dance', which I had addressed earlier in the chapter, became a more vivid issue in the larger context of the forum. One was alerted not only to the connection between dance and numbers in *Lilavati*, but to the interplay of forces and energies in nature which make this dance possible in the first place.

Indeed, as *Lilavati* gets increasingly popular, it will be imperative to hold on to the lessons of nature which are inscribed in the so-called 'grammar' of its idiom. Without a constant exploration of the energies contained within its spectrum of movements, *Lilavati* could easily become cosmetic, a mere show, a money-spinner, even a 'lollipop' of sorts. To retain the integrity of the work, one can never afford to forget that the questions in *Lilavati* are perhaps more precious than the answers, because they contain the secrets of nature which are eternally alive. In her own way, Chandra has tried to keep these questions alive through the radiance of her choreography and her ceaseless attempt to relate the energies of art to the enigmas of life.

27

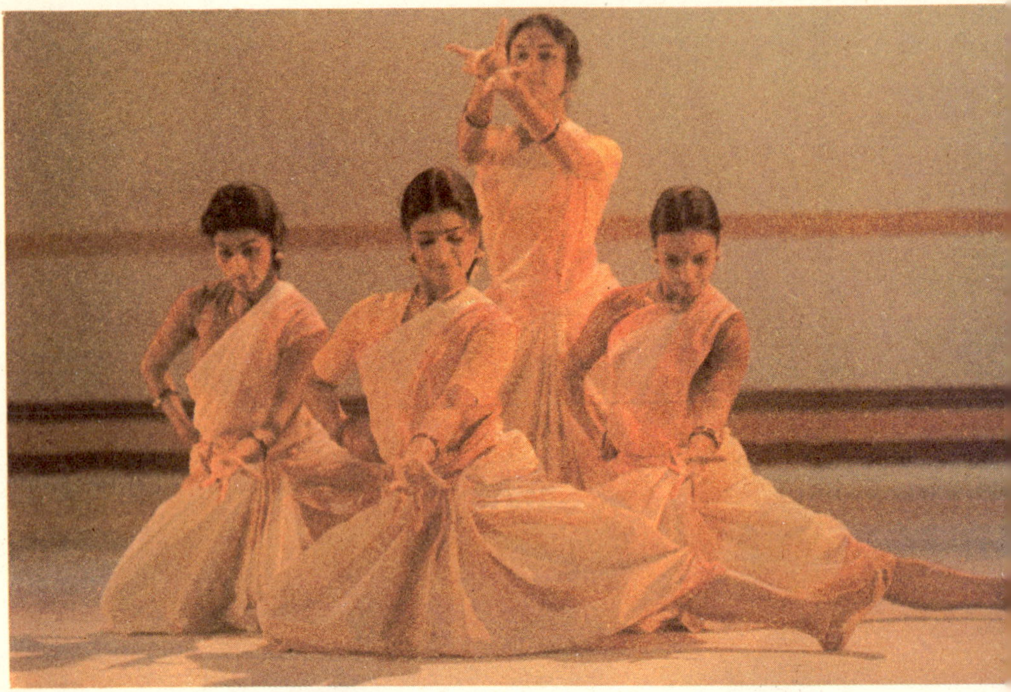

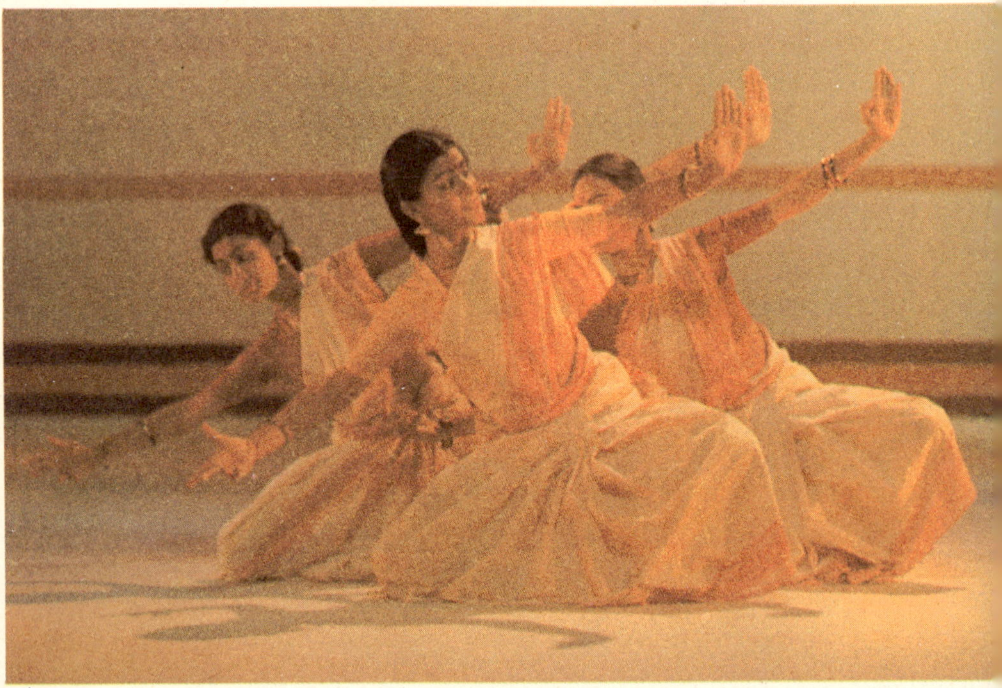

30

31

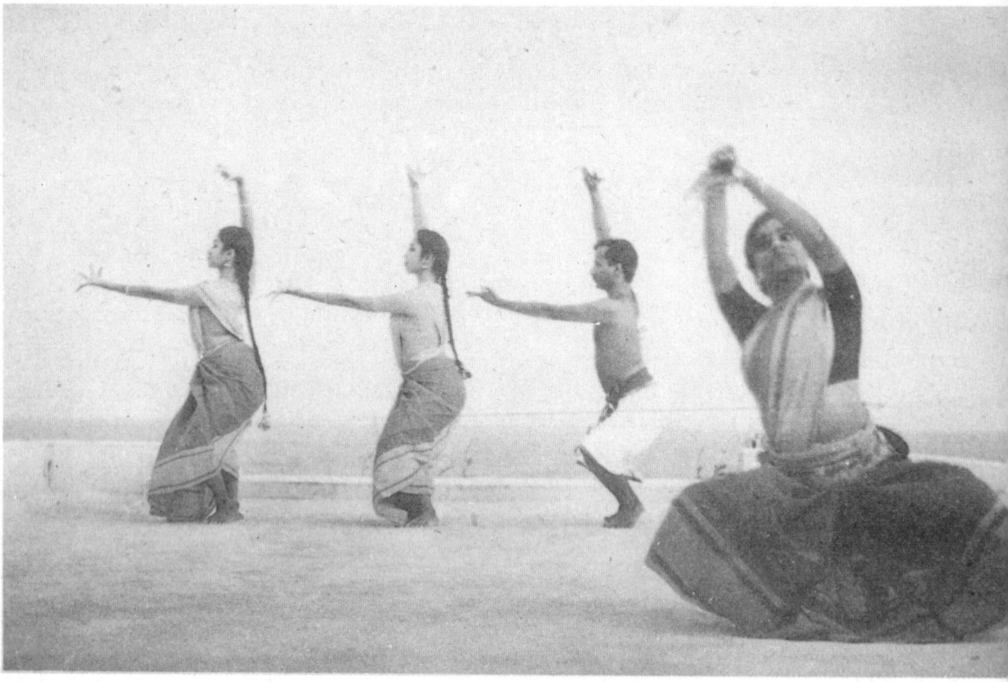

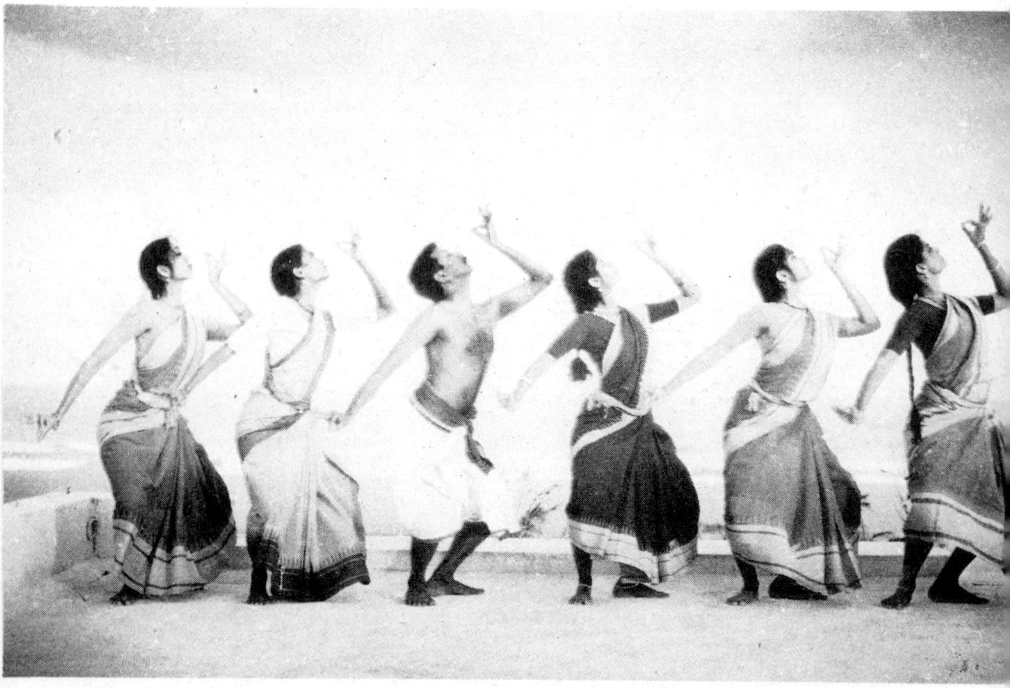

34

9

35

Homage to Breath

If the sheer effervescence of *Lilavati* succeeded in disarming criticism, the production did not leave Chandra with a false sense of reassurance. Within a year she produced yet another substantial work which could be regarded as the quintessence of austerity in dance. *Prana* is Chandra's homage to breath, that vital force which keeps us alive and of which we are so ignorant. Indeed, at a time when the 'world is short of breath' (to use Chandra's words), it becomes almost mandatory to reclaim the art of breathing.

Ironically, though one would have imagined that dancers would be more conscious of this 'art', the reality is that they too are distanced from the vital forces of *prana*. Confronting this problem within the immediacies of her own dance work, Chandra deepened her own 'search for breath' through *Prana*, which attempts nothing less than a correlation between Yoga and Bharatanatyam, or more specifically, their *asanas* and *adavus* which may be structured differently, but which are, nonetheless, connected through common principles of energy and breath.

Breathing is so seemingly invisible and 'basic' an activity that one is almost tempted not to question it at all. However, among the many invaluable sources of knowledge in our culture, *Pranayama* could lie at the foundation of many intellectual and physical disciplines. Generally viewed as the fourth stage of Yoga, this 'science of breathing' is said to initiate the *antaranga sadhana* or inner quest for Self, whereby the 'senses can be freed from the thraldom of the objects of desire.'[1] In the supremely clear prose of the yoga master, Sri B.K.S. Iyengar, we learn that:

> *Prana* means breath, respiration, life, vitality, wind, energy or strength... *Ayama* means length, expansion, stretching or restraint. *Pranayama* thus connotes extension of breath and its control. This

control is over all functions of breathing, namely, (1) inhalation or inspiration, which is termed *puraka* (filling up); (2) exhalation or expiration, which is called *rechaka* (emptying the lungs); and (3) retention or holding the breath... which is termed *kumbhaka*.²

One could enter many metaphysical subtleties and discriminations about *Pranayama,* but what needs to be emphasised at the very outset is that Chandra's production is not about *Pranayama*. Indeed, one could justifiably question whether *Pranayama* can ever be 'represented' on stage. It is one of the most difficult and interiorised states of consciousness that very few students of Yoga can claim to know with any degree of honesty. In Chandra's group, only Nandakumar has investigated Pranayama at a fairly advanced level. The other dancers are still exploring the so-called 'third stage' of Yoga which focuses on *asanas* (postures), which are the primary focus of attention in the production. Needless to say, even at this stage, the appropriate breathing is a vital factor for facilitating a 'mastery' of the *asana* in which the body is 'conquered', in Iyengar's words, and made into 'a fit vehicle for the soul.'³

At a purist level, there are traditionalists among *yoga* masters who prohibit any kind of interaction between Yoga and dance. Chandra, too, firmly believes that the disciplines, which are distinct, should not be 'mixed' arbitrarily. Nonetheless, there is much to learn from a close and rigorous study of their interrelationships. In this context, she often likes to counter the prejudice of traditionalists by reminding them of a famous story in which we learn that 'when Shiva as Nataraja danced on Kailasa, he had before him an august audience. There was Bharata who was inspired to create the *Natyasastra*. There was Panini who was inspired to write the *Vyakaranashastra* (grammar). There was Vyaghrapada who inspired martial arts. There was also Patanjali who was inspired to write the *Yogasutras*.⁴ Without seeking historical 'authenticity' for this story, it is possible to realise its acknowledgement of the interrelatedness of different philosophical, physical, and linguistic traditions in India.

Indeed, if there is one lesson that is illustrated from observing the process of *Prana* (which I was privileged to watch from its earliest stages), it is simply that Yoga practitioners can learn as much from dance as dancers can learn from Yoga. It is the reciprocity of these disciplines that Chandra explores in *Prana,* not the superiority of one over the other. Indeed, the entire production is most harmoniously balanced in its almost measured distribution of time with the *asanas* of Yoga being interspersed with the *adavus* of Bharatanatyam, both given their due respect in the overall time-space continuum of the production.

Asanas/Adavus

Representing the more corporeal stage of Yoga, *asanas* should be sharply differentiated from 'poses' and 'gymnastic feats.' In these still postures, where the limbs of the body are coordinated to form particular conglomerates of energy, one can attain 'a complete equilibrium of body, mind, and spirit.' Or to put it more realistically, one has to work towards this 'equilibrium' which could be a lifetime's undertaking. As Nandakumar puts it ruefully and with all the humility of a *sadhaka,* 'I have not yet seen the *padma* in the *padmasana* — and that is supposed to be the most rudimentary of forms.'

When I question him about the word 'see', I begin to realise some of the complexities involved in realising the images embodied in the *asanas.* As is well known, the *asanas* are almost emphatically grounded in the particularities of nature and everyday life, which are specifically named. As in the stylised gaits of Bharatanatyam there are specific references to the *mayura* (peacock) and *hamsa* (swan) as well as more 'rare species' like the *kapinjala* or partridge, 'the *chataka* bird which is supposed to live only on raindrops and dew.'[5] Similarly, Yoga offers its own visual complements to the martial postures of the horse, the lion, among other quadrupeds, including more domesticated animals like the dog — and not just a dog but a 'downward looking one' which is seen in the *adho mukha svanasana*. Along with the *bhujanga* or serpent which is invoked in both the vocabularies of dance and the martial arts, Yoga even incorporates the most seemingly insignificant of insects in its pantheon of movements, like the *salabha* (locust).

It even vivifies inanimate objects like the staff of a Yogin as in the *yogadandasana* as well as the most intimate of organisms like the human embryo as in the *garbha pindasana*. In its celebration of life embracing mountains (*tadasana*) and trees (*vrksasana*), its homage to mythic figures and deities ranging from Hanuman to Vishwamitra, it does not forget to include death in the *savasana*, where the body resembles a corpse in the most seemingly simple, yet 'difficult' of postures to 'master.' In order to master death in the form of an *asana*, the mind has to be stilled, which necessitates a total control over one's *prana*.

Counterpointing the density of stillness explored in particular *asanas* in *Prana* are the *adavus*. These combinations of hand, foot, head and eye movements in different sequences are performed with an almost divine clarity to *vilambit kaal*, the slow tempo that provides the pulse of the production. Each measure of movement resonates so powerfully that after a point, in my experience at least, the *vilambit* becomes part of one's heart beat, as the journey of *Prana* takes one inwards into unexplored areas of our consciousness. Sustained from beginning till the end in one uninterrupted span of time, it is the sheer power of *vilambit kaal* that brings the *asanas* and *adavus* together in a rare harmony, one tuning into the other, reinforcing the most basic principles of energy that help us not only to dance but to live. Quietly, yet rigorously, *Prana* urges us to hear our own breathing.

Returning to Navagraha

While the *asanas* and *adavus* constitute the basic elements of the choreography, the larger structure of *Prana* is inspired by one of Chandra's recurring images in dance — the Navagraha. Almost eighteen years after her production with Kamadev on the same subject, Chandra now returned to the iconography of the nine planetary deities to provide her with the basic 'grid' for the production. Now at long last she did have trained dancers to represent each *graha,* unlike her earlier disastrous experience with nine boys in the opening show of *Navagraha* in Pondicherry where she realised the impossibility of working with non-dancers. In *Prana,* with the support of her dancers and Yoga exponent, Nandakumar, she was finally able to realise her vision of the Navagraha in what could be considered her most definitive work as a choreographer.

Though the iconography of the Navagraha varies considerably from temple to temple, it is the square mandala of the *Navagraha* that was the primary source of inspiration for the production. The one central principle that Chandra retained from the original iconography concerns the multicentricity of the *grahas,* who face in different directions. Translated into dance terms, this means that the individual dancers representing each *graha* are limited by the space allotted to them — literally one-ninth of the total square — but within that space they are free to revolve around their own 'centre' in any number of directions and deflections inspired by the multidimensionality of the Bharatanatyam idiom.

While the *navagraha* are traditionally represented by specific colours, gems, grains, metals, minerals, Chandra focused on two of its correlations — the numbers and *yantras* (cosmic diagrams) — which enabled her to structure her choreography in a specific way. Incorporating some basic knowledge of the *grahas* as a 'take-off point', Chandra used a specific number of dancers to represent the numeral traditionally associated with each *graha*. She also shaped the *asanas* in accordance to the visual symbols of the particular *grahas* as noted below:

Surya (Sun)	1	●
Soma (Moon)	2	∪
Angaraka (Mars)	3	▲
Budha (Mercury)	4	⬥
Brihaspati (Jupiter)	5	—
Sukra (Venus)	6	⬟
Sani (Saturn)	7	∪
Rahu (Eclipse)	8	≡
Ketu (Eclipse)	9	>

Each of the *grahas* is evoked through a cosmic diagram created by the dancers, one dancer representing Surya leading to nine for Ketu. All the dancers participate in the *adavu* sequences as well which intersperse the visualisation of the specific *grahas* through *asanas*. And thus, the choreography of *Prana* oscillates between the meditative interiorised states of Yoga and the crystallised forms of Bharatnatyam in which the dancers appear like a constellation of stars.

Navagraha Kritis

One further source of power that has contributed to the realisation of the Navagraha is the most inspired — and one could say, radical choice of the *navagraha kritis* composed by Muthuswamy Dikshitar (1775-1835), who is one of the legendary figures of the 'Trinity' in Carnatic music along with his contemporaries, Tyagaraja and Shyama Shastri. Apart from his mastery of *raga*, Dikshitar also excelled in his profound exploration of *vilambit kaal,* which was the most appropriate tempo in his musical vision for an evocation of *shanta rasa.*[6] This is the *rasa* which permeates the experience of listening to the *navagraha kritis,* which almost actualise the state of *vishranti* or 'rest' in which the state of absorption in a particular aesthetic object (in this case, the *kritis*) is so complete that there is almost 'no extraneous movement or desire to break that state of consciousness.'[7]

At a more factual level, it is said that the *navagraha kritis* were composed when Dikshitar was staying in Tiruvarur where there was scarcely a deity, or shrine or temple which he had not addressed through his musical devotion. On a more mundane note — and it never fails to move me how the greatest of seers can respond to the smallest of matters — the *kritis* were composed to alleviate an acute stomach pain suffered by one of Dikshitar's students, Tambiappan, whose malady was associated with 'a bad period in his horoscope.'[8] It is said that after composing seven *kritis* from Surya to Sani, Dikshitar urged his student to sing these compositions regularly. The student followed this 'prescription' and was cured.

Set in the seven Suladi-*talas,* the series of *kritis* 'begins with the song on the Sun in Saurashtra and ends with the one on Saturn in Yedukula Kambhoji, including the rare Paras on Venus.'[9] The *kritis* on Rahu and Ketu were composed later. So we learn from V. Raghavan's authoritative study of Dikshitar in which we are informed that the *sahitya* or text of the *navagraha kritis* follows in the tradition of the *Mantra Shastras.* From these texts, with which he was intimately familiar, Dikshitar derived his model of describing 'the forms of the deities to be contemplated, the posture (*asana*), the expression on the face, the gesture of assurance (*abhaya*) and the various kinds of weapons (*astra*) held in the hands.'[10]

For Chandra, it was not so much the rhetoric of the *sahitya* in the *navagraha kritis* that mattered but their profound sense of flow. In her earlier production she had performed her adaptation of the Surya Namaskar to Dikshitar's '*Suryamurthe...*' that begins the series of *kritis*.

Even at that stage she had realised that it was almost impossible to dance to the sheer 'weight' of the *kritis*. The only movement that was appropriate had to be as still and concentrated as possible closely related to yogic principles. Unfortunately, this was not initially understood by most classicists and performers who ridiculed the idea of 'dancing' to Dikshitar's music. Only gradually did Chandra manage to convince them of her particular way of embodying the *kritis* through movement.

These *kritis* are now used in *Prana* during the *asana* sequences in which the particular *grahas* are visualised. They are interspersed with the *adavu* sequences incorporating live percussion and *sollukattus* provided by Udupi Lakshminarayan. Thus the entire score of *Prana* moves back and forth between Dikshitar and Bharatanatyam *sollukattus*, recorded music and live sound. While this requires very sensitive balancing, it also adds considerably to the 'movement of sound' in the entire piece, at once moving inwards and outwards, resonating on stage and suffusing the entire space from beyond.

The Opening of 'Prana'

Prana begins on a totally still visual: Nandakumar holding the *parsva sirsasana* or head-stand in the centre of the stage.[11] In this 'zero position' as Nandakumar likes to describe it, the legs are thrust in the air, ram-rod straight, evoking a sense of weightlessness. In this pure verticality, where the elbows are totally aligned to the points on the shoulders, there is the most exhilirating sense of equilibrium, a means of holding the body still while looking at the world upside-down.

In the total stillness of the movement, punctuated by the drone of the *sruti*, the dancers gradually come on stage in different combinations with a very matter-of-fact dance walk. Arriving at their respective positions in the square-like grid with Nandakumar as Surya in the centre, the dancers slowly lower themselves to the ground and very gradually move into *salabhasana*. It is a most arresting movement to watch particularly since we see it performed simultaneously by the eight dancers in multiple directions. What contributes infinitesimally, yet powerfully to the overall energy is the undertone of '*ta ka dhi mi ta ka dhi mi*' which the dancers voice under their breath, creating a most vivid sense of the coordination between breath and movement.

As the dancers gradually lower their bodies to the ground, there is a totally unexpected shift of energy in the centre as Nandakumar twists his legs in the *parivrttaikapada sirsasana,* his trunk turned sideways, the legs splayed in the air in the shape of some pre-historic bird. All the while he continues to balance himself on the head.

While admiring the sheer risk involved in performing this movement on stage, I simply cannot forget the wonder of it when I saw it for the first time. Perhaps, this was simply because I was not anticipating anything, but when Nandakumar twisted his legs in the air, it almost seemed as if the entire stage (and with it, the earth) was moving. It is the closest I have ever come to experiencing a 'cosmic movement' on stage. It was not just Nandakumar's legs that were twisted, but the entire space with it.

As the dancers stand up slowly, there is yet another charge in the entire space which is provided by the sudden beat of the *mridangam* to which the dancers move in a circle, almost like a galaxy of planets. Then they line up at the back of the stage in a cluster holding strong *mandala* positions.

Meanwhile Nandakumar slowly lowers himself and, with split-second transitions, moves into the *virabhadrasana,* which is shaped almost like a 'missile' with the entire body suspended in the air on one leg. From this quintessence of poise and force, which suggests a potential of explosive energy, Nandakumar moves into the *hanumanasana,* which resembles a split with both the legs stretched on the floor but vertically rather than horizontally. The only variation is that Nandakumar does not bring his hands to his chest but slowly lowers his hands from top to waist-level stretching them on either side.

As he does this, with his eyes 'making holes in the space'

(as Chandra likes to describe it), the dancers move forward in a mass, sliding their feet on the ground with their legs outstretched in a Kathakali position. As they hold this martial stance behind the *hanumanasana,* the lights fade on the first sequence, leaving a most vivid after-image of the homage to Surya.

Planetary Yantras

a) *Surya*

A single beam of light falls on the exact spot where Nandakumar had been positioned. Only now we see Geetha who evokes the power of Surya through an exploration of the *utthita parsvakonasana.* In a slow flow of movement that radiates a sensuous power, Geetha stretches her entire body with one hand resting on the ground, the other covering the ears in a straight line. In this position, which is subtly highlighted through the upward thrust of the head, one can actually see the skin on the sides of the body being stretched almost like a fabric. And almost magically, Geetha becomes a 'bird in flight.' That is how Chandra envisioned the *asana:* the Sun as a fire-bird.

b) *Adavu Sequences*

As the *kriti* to Surya fades, the live music begins with *mridangam, morsing,* and the *sollukattus* voiced by Udupi Lakshminarayan. Then begins the first sequence of *adavus* which is performed in *vilambit,* each beat amplified by the simultaneous movement of different leg and arm positions. The dynamism of the choreography lies in the simple fact that while all the dancers perform the same group of *adavus,* they begin it at different points, so that one dancer could be bent downwards from her waist, while the other could be looking sideways at an outstretched hand, while yet another could be looking upwards in the direction of her fingertips. The overall effect is that of a multicentric kaleidoscope of pure movement, with the dancers' bodies cutting into each other, at times superimposed on each other, at other times almost colliding into each other, then drifting past one another. It is a most crystalline evocation of galactic movement, the planets at play in the cosmos.

Among the other features in the *adavu* sequences, one should emphasise the strategic way in which Chandra incorporates the *adavus* within the exits of the dancers before the next *asana* sequence. This creates a sense of a 'controlled scattering' of bodies in space, where the physical connections between the dancers are sustained but through tangents and distances rather than determined proximities.

Another way in which Chandra incorporates the *asanas* into her choreography is by 'clearing the space' in the manner she had explored in *Angika* with the dancers separating in two groups, gliding past one another and then moving to the extremities of the stage.

In one of the sequences, Chandra also explores the principle of 'arrested movement' by making one of her dancers or a group of them 'walk' within the grid while the others hold their still positions. This creates tense and disjointed configurations, with some dancers almost colliding against each other, while others seem to be isolated.

One way or the other, the purpose is to explore multiple combinations of energy through asymmetry rather than symmetry, unpredictability rather than causality, risk through assertion of individuality rather than safety in numbers, nuance of specific details rather than 'quantitative' effects. It is not surprising, therefore, that all the dancers (even those whose faces are not clearly seen because of their back positions) register their own presence on stage. In this 'galaxy', one could say that there are no 'stars' but individual beings.

c) *Soma*

Having provided a general perspective on the *adavu* sequences, which acquire an almost hypnotic quality through their repetition and subtle differentiation, we can now focus on the *asanas* used in the creation of the *yantras*.

For Soma which follows Surya, two dancers create the crescent-like shape of the moon through a strangely intimate sequence. It begins with both of them lying on the floor looking at each other, a distanced couple.

The *asana* used in the sequence is an adaptation of the *vasisthasana*, where the entire body is suspended sideways balancing on a single hand with the feet held tightly together like a fulcrum. The effect is heightened when, with an almost glacial stealth, the dancers swivel their bodies so that the same *asana* is seen in reverse perspective, one dancer looking outwards, the other facing inwards.

What needs to be pointed out about the performance of the *asanas* in general is the subtlety with which they have been 'adapted' and 'transformed.' The most important consideration concerns time. While an *asana* performed in the privacy of one's room can be continued or stopped according to one's will or state of preparation, the *asanas* on stage have prescribed durations of time. Moreover, they are performed not in silence but to Dikshitar's music, which has its own energy and immediacy. To maintain the flow of their movements, the dancers continue to count silently maintaining their own dance-beats within the framework of the *asanas*.

The second difference that needs to be highlighted concerns the very basic point that an *asana* is generally preceded by a warm-up or by another *asana*. While the entire opening sequence of *Prana* could be viewed as a warm-up, it is not so in an entirely technical way. Also, in performing an *asana,* one may need to 'begin' at a very different point from the prescribed beginning in the yogic *shastras*. For the larger concentration of 'flow' in the performance, as well as for the general visual effect, it is necessary for the Soma sequence, for example, to begin with the dancers lying flat on the ground, face downwards, from where they move into *bhujangasana,* and then gradually work their way into *vasisthasana,* which is the primary *asana* of the sequence.

Despite these small changes which have emerged through the performance of the *asanas,* Chandra has tried very hard to be 'true' as far as possible to their inner principles. Faking an *asana* was simply not allowed. Rather, the dancers were constantly urged to stretch their limits, if necessary by revealing their own inadequacies in the process. The purpose was not to exhibit 'perfection' but to show the struggle involved in realising this goal.

d) *Angaraka*

In the visual evocation of the planet Mars represented by a triangle, three of the dancers perform the *prasarita padottanasana* in a triangular formation with their legs stretched in a standing position, the palms placed on the floor with the head looking straight out. Of course, this movement is performed so slowly that it takes almost three to five minutes to complete. In the original *asana*, the 'destination' is to touch the floor with the crown of the head so that the entire weight of the body is supported by the legs. In *Prana*, what registers most powerfully is the slightly upward surge of the body after the head is raised from the ground and thrust forward almost at eye-level with the audience.

Visually, the most startling feature of the *asana* lies in the defined use of the buttocks, a part of the female anatomy that is normally camouflaged on stage. Here the power of the image lies in the very disembodiment of the form. Each of the dancers is part of a larger triangle and each creates a triangle in her own right with the two extremities of the legs forming the base ends of the geometric form. In addition, if one looks very carefully, one can see a shadow on the ground created through the bodies of the dancers. 'This is', to Chandra's delight, 'a most perfect triangle', almost an ethereal sign of Angaraka itself created through light.

e) *Budha*

In this sequence, four dancers create the image of a 'droplet' holding what would seem like the easiest and most familiar of *asanas* — the *vrksa* or 'tree'. In the initial stage of its exploration in the open-air Mandala theatre, nothing could have been more sublime. The dancers would be suspended in their one-legged positions, their hands drifting slowly upwards, then lowered, so that at certain points their arms would intercut into each other, creating a criss-cross of images. No one could have imagined that there would be a problem with this sequence. The dancers seemed to have fully understood the basic principle of *vrksasana* which necessitates a downward pull of the leg and the upward thrust of the hands so that the body seems to be pulled in opposite directions.

Significantly, this was the one sequence (so 'perfect' in rehearsal) that proved to be disastrous on the opening-night performance when not one of the dancers could hold the *asana* that they imagined they had 'mastered.' There were, of course, unprecedented practical problems relating to the performance itself. A performer's silk *dhoti* was too slippery for the suspended leg to get a firm grip on the thigh of the other leg. Then there was the glare of spotlights which had not been sufficiently anticipated, apart from vibrations on the stage floor which persisted after the previous *adavu* sequence had been performed. Perhaps, in addition to all these *vighnas* (obstacles), Nandakumar says that the dancers were possibly assailed by 'demons of doubt' which had emerged through over-confidence.

Today, the *vrksa* is more controlled in performance, but it has never achieved the grace of its rendition in those early rehearsals, when one could get lost in the magical stillness of the movement. One obvious problem that could account for its difficulty in performance has to do with its duration: five minutes. This is an 'eternity' in terms of performance time, and even Chandra is compelled to acknowledge that she is perhaps asking too much of her dancers to hold the *asana* for the entire time.

So now, there is a more gradual breakdown of the movement which begins with the dancers simply standing and raising their hands; the *vrksa* follows. At long last the dancers are beginning to realise that the point is not just to balance on one leg, but to sustain the entire flow of movement from beginning till the end. If they cannot sustain their balance, it is no longer 'the end of the world' for them. They simply lower the suspended leg and *stand,* holding on to the cycle of energy created through the other bodies on stage. In the meanwhile, Dikshitar's *kriti* dedicated to Budha continues in the background, seemingly indifferent to the minor mishaps on stage.

f) *Other Yantras*

The journey of *Prana* continues in its measured oscillation of *asanas* and *adavus* in which the remaining planets are visualised through the austere 'lines' of Brihaspati, the nuanced feminity of the 'star-like' Sukra, the 'rings' of Saturn and the 'arrow' of Rahu quivering with taut intensity.

Finally, in the concluding evocation of the eclipse Ketu, the dancers cut across the stage on a diagonal like a flash of lightning. This is the only moment in the entire production in which the sheer speed of the dancers consciously breaks the relentless use of *vilambit*. Displaying her keen sense of minimalist effects, Chandra insists that this fast movement can be the only conscious use of speed in the production. To repeat it could only result in a negation of its power.

Having entered in fast speed, the dancers then hold their positions on the diagonal and return to *vilambit* as they slowly sink to the floor in unison and shape the *dhanurasana* with their bodies. From this bow-like structure of the body, the dancers simply lower their heads and feet on the floor and relax for a few moments, the stage seemingly strewn with still corpses facing downwards.

Then, they gradually arch their torsos from the waist up in the *bhujangasana,* their eyes focusing upwards towards a still point. This is a moment of total synchrony of mind, body, and being. Nothing is pushed. The *asana* is allowed to be what it is. Then, maintaining total coordination in movement, the dancers rise to their feet and simply stand, slowly raising their hands to the waist. It is in this most ordinary of gestures, neither strictly related to dance or

Yoga, that the dancers radiate their greatest strength. From Surya to Ketu, they have 'journeyed' within their bodies and this inner 'journey' registers in their stillness.

From 'Namaskar' to 'Shanti'

Having completed the entire cycle of the *navagraha*, the dancers now perform the Namaskar sequence of movements described earlier in the book (see Chapter Seven). With this sequence, there is a total change in the vibrancy and colour of the musical score, contrasting sharply with the dry resonance of the *sollukattu* patterns. Now there is an assertion of martial as opposed to yogic or dance energies, but so elegantly constrained within the limits of the choreography that it radiates a militant grace rather than mere power. Celebratory, yet taut in its total coordination of movement, which is held through sculpturesque body-clusters, *Namaskar* presents an efflorescence of energies, which is a fitting tribute to the elements that have been celebrated in *Prana* so far.

Significantly, however, Chandra does not end on this celebratory sequence whose 'climactic' possibilities she consciously negates. Once again there is a swift transition to the *grahas* themselves, who line up at the far end of the stage in a straight line — all eight dancers silhouetted on the darkening stage, resembling a distant row of deities. Joining them in front is Nandakumar who has reappeared as Surya as in the opening of the production. Now under a single shaft of light, he holds the *garudasana*, his legs interlocked, his hands entwined, the tips of the fingers rising above his head like a tongue of fire.

In the meanwhile, the dancers continue to radiate stillness as silence descends on stage punctuated only by the strangely primitive and eerie sounds of the *morsing*. Then, in one unobtrusive movement, the dancers move forward and create a square grid around Nandakumar, much more concentrated than the opening *mandala* of the production so that it acquires additional density. In this perfect square, the dancers hold various *mandala* positions in different directions, one leg raised above the ground, hands outstretched in clearly defined *hastas*, with the *garudasana* still barely perceptible through the cluster of bodies. In this final image, it seems as if the *navagraha* are levitating, yet firmly grounded to the earth. As the dancers hold their sculpturesque positions, Lakshminarayan chants a *sloka* invoking the aura of Shanti which brings the production to a very deep and restful end.

And yet, this is not how Chandra had originally wanted to end the production. The 'Shanti sloka' has been included primarily on Lakshminarayan's insistence. This could partly be ascribed to his conviction that the Navagraha need to be appeased during performance. Chandra herself had wanted to end the work on pure silence, punctuated only by the *sruti*, echoing the silence with which the production begins. She had argued at length with Lakshminarayan about the power of this choice and even criticised the use of '*Shanti*' as a cliché. But in this particular case, Lakshminarayan was not willing to budge from his decision, and even Chandra had finally to accept that his beliefs had to be respected in their own right. However, she has not yet given up the possibility of finding the opportunity and courage one day to end *Prana* on a note of pure silence without the mediation of any *sloka*. For her, this would be an even greater tribute as an artist to the cosmic energies of the *Navagraha*.

Beyond the Disaster of Opening Night

In retrospect, the first show of *Prana* at Auroville was something of a disaster. Clearly, this was not on account of lack of rehearsal. If anything, *Prana* has been more consistently rehearsed than most of Chandra's productions. The opportunity to perform in Auroville was viewed positively as a way of testing the dynamics of the work with an unknown audience. But from the start, the production verged on total collapse. Nandakumar just about survived from 'crashing to the ground' in the *sirsasana* sequence. A feverish Chandra (whose temperature increased to 103 degrees during the course of the day) totally failed to 'find her centre' on stage in the *Surya Namaskar* sequence which had originally been included in the production. The dancers themselves failed in their strongest moments. As for the lighting, controlled by the ever-reliable Sadanand who radiates positive energies in the worst of crises, it was almost sadistic in its abrupt fluctuations of power. And yet, through all this disorientation, I could not help marvelling how the dancers managed to hold themselves together as far as possible and go through with the production.

Many productions later, during a performance in a make-shift theatre space in Mysore, we faced a near calamity that could have resulted in an accidental death. Geetha was performing her *asana* in the opening homage to Surya, when the spotlight directly above her fused so violently that a live wire snapped and almost landed on her body. Seemingly oblivious of the danger, to which the audience responded with audible gasps, Geetha simply moved behind the dangling wire and continued the rest of the sequence, maintaining its flow with an unreal calm. Needless to say, the performance had to be stopped for a few minutes while the spotlight and wire were removed.

But in retrospect, I cannot help wondering about the incident at levels that one does not 'normally' consider as a theatre practitioner or critic. It seems to me that Geetha was 'protected' that night from a nearly fatal accident through a particular resilience contained within the energy of the *asana* itself. It was the very stillness and concentration with which the *asana* was performed that enabled Geetha to be so utterly calm, when in 'normal' circumstances, as she herself admits, she gets quite hysterical if something touches her accidentally like an insect or an unknown object. In the 'flow' that she achieved during the Mysore performance, one saw how Yoga had not just given her a certain poise as a dancer, but a way of protecting herself against disruptions.

For some of the dancers in Chandra's group, who happen to be more religious than the others, the performance of *Prana* cannot be entirely separated from some vaguely defined personal connection to religious experience and faith. Though this is not a major issue or source of debate in the group, it is a reality for some dancers that should be acknowledged. As for Chandra, who is perhaps more assertively unorthodox than the other members in the group — there are no gods or goddesses worshipped in her house, no daily *puja* — there is, nonetheless, a very personally investigated and fantasised relationship with an entire spectrum of elements and energies relating to nature and cosmos. The Navagraha are simply part of her larger awareness as an artist of a 'universe' that cannot be easily rationalised. At no level can her response to the Navagraha be considered 'religious' in a formal sense. I would prefer to describe it as a connection that she has created for herself to the larger realities of ecology and search for self.

Prana embodies this search for self in a very real way. For me, it is a journey each time in which I am alerted to the sound of my own breath and the *vilambit* which merges with the beat of my heart. No work by Chandra has moved me more deeply. It is a new experience each time that convinces me of the transformative power of her art. As the dancers themselves have grown through performing the work, the entire experience of doing and seeing *Prana* becomes more and more crucial for the entire group and the growing number of spectators who have interiorised the production in their own ways.

To end on a more down-to earth note, I am reminded of Chandra's informal meeting with the dancers following the Auroville disaster. There were no 'spiritual reflections', just a candid post-performance analysis. Chandra was still recovering from flu, but she had sufficient energy to ask cheerfully: 'Where did we goof?' And one by one, all the dancers began to recreate their 'goofs' with much solemnity interspersed with bursts of laughter.

It was clear to me on watching this group that they have learned how to support each other. The vulnerabilities are shared, and this is what enables them to deal with occasional disasters and accidents with or without the intervention of the Navagraha among other forces. It would be only appropriate at this point to investigate the inner dynamics of the group by exploring the relationships between the dancers and Chandra. I shall deal with this subject in the next chapter along with Chandra's working relationships with musicians, collaborators, and foreign artists. Her search for self continues through these relationships.

BUDHA ← MERCURY	SUKRA ↑ VENUS	SOMA ← MOON
GURU ← JUPITER	SURYA ↓ SUN	ANGARAKA ← MARS
RAHU ↑ ECLIPSE	SANI ↓ SATURN	KETU ↓ ECLIPSE

37-45

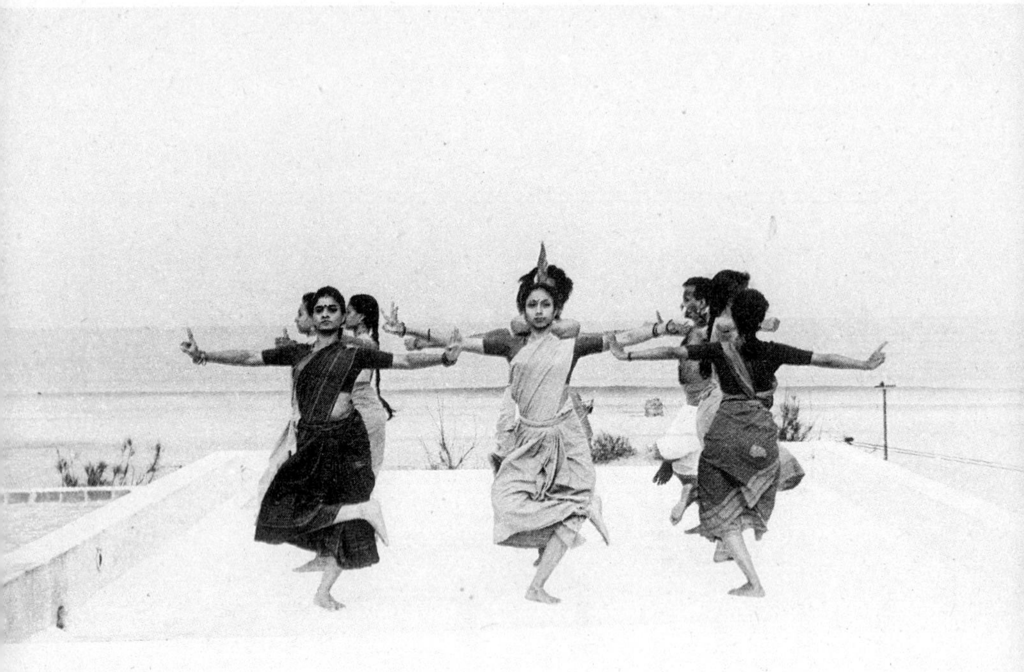

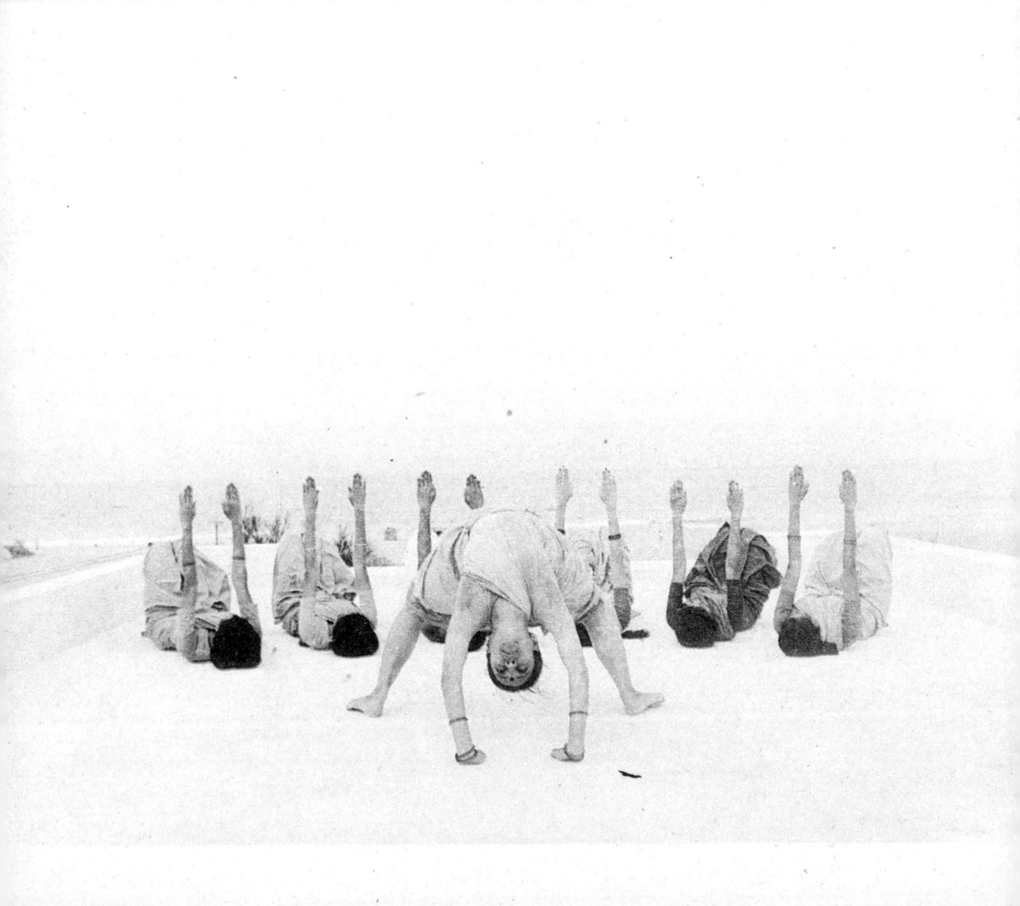

48

49

10

'I am not talking about dance all the time.
I am talking about your bodies, your lives,
your consciousness.'

Relationships With Dancers

Chandra never fails to remind her dancers that there is a world beyond dance. Over the years she has interacted with them less as a choreographer, and definitely not as a guru, but more like a wise friend. She has been candid both in her criticism and praise, adopting a very direct style of address and communication no different from her relationships with people in general. Despite her obvious influence on her dancers' lives, it is significant, however, that she has no particular hold over them. Dancers have come and gone since *Angika*. The few 'regulars' meet once a week to keep in touch with the productions. In these thoroughly unprofessional conditions of work, where no one receives a salary, it is only obvious that the dancers cannot be persuaded to stay on if they find a job in another city or if they get married or if they simply cannot find time to rehearse. Despite these obvious problems, which are proving to be increasingly difficult, Chandra has learned to accept them as part of her continuing resistance to institutionalisation.

So strong is her faith in self-sufficiency that she believes no one is indispensable. She has found that if some of her dancers leave, the others immediately assume new responsibilities to sustain the overall energy of the work. And in this process, Chandra has found to her joy that the so-called 'weaker' dancers have actually gained in strength.

Besides, she firmly believes that people have to go their own way. Ultimately, no one can determine the journey of a dancer's life but herself. Speaking about her own love of solitude, she is disarmingly frank when she admits, 'It's so good to have the dancers around, but it's also such a relief when they leave.' Clearly, Chandra continues to hold on to her continuing quest to find space and time for herself, which she desires for all her dancers and friends as well. 'Let us be together, but let us also be free of each other': this would seem to be one of the general principles underlying Chandra's relationships, both in work and life.

In the absence of a professional infrastructure, Chandra has never auditioned or advertised for her dancers in a formal way. She has somehow got in touch with them through other dancers and friends. Sometimes they have searched her out. This was the case with Sumitra Gautam, one of the first female dancers who worked with Chandra from the first production of *Angika*. After training in Bharatanatyam at Kalakshetra for seven years, Sumitra found herself dissatisfied with the 'traditional dance repertoire and methodology of learning.'[1] There were too many 'do's and don'ts' which ultimately did not help her to address any of her own 'experiences' or 'personal values' as a woman. Despite her arduous training at Kalakshetra, Sumitra found herself left with a 'burning desire' not just to dance or compose, but as she puts it so movingly, 'to be honest to myself, work with my body, and most vitally, discover my spirit in and as myself.'

Understandably, this 'desire' was not likely to be met through joining a professional dance company. It was Sumitra's luck — or more accurately, her own perception — that led her to approach Chandra herself. 'Meeting Chandra', as Sumitra reveals, 'was like a breath of fresh air, a scope to *be*.' At that time Chandra was just beginning to articulate her fantasy of *Angika* as a 'personal voyage of self-discovery' in which Sumitra found space for her own questions and exploration.

Apart from the physical lessons to be learned from the martial exercises conducted by Sri V. Pandian and the theatre exercises and improvisations directed by Bhagirathi Narayan, it was the general 'openness' of the group that moved Sumitra — an 'openness to other people, other views, other values.' In this context, it is significant that Sumitra had the courage to confront her own brahminical values which had conditioned her body through so many 'compulsions and codes.' At Skills, in a mixed group of predominantly male martial artists and two female dancers (Sujata and Vasanthi), Sumitra was compelled to question her conditioning by 'relating', in her words, 'more naturally to her body.'

Perhaps, the depth of her association can best be expressed in the moving acknowledgement of what she was 'given' through *Angika*:

> The value of Chandra and *Angika* in my life is not a commitment to perform or even to create — it is just a commitment to be honest with myself and my body and values, not in indulgence or excess, but in vitality, alive — to be true to myself, not as a myth or with borrowed strait-jackets but in my own guts and deepest predilections; to give, perhaps, as I have been given — with no demands, no guru-ship, just as one friend to another, in a human context.[2]

This eloquent tribute comes from a dancer who, as a matter of fact, no longer dances, but who has chosen to be 'honest' in her own life which, at this point in time, focuses on her role as a mother. At one level, one could say that Chandra is disappointed that Sumitra is no longer with the group, but she also has a tacit admiration for Sumitra's own search. Motherhood, as we will discuss later in the book, happens to be Chandra's *bête noire*. But if a dancer like Sumitra chooses to be a mother with full consciousness, Chandra realises that the choice is significant in its own right, even though it may contradict her own values.

The Body Freed and in Pain

Along with Sumitra, Sujata also worked with Chandra in the very first production of *Angika*. When she joined the group, she was by her own admission awkward, shy, and very resistant to the martial and theatre exercises. Her training at Kalakshetra had left her with tremendous blocks that prevented her from 'freeing' herself as a woman and performer. After remaining an 'outsider' for a long time,

Sujata finally made a breakthrough during one workshop session with Bhagirathi when she unselfconsciously carried one of the male participants on her back. This was the first time that she had been able to confront her taboo concerning touch.

This was followed by a long process of freeing herself from inhibitions that continued beyond *Angika*. For a long time, for instance, Sujata was unable to dress in front of the other dancers. She always felt obliged to shut the door while changing. Now she no longer feels this compulsion to conceal herself (and her body). This became particularly clear to Chandra after one rehearsal of *Prana*, a production which has necessitated the use of shorts rather than pyjamas to facilitate the stretches in the movement. As Chandra observed:

> After rehearsal I saw Sujata in her shorts and blouse. She was so free in her movement. So I said: 'Sujata, let me take a good look at you.' She stood freely. I said: 'Do some *adavus* for me.' She did and the lines of her body were so clearly revealed. I realised that Sujata had come a long way from the time she had joined the group. She was now free in her body.

And yet, there is a different episode in Chandra's relationship with Sujata which reveals a very different perspective on the 'body in pain' (to borrow Elaine Scarry's phrase)[3] rather than the 'body liberated.' Some time ago Sujata had fallen from a motor-cycle just two days before a performance. 'It was a case of false modesty', as Chandra puts it candidly. 'She didn't pick up her *sari* so that it got caught in the wheel and she fell.' Badly bruised and hurt, Sujata could scarcely move. So she stayed away from the rehearsals but insisted on doing the final performance. In the very last rehearsal on stage, Chandra insisted that she perform: 'You must participate.' Whereupon, Sujata promptly started to 'howl', making Chandra feel 'very guilty.' 'All the dancers clustered around her', Chandra remembers, not without a sense of humour. 'All sympathy for the injured, the wronged party. I was sitting alone being made to feel guilty, the one who made Sujata cry.'

The point is, as Chandra elaborates on the logic of her decision to make Sujata dance in spite of the pain:

> It is wishful thinking that you are in control of your body when you are in pain. At such moments, you have to make an additional effort to walk, stand, balance. You need to find out if there is any movement that needs to be changed, modified. The dancer has to figure out her exact capacities when her body is in pain.

In making this statement, Chandra is not just conceptualising in the abstract, but speaking from her own experience when she herself had accidentally fallen into the orchestra pit of a theatre during a rehearsal. Recalling this incident, Chandra says;

> My first thought was how I could make my entrance with the minimum of pain. I asked my body: How will you move today? What foot do I use? Which hand? In what direction? I kept on making this effort till I was able to conquer the pain.

According to Chandra, Sujata was able to dance after she had been injured, but the pain was visible on her face. 'I, on the other hand', says Chandra, not without a certain pride, 'was able to conquer pain. To be a dancer, you must have a will, endurance, stamina and courage to confront any kind of problem. There's no point aspiring to be a dancer otherwise.'

This is the kind of advice that Chandra gives her dancers. In this context, she is known to be very firm with them when they run a temperature or if they have aches and pains. Categorically, she states: 'I don't accept fevers and headaches. I think that this is some kind of indulgence and self-pity. Even if you have a temperature of 103 degrees and you dance, you can feel fine.' In a lighter vein, she likes to remember one of her *'68 Poems* which summarises her attitude to pain:

>How are you
>I am alright
>only
>my joints
>are
>stiffffff
>ffff
>fff
>ff
>f

Dancers on Chandralekha

One of the strongest signs of the group's vitality lies in the dancers' ability and freedom in reflecting on Chandra's work. Unlike most established dance-schools where, to use the jargon of dance, the *adavus* are *'chittified'* (i.e. learned by rote) without any questioning or self-reflexivity, Chandra's dancers are now in a position to reflect on what they have learned and are in the process of discovering.

Among the dancers it is Tripura (or Tippi as she is known in the group) who had an opportunity to work with Chandra even before *Angika*. This was when she was still studying dance at Kalakshetra when Rukmini Devi allowed Chandra to use four of her dancers to revive *Tillana* for the first East-West Dance Encounter. Recalling her earliest rehearsals with Chandra in 1984, Tippi clarified some basic characteristics that distinguishes Chandra's style of dance from the Kalakshetra method:

>For one thing I remember working much harder at Skills than Kalakshetra. Chandra was particularly strict about the *aramandi*. We had to get down much lower from our knees than at school. Also the question of power became clear to us for the first

time. Chandra urged us to stamp the floor much harder.

Following up on these observations, the other dancers also contribute to the discussion with specific observations.

'The spine is of primary importance for Chandra — it has to be stretched to the maximum limit.'
'The extensions of the movement have to be as complete as possible.'
'The origins of the movement have to be explored. It's not enough just to do it, you must know where the energy comes from.'
'The relationship of dancers to musicians is important. But most of all after working with Chandra, we have started relating to one another. We no longer do our own thing.'
'You just have to keep in line. Also, we have become much more aware of the overall dynamics of the space — diagonals, verticals, horizontals.[4]

In addition to these specific principles of dance, the dancers also acknowledge the differences in socialisation between the way Chandra relates to them as women and the more formal attitudes of former teachers and colleagues. To begin with, Chandra rejects the authority of the guru. This created some embarrassment for the dancers when they first met her because they did not know how to address her. Clearly, she was no one's '*amma*' but nor could she be addressed as '*athai*' or 'ma'am' or 'madam' or worse still, 'aunty' (which is how Meera addressed Chandra the first time only to be snapped at). Chandra made it clear to all of them that she wanted to be called 'Chandra' and nothing else.

After accepting this informal address, the dancers learned that, despite the discipline of the dance sessions, there were no rules as such about how one was expected to behave. There was no question of touching Chandra's feet at the beginning of the rehearsal. Indeed, to this day, Chandra does not allow any of her dancers to genuflect or prostrate themselves in front of her. One of her increasing horrors is that, as she becomes more famous, she finds dancers 'diving at her feet.' Invariably, Chandra has to stop them from doing so, suggesting instead that they greet each other with an embrace.

Significantly, it is only before a show that the entire group of dancers (including Chandra) performs the *Tatti Kundikal* before Udupi Lakshminarayan, the ritualistic salutation to earth which culminates in seeking the blessings of the teacher. Though Lakshminarayan is not really the teacher of the group, he does the *nattuvangam* for the performance. Moreover, as a senior artist who believes in the sanctity of ritual, the dancers touch his feet in deference to his belief. Chandra, however, does not allow this for herself. Her way of showing support to her dancers is by going to each one of them before the show and hugging them with a few words of encouragement.

In addition to the informality of address and exchange of emotion, the dancers have also discovered other aspects of the socialisation at Skills which differentiates it from traditional institutions. For one thing, there are no hierarchies among the dancers. This becomes particularly obvious as the dancers assume full responsibility for marking their positions on the stage floor and checking out the sound levels. Sometimes, it seems as if too many people are making decisions at the same time, which is a source of great irritation to Dashrath in particular, who firmly believes in the authority of a single director. Nonetheless, there is a very real sense of sharing responsibilities, even though Chandra continues to lament the lack of initiative in the group to rehearse entirely without her, despite some progress in this direction.

Recalling the hierarchies to which she had to submit as a student at Kalakshetra, one of Chandra's dancers, Krishna, recalls how some of her senior colleagues were 'bossy.' At times they would force the juniors to jump one hundred times early in the morning or do some other arduous exercise. Needless to say, they had to be addressed respectfully along with the teachers whose judgement on a student's progress was unquestionable. In addition, there were other unspoken rules like not wearing black in class. Ironically, this happens to be one of Chandra's favourite colours. At a more petty level, there were rules in performance like 'never show your back to the audience', which, of course, Chandra greatly relishes in debunking as a choreographer apart from making her dancers do other 'unmentionable' things like leaping in the air and lying on the floor.

Apart from the absence of these 'rules' at Skills, Chandra's dancers also value the rejection of any false sanctimony or sense of morality. Dance is something to be enjoyed, not worshipped: this is the message that they have got from Chandra, which has encouraged so many of them to keep returning to Skills despite practical problems and family pressures. At Skills, the dancers feel free to explore themselves and socialise with other artists. Men and women share the same space in a spirit of creativity and fun rather than repression.

Now it is possible for the dancers to look back on their early days with Chandra and examine their own process of understanding her principles. As Meera puts it very candidly, 'The very first day we met her, she said: *Spine*. I honestly didn't know what she was talking about. Now I am beginning to.' This knowledge is now being extended to an understanding of Chandra's choreography and not just the individual movements of dance. As Krishna observes: 'I now know the enormous work that Chandra puts into every show. There are changes everyday. She prepares. Once I peeped into the room while she was preparing for rehearsal. I saw that she was working on herself. Later, she works on individuals, and finally with the group. She tests all her ideas on her own body. That comes first.' Pausing in her astute reflections, Krishna adds: 'I am learning from Chandra that choreography is not just an illustration of an idea. It is an entire process of thought that has taken years and years of work on one's self.'

Such is the dynamism of the work-process in Chandra's group that newcomers get integrated very soon. In fact, in one of the latest productions *Sri,* some of the more demanding martial movements have been given to Jasmine and Padmini, who have imbibed Chandra's principles of movement in an astonishingly short amount of time. Jasmine, of course, had studied *kalari* for six years before joining Chandra's group. After initial stiffness due to her relative lack of exposure to dance, she has now grown into one of the most vigorous dancers in Chandra's troupe. Reflecting on her own growth, Jasmine says that what she most liked about being at Skills from the very beginning was its 'openness to women.' In the *kalari* her guru was always singling her out. Then there were all kinds of pressures: 'A woman shouldn't do this. She shouldn't look at men.' At Skills, she found a forum where her own assumptions of femininity could be nurtured and questioned.

As the dancers have come to know Chandra, it goes without saying that she, too, has internalised each of them. She is keenly aware of their individual capacities and qualities of movement: 'Geetha has power. Radhika has a challenge in her stance. Tippi has lightness. Sujata has flow...' These are the innate qualities of the dancers that Chandra is fully conscious of in her choreography. When a senior Bharatanatyam dancer from Kalakshetra once told Chandra rather dismissively: 'You are working with rejects', Chandra pointed out the potential of so-called 'rejects.' Among her dancers, Chandra may have no stars, but she has individual members of a *company* who are able to contribute to each others' energies without displaying their egos on stage. This, in itself, is a major achievement, and contributes substantially to the integrity of her choreography.

The Male Dancer

Among the dancers in Chandra's troupe, there is just one male dancer who may not be as conspicuous on stage as Nandakumar or any of the martial performers, but something would definitely be lost in his absence. It is through Sridhar that Chandra consciously breaks the dominant femininity of her dance compositions, and at the same time, reveals the 'feminine' in the male presence.

It is worth addressing Sridhar's history as a dancer separately because it encapsulates some of the challenges and dilemmas faced by male dancers in India today. For a start, they belong to a very scattered minority, especially in the classical dance world. Unable to sustain their careers as solo performers, most of them become teachers, or join the film studios, or opt out of dance altogether. Sridhar could be one of the few male dancers attached to a company in which he is frequently the only male presence. But the point is that he is so fully integrated within the group that he is compelled to emphasise: 'I don't think of myself as a male dancer. I'm just a dancer.'

In his early exploration of dance with several dance teachers, Sridhar remembers reaching a point when he began to 'hate' the milieu. He felt 'exploited' by his peers and elders. He was particularly sensitive about the adverse criticism he had received when he had choreographed a short piece in 1983 where, somewhat naively, he had used *karate* movements for the *rakshasa* characters. There was almost no room for exploring anything new in the language of dance.

At home it was even worse. His father's side of the family 'cursed' him for being a dancer. When I attempt to probe the situation, it becomes clear that Sridhar does not want to be reminded of those days. One can infer that he was (like most male dancers) branded as a 'pansy' and a 'waster.' Ironically, while receiving this kind of criticism, Sridhar continued to do whatever a 'man' from a respectable family is expected to do — he passed his B.Com., M.B.A., and then got a good job as a Marketing Development Officer at LIC where he was 'miserable.' However, when he was not given leave one day for a particular performance, he promptly left and got himself an even bigger position at the Apollo Hospital, where he was, till quite recently, an Insurance Manager.

Now the family was a lot more adjusted to Sridhar's attachment to dance, and he too could 'call the shots' in his office since he had a senior position. The schism, however, remained: at the job he was one person, an executive who was 'suited and booted', appropriately diplomatic, but at Skills he was a dancer who had to get his *aramandi* straight. This occasionally resulted in some 'ego problems', but over the years, Sridhar has learned to confront the strictures of his masculinity by responding to Chandra's particular understanding of 'male' energy. In the duet episode of *Lilavati* in particular, where he is 'pushed against the wall' by Geetha (and earlier by Radhika), Sridhar learned that being 'male' is neither 'macho' nor 'arrogant' but something associated with 'a deep, serene strength.'

On a more familial level, he was surprised and happy to see how his own father responded to the 'dignity' in the representation of sexuality in Chandra's productions. As for his mother (like most mothers of the dancers in Chandra's group), they have been completely won over by the use of cotton saris and the unaffected grace of the women on stage.[5] Therefore, one should keep in mind that Chandra's influence has extended beyond her dancers to their families as well. As Sridhar puts it rather movingly: 'The family started talking to me at home the more I worked with Chandra.' Echoing Sumitra's comments on the human context of Chandra's work, Sridhar adds:

> The values I have learned from Chandra are ultimately human. They pertain to everyday life. 'Respect yourself... Have faith in yourself'... I mean these are things that we have heard for a long time. But now we are beginning to confront them through Chandra.

What Sridhar among the other male performers in Chandra's group has yet to problematise is the femininity of their own energies. For a start, it should be emphasised that Chandra does not classify bodies on the basis of gender. Indeed, she never speaks of the 'feminine body', but simply the individual *bodies* of dancers. Thus, she never makes an issue out of differentiating between what men and women are capable of doing on stage. Just as Sridhar performs all the dance movements along with his female colleagues, so also do the women in the group perform the martial exercises as executed by the *kalari* artists from Kaduthuruthy. If the women are not able to do a particular movement — for example, the 'crocodile' walk from *Kalarippayattu* — this is not justified on the ground that they have 'feminine bodies'. They simply have to work harder at the movement, just as the men have to work on certain movements that counter their social and physical conditioning.

So, at a fundamental level, Chandra totally rejects the notion of the 'feminine body' along with the 'biologistic' assumptions of femininity itself. In this regard, I remember receiving a clue from a casual statement made by Chandra during rehearsal. Both of us were watching a male gymnast on stage, who had once contributed very dynamically to the orchestration of movement in *Angika*. Now it was only too clear that his movements were dry and mechanical. I turned to Chandra and asked: 'What's wrong with him?' And without pausing to think, she simply said: 'He's lost his femininity.' In retrospect, I am now clearer that when Chandra uses the term femininity, she views it as a creative principle which draws its sustenance from a sensuous and pliant energy, which animates the body within a circular form rather than through rigid lines.

At its deepest levels, the femininity of the male performer can be almost invisible. Such is the case with one of the youngest members in the group, Kuttishaji, whose sheer mastery of Kalarippayattu has enabled him to achieve a gravity beyond his years. Sometimes he resembles a Buddha-like figure, an ancient youth. Such is the perfection of his movement — and this is confirmed by most martial *gurus* — that he has the capacity to 'disappear' when he moves. We don't see him, we see the movement. Personally, I would have to say that he is possibly the only performer I have seen whose ego is almost completely absent on stage. Sometimes this can prove to be a problem from a 'performative' point of view because Kuttishaji does not 'project' or 'express.' He does not represent the movement.

He *is* the movement. Or more simply, he *is*.

The deepest core of spirituality in the group is felt moments before any performance when the entire company including Chandra, Sadanand, the dancers, the martial artists and the Yoga practitioners meet backstage to share their solidarity. This is, perhaps, the most private moment for the entire group when they explore a *communitas* of their own making, sharing their silent energies in slow, meditative, improvised movements in a circle of harmony. This is the closest that the group has come to exploring 'ritual' — but a ritual that emerges out of their own needs and sensibilities, not a submission to any prescribed set of rules.

During this 'ritual', there is a profound meeting of various participants as individuals and performers, whose social, cultural, and linguistic specificities seem to dissolve into a common pool of energies. At this level, the disciplines of Yoga, Kalarippayattu, and Bharatanatyam meet, reinforcing the commonalities that underlie their respective traditions. Within moments, this harmony of movement gets translated into the performance as the dancers appear on stage radiating a totally centred energy and group ethos.

'Foreign' Connections

Apart from working directly with Chandra, the dancers have gained enormously from workshops with outstanding international artists like Susanne Linke from Germany. Strikingly individual in their ways, Susanne and Chandra are, nonetheless, bound through a core of principles which extend as much to their everyday lives as to their work as dancers. If Chandra's struggle in dance has been catalysed through her very real resistance to the religiosity, mindlessness, and cant of the established dance 'tradition', Susanne's struggle has been to find a language entirely within a contemporary idiom.

Both women have fought all kinds of 'battles' in life. In Chandra's case, we have examined her very real confrontation with the legal system when she was charged with sedition. In addition, of course, she has faced a great deal of suspicion, if not hostility from the dance establishment, which is only now beginning to take her seriously. In Susanne's case, the 'battle' began even earlier with her life itself. After suffering in her childhood from meningitis which left her almost without speech or hearing, she found that she could only express herself through 'movement.' It was through the inspiration of the great German dancer, Dore Hoyer (to whom Susanne has recently choreographed a *'Hommage',* which Chandra's group saw in Germany), that she pursued dance almost like a 'religion.' But this 'spiritual quest', as Susanne emphasises, has nothing to do with 'God' as such. It simply means 'being honest' to yourself.[6]

Honesty: that is what brings Susanne and Chandra together. That is also what was most clearly revealed in their statements and productions when they met at the first East-West Dance Encounter, where they clearly left the deepest impression in the audience. Almost a year after the Encounter, Chandra and Susanne had an opportunity to probe this 'honesty' more deeply *in the language of dance* as they jointly conducted a workshop held at Skills in October 1985. Instead of focusing on any particular theme, the purpose of the workshop was simply to 'free' the bodies of the dancers as far as possible from their conditioning, determined as much through social pressures as through the training of dance itself.

It is said that on the very first day of the workshop, Susanne focused on those 'taboo areas' of the body which are neither meant to be touched nor explored.[7] Almost fiercely, she went about yanking the bottoms of the dancers (both men and women) exhorting them to 'move your popos; feel your popos, don't move about as if you only have hands and legs and no bottoms.' Consciously breaking the decorum of the female dancers so visible in their mechanised gestures and movements, Susanne urged them to work on their entire bodies and not just the individual limbs ('the spare parts' as Chandra likes to put it). To energise the body necessitates an exploration of the lower part of the spine, the lower stomach, hips, and 'popos' which the dancers had clearly neglected in their seemingly rigorous training in various dance institutions.

Another vital aspect of the workshop concerned the socialisation of movement. Not only was Susanne able to reveal the close links between the mechanisation of the body and 'middle-class' inhibitions and prejudices, she also showed the dancers the value of confronting the 'small things of life' in everyday household activity. These parts of our everyday routine can become tyrannical if one has no perspective on them. It is only through social consciousness that the 'drudgery' of life can be transformed into 'art' as she herself demonstrated so memorably in her much-acclaimed piece on *The Bathtub*. This *tour de force* of movement centering around a bathtub began with fundamental explorations of cleaning and scrubbing the floor. It was from this 'ordinary' action that Susanne found both the concept and the energy for her dance. As she described it so clearly to the dancers:

> The drudgery of life is that everything repeats itself. But if you are creative, in every repetition you begin to discover new meaning. Like the movement of looking up is so simple and all of us do it all the time. But only when we realise that the impulse for looking up comes from the bottom of the spine will that movement begin to make any meaning for us. Otherwise, we're floppy. Like kitsch. To move the space with understanding, with bodies and with imagination, is what we as dancers can do.[8]

One can understand why Chandra responds to Susanne's capacity to confront her social consciousness within the discipline of her body. This is a very rare quality among dancers today whose knowledge of the body so often exists in a vacuum, or in an overly technical context with the body being reduced to an 'anatomy.' Susanne is different because her understanding of the body is integrally related to an overall attitude, and more specifically, a resistance to the mechanising forces in our society. It is with this context in mind that Chandra summed up the lessons of the dance workshop with the statement: 'We're not only talking of dance today, but of certain principles which help us to be free, principles which are as important for art as for life.'

The Walk Workshop

The continuing quest to forge connections between art and life through dance was the primary stimulus behind the Walk Workshop, which was conducted jointly by Chandra and one of Susanne's colleagues, Claudia Lichtblau, who is presently a leading member of the Folkwang Tanzstudio in Essen. The concept of the workshop came from Chandra who had envisioned a very wide canvas of 'walks' in a larger social and political scenario. The limited two-week span of the workshop however, necessitated a concentration on the basic principles of 'walking' in multiple traditions of dance.[9]

Along with three members from the Folkwang Tanzstudio, there were Chandra's Bharatanatyam dancers as well as performers from different physical traditions like Kalarippayattu, Kathakali, Chhau, Theru-k-koothu, Devarattam, Paraiattam, and two actors from the contemporary Tamil theatre group, Koothu-p-pattarai.

The point of the workshop was to provide a forum in which the dancers as individuals could question their own resources, mechanisms and possibilities. The focus of investigation was 'walking', nothing more, nothing less. By juxtaposing their own 'walks' with those from other traditions, the dancers were compelled to re-examine their perceptions of centering, balance, direction, rhythm and line. In the process, they confronted their own conditioning and learned not to take their bodies for granted.

One could say that each performance tradition in the workshop functioned as a catalyst. It was not just the Germans who operated as 'foreign' elements, triggering off new connections within the bodies of Indian dancers. When the Bharatanatyam dancers attempted to follow the intricate footwork of the Devarattam performers, they were confronted with a different kind of 'foreign' intervention. Only this one came from their own state of Tamil Nadu.

The hierarchies of the Indian dance world were, perhaps, most blatantly challenged through the intervention of the Paraiattam performer, Rangaraj, whose 'walks' exploded into dance. I believe it is of some historical importance that this was the first time a Paraiattam performer, generally categorised among the 'lowest of the low', was invited to share the performance space with a group of 'cultured' Bharatanatyam dancers trained in the Kalakshetra style. 'Good' brahmin girls participated in his dance with gusto and there was a total absence of caste prejudice.

Inevitably, the question arises whether Rangaraj was not decontextualised from his tradition in order to participate in the workshop. After all, Paraiattam is performed in funerals, an occasion far removed from the seeming triviality of a workshop. But I learned that it is also performed in processions, festivals and, sometimes, in political rallies as well. The rhythms of the performance vary according to the shifts in social context. Without making an issue of it, Rangaraj seemed to know how to adapt his skills to the situation in which he was placed. He knew what he was doing on that stage, not just when he led the other dancers in his own tradition, but when he learned to 'walk' in theirs as well.

Walking can be an intensely vulnerable experience, as all the dancers discovered in one of the first exercises devised by Claudia, who led most of the workshop sessions. Astutely, she had the dancers walk to three points on the stage all by themselves with the entire company watching them. Almost immediately, it became clear that dancers don't walk; they dance 'walks'. Accustomed to performing highly evolved *charis,* where all the details of hip, neck, heel and leg are worked out, the Bharatanatyam dances, in particular, felt somewhat 'naked' as they walked from point to point without the elaboration of dance.

Inevitably, there was a tendency to fill the vacuum of the movements with the burden of motivation. If a dancer's neck drooped, did that mean she was sad? Or was she looking at something? When her gaze wandered in the distance, was she searching for someone? All these motivations, we realised, were essentially fictions created to dissimulate the basic problems of walking.

'All I want you to do is to push against the air', Claudia advised the dancers in her attempt to free motivations from the basic movements of walking. Trained to think of 'walks' as units in a dance, fully worked out, the dancers now had to investigate 'walking' as a process of movement. Unfettered by a specific code, they had to become more alert to the inner connections within their bodies that compelled them to move right rather than left, on a diagonal rather than backwards.

In this regard, Claudia used an interesting (and elusive) phrase to describe the pre-condition of walking: 'cleaning the body.' One cannot walk with any sense of clarity if the body is cluttered with stereotypes and mechanisms. The essential centre of any walk has to be located in the small of the spine, where our energy is, at once, most dormant and potentially explosive. It is from this base that the spinal column can be energised, and thereby stimulate the walk. 'Cleaning' the body does not mean erasing it of energies; rather it involves the redefinition of our sources of energy, enabling us to develop a new sensitivity to what is essential.

One of the most frequent gestures used by Claudia in her pedagogical process was to touch the top of the dancer's head, almost as if she wanted the body to lengthen in a puppet-like movement. Unquestionably, her colleague, Mathias Hartmann, had mastered this total centredness and linearity of the spinal column. At times, he almost seemed to become a line, a vertical one stretching upwards, defying the laws of gravity.

Predictably, this linearity was difficult for our dancers to attain, because our sense of line in India is decidedly non-linear. Indian lines are more like a continuous series of dots; they incorporate a multitude of infinitesimal curves and deflections. Our necks have a natural flexibility, following the movement of the eyes. And our hips can always be relied upon to sway.

Apart from exploring different conceptions of 'line', the

workshop also presented other enigmas of movement. Why was I, for instance, so throughly discomforted by the sight of Indian dancers moving forwards in a precise group with an almost disembodied walk, like faceless figures in a crowd? The movement seemed to prefigure a kind of mechanisation that we have (fortunately) not yet acquired, even in our metropolitan centres. Also, the very idea of walking forwards in a decisive line is bizarre for anyone who has lived in a city like Calcutta, as I have, where walking on a street demands a constant negotiation, if not circumambulation of other peoples' bodies.

Another uncanny sensation emerged when I watched the dancers walk backwards. It was like watching the slow rewind of a tape-recorder. In this case, the source of fear (cutting across all cultures, I suppose) is that, in walking backwards, a norm is reversed. The body is made to face an unknown space. The eyes of the dancers seem to be in the wrong place.

Strangest of all phenomena were the varying impulses of moving from left to right and from right to left. Entrances, as we know, can be made from either side of the stage, but they have distinct significations. At one point in the workshop, Chandra demonstrated the ambivalences of the principle by repeating the same entrance from either side of the stage; one felt strong, the other didn't work.

All these speculations about entrances were made, of course, within the unconscious framework of the rectangle — the stage on which we performed. I learned how much we take for granted in our seeing of performances, for instance, the blackened space that hovers above the heads of the dancers and the top edge of the proscenium. In almost every performance, we seem to be conditioned by our own gravitational impulse to focus on the bodies of the dancers from head down.

Grounded as our dance tradition are in earth-energies, they also incorporate an abundance of abstractions. When I hinted at the rarefication of Indian 'walks' in the workshop, Chandra defended the 'homage to ordinariness' found in our dance traditions. Spontaneously, she demonstrated the cow's urine walk' from Chhau with a skipping movement in a zig-zag path. Yet, as Claudia pointed out, if one didn't know what the 'walk' was supposed to signify, one would scarcely be thinking of cow's urine. The 'reality' contained with the movement has been sublimated.

Therein, I believe, lies both the richness and limitation of our classical forms. They are so highly evolved that their referentiality to our world seems slight (or, perhaps, this is a problem of our perception). This is not to deny the deep layers of the 'real' in our performance traditions but they have to be perceived through abstractions. The problem is that many of our dancers no longer seem to be in touch with the primary energies of their dance, preferring the virtuosity of forms to an investigation of their content.

Consciousness, as Chandra never fails to emphasise, is as necessary for a dancer as anyone else. To walk without a philosophy of the body is to simplify the act of being on stage. More so than the other participants in the workshop, it became clear that for Chandra the vitality of the spine is linked not only to dance energies, but to issues of life and resistance as well. Techniques become meaningless if they are not situated in a larger awareness of the cosmos, of which we are a part. The *brahmasutra*, after all, is not just a line, it is a *mandala*. *Kundalini* is not another 'centre'; it is the most potent source of psychic energy. Within the larger context of such concepts, so strongly echoed in the very space of 'Mandala', Chandra's open-air theatre, where the moon and stars are perennial spectators, *what does it mean to walk?*

Perhaps, as Chandra put it, with that half-seriousness which is the mark of her wisdom, 'We are simply walking towards ourselves.' Walking towards a deeper understanding of those subtle bodies that lie concealed within our mechanical frames. Gradually as the days of the workshop flowed into one another, the dancers seemed to shed their mechanical selves and develop a new radiance on stage.

One deep regret, of course, was that the social and political dimensions of 'walking' were not explored in the workshop as Chandra had originally planned. This would have necessitated not just a larger time-frame for the workshop, but a shared consciousness about the state of the world with specific reference to the possibilities of resistance through the body. With Susanne it had been possible for Chandra to confront the larger social dimensions of mechanisation and their direct effect on the flexions and tensions of the body, but with Claudia the concentration was almost entirely focused on the technicalities of dance.

Undeniably, this was somewhat disappointing to Chandra who can never conceive of any movement on stage without linking it to a larger social statement. Even more disappointing was Claudia's reticence in confronting the fundamental differences within the respective body-structures of the dancers. She was more concerned with shaping an overall orchestration of movement in which differences could be subsumed within set norms. This resulted in a kind of imposed virtuosity, where Mathias, for example, imitated the Chhau movements without really grasping the principles of circularity in the body, while the Chhau dancer, Sadasiva Pradhan, was compelled to walk in a straight line which his body clearly resisted.

If these differences could have been observed within larger concepts and philosophies of the body, this could have illuminated the specificities of physical cultures, both within India and in relation to western 'schools' of dance. In the absence of a conceptual base for a cross-cultural perspective on dance, however, the search for a 'perfect line' in the bodies of the dancers became somewhat too technical in its monochromatic drive.

Against Aridity

In the aftermath of the Walk Workshop, Chandra was compelled to speculate on the resources of her own dancers in a wider, intercultural context. While admiring the perfection of line, the precision of movement, the scale of the choreography, and the synthesis of sound and light to be found in the numerous European dance productions that she has seen over the years, Chandra was nonetheless compelled to admit that most of them radiated a 'terrific aridity.' She was not being cynical, but genuinely puzzled: 'I have often wondered why these fantastic dancers are creating dryness on stage? Does it come from over-perfection, precision taken to the point of mechanisation?' At the same time she was compelled to reflect on our own dance traditions in India:

> We are not so rehearsed. We work with almost no organisation or regularity. Yet there is a glow on stage. The vitality of the concept comes through our limbs. And this physicality is understood both in the totality of the body as well as in the individual parts of the body, in the *angas* and the *pratyangas,* in a total flow of movement.

One should qualify here that Chandra is not justifying the lack of professionalism in our dance culture, nor is she making any false causality between 'amateurism' and 'vitality.' What she is emphasising, however, is the value of having concepts of the body which are rooted in the very lines, energies, and sensuality of our dance traditions. Even the most codified and familiar of *hastas* are steeped in 'physicality, life, nature.' Daily behaviour and the ordinary patterns of life get transformed through a process of abstracting the movements of life into codified gestures. In performance, these gestures are further invested with 'a life of their own'. And it is through these intimate connections linking nature, life, and dance that our dance traditions continue to be animated, despite the increased commodification of performance. 'Our dance', as Chandra says with deep conviction, 'is still capable of *humanising* us. Ultimately, the criterion for art/dance/being human is the same. Can we create *rasa?* Can we humanise our art? Against aridity.'

One of the greatest tributes to the vitality of Chandra's dance work came from Pina Bausch, arguably the most radical choreographer of our times, who saw a production of *Angika* in her home-town of Wuppertal. One particular quality that impressed Bausch was the strong individuality of each of the members in Chandra's company. 'Each one of your dancers registers on stage', Bausch told Chandra in an intense discussion following the production. One could see that she was moved by this seemingly simple reality. Indeed, at a time when most western dancers are becoming increasingly anonymous, if not clone-like on stage, one can understand why *Angika* has received such a deeply emotional response from European audiences.

In addition to the individuality of the members in the ensemble, there is also a very perceptible interplay of male and female energies in Chandra's productions that totally counters the neutering of sexuality in most contemporary Euro-American dance performances. The sensuality of a production like *Angika* cannot help being contrasted to the cultivated androgyny that is so much in vogue these days. However, one should stress that this 'sensuality' is not contrived in the tradition of Martha Graham, for instance, who turned to Greek myths in order to dramatise primal energies on stage with an excess of heterosexual heat (or so it would seem today as we witness her bold, yet dated choreography). Even Chandra is compelled to admit that she finds the male-female interplay in Graham's work at once archaic and self-conscious. Where *Angika* scores is in its very *direct* celebration of male-female energies, which are rooted in primary principles of the body and everyday actions relating to sitting, standing, and walking, rather than a theatricalisation of myths.

Once again, it is the interrelatedness of dance and life that makes the productions 'glow' on stage. The power of the work lies in the fact that for all the brilliance of its conception, it is Chandra's language of dance that 'breathes' with life. For all their meticulous coordination, her dancers are neither regimented nor homogenised but disciplined within a framework in which they are free to be themselves.

Outside Professionalism

The problem with Chandra's group does not have to do with 'aridity.' More prosaically, one could say that as its reputation grows with more performances and foreign tours, the real problem has to do with the absence of a professional infrastructure. When *Angika* started off in the mid-eighties, the dynamics of the group could be sustained within an amateur framework with no provision for a permanent company, fixed salaries, administration, or regular hours of work. What mattered was a concentration of energies and camaraderie, a combination that could be felt in the immediacy of the performances. When some critics complain that Chandra's work is 'amateur', they fail to realise that this very spirit, animated by individual skills and a vibrant choreographic scheme, is what distinguishes the work from more seemingly 'professional' productions.

In recent years, however, one must admit that the absence of 'professionalism' in Chandra's group has created tensions. Significantly, they have manifest themselves most acutely on foreign tours which necessitate a pragmatic attitude towards the signing of contracts, scheduling, advertising, among other priorities of the international dance world. One cannot be 'slotted' in such a professional circuit and continue to uphold amateur norms. The approach has to be more businesslike and realistic if only to protect the values of love and trust with which Chandra has worked so far. In addition, one needs to protect one's work from being misrepresented in the wrong forums over which one may have no artistic control.

While most of the foreign tours in Germany, Italy, and the erstwhile Soviet Union proved to be creative learning experiences for Chandra's group, the more recent tour of the company to England in October 1992 was a largely negative experience. Ironically, this was precipitated to a large extent through the unprofessional organisation by the English sponsors. There were glaring lapses in the lack of correspondence, payment of fees, and last-minute signing of contracts and issue of work-permits, which created any number of tensions within the group. To my mind, it would have been better if the tour had been called off. Instead, Chandra continued to function on a word-of-mouth trust that was systematically negated through the tour, compounded by the cliques which were created within the group for the first time in the history of *Angika*.

In retrospect, one can say that there were many lessons to be learned from the England tour. Indeed, the tensions erupted at a very strategic point in the development of Chandra's career which was all set to enter an international circuit. The tour, however, compelled Chandra to reassess her attitude to the larger phenomenon of 'multiculturalism' for which there are substantial funds in the West, increasingly manipulated by 'middlemen' who claim to represent non-western cultures with greater sensitivity than the more established and allegedly 'racist' organisations based in western capitals. What may need to be acknowledged is that these new structures of representing 'South Asia' are 'racist' in their own right, perpetuating different modes of domination through a new rhetoric of representation.

This is not to deny the necessity of remaining open to creative interactions with western audiences and artists. Chandra's close relationships with Susanne Linke, the dancers of the Folkwang Studio, and the members of Premio Gaia in Palermo are just a few examples of the kind of bond she has established and continues to explore with western collaborators. Indeed, for her most recent production *Bhinna Pravaha* based on the concept of a 'confluence of differences', she involved both western and non-western participants in her first staging of the project.[10] Drawing from Kalidasa's *Raghuvamsham,* which depicts how the waters of the Ganga and the Jamuna meet while retaining their distinct energies, colours, and tonalities, this most consciously hybrid of Chandra's productions challenges the absolutes of Hindu fundamentalism so dominant in India today.

For this piece, Chandra renewed her contact with Claudia Lichtblau of the Folkwang Studio who in turn had an opportunity to dance with three of Chandra's most experienced dancers, Meera, Krishna and Padmini. Their juxtaposed idioms of Bharatanatyam and expressionist modern dance were further complemented by Chandra's ingenious interplay of Chhau and Bharatanatyam, as represented by Ileana Citaristi (an Italian dancer based in Orissa) as well as Shangitha Namashivayam (a Sri Lankan dancer based in Australia), who evoked the auras of Ganga and Jamuna with their distinct sensualities. In addition, Chandra incorporated a counterpoint of voices by inviting two singers from distinct traditions to create a combined score — Aruna Sayeeram, a Carnatic vocalist based in Bombay, and Chantal Herder, who is an opera singer based in Vence in the south of France.

With such a rich tapestry of cross-cultural inputs, it is scarcely possible to deny Chandra's openness to collaborations despite her increased vigilance about the politics of multiculturalism. One factor that has invigorated her since the England tour is her renewed realisation that 'it is always possible to fill up the holes' in her choreography. In the revival of *Sri*, for instance, in preparation for the Kalanidhi Dance Conference in Toronto in February 1993, it appeared at first that the work would suffer in the absence of Geetha, who is now married and settled temporarily in Glasgow, and Sujata, who is back in Calcutta. But what was astonishing even in the first week of rehearsal is how the existing dancers and the new ones managed to 'fill up the holes' in the production with their individual energies.

At one level, this speaks flatteringly about the capacities of the dancers and their commitment to the work. But it also reveals the resilience and integrity of Chandra's choreographic framework, which in the spirit of *mandalas*, has a tensile flexibility, capable of moving inwards and outwards, absorbing new elements and surviving without others. It is through this dynamic of energies — ever-renewing and always open to the possibilities of change and questioning — that Chandra has learned how to transform limitations and temporary setbacks into new potentialities of strength. And the dancers, too, continue to find connections to themselves and others through the inner vitality of the work itself.

The limitations could be that this process of consciousness seems ultimately restricted to dance. Sadly, Chandra is beginning to acknowledge that while she continues to care for the consciousness of her dancers — a consciousness that she would like to extend beyond dance to social and political commitments in life — she also realises the task involved in confronting the larger realities of consumerism and the negation of ideology. Ultimately the lives of her dancers lie beyond her influence and there is not much that she can do beyond stimulating their creativity in her brief, yet intense interactions with them.

For her own part, Chandra knows that consciousness cannot be assumed through the mastery of a particular form or set of techniques (assuming that such 'mastery' is possible in the first place). Consciousness is a process that is at once nurtured through the principles of dance, and yet challenged through larger social and political movements that animate the world. For a more detailed study of these processes, let us turn to the next chapter in which I will attempt to contextualise Chandra's creativity within a spectrum of ideas relating to feminism, ecology, and the transformation of self.

INDIA WORSHIPS ITS WOMEN

In Search of Freedom

The search for freedom is a continuous quest for Chandra. As boldly as she seems to have countered various social norms and modes of regimentation, she is only too aware that 'freedom' can never be taken for granted. It is something that demands constant vigilance and re-definition not only in relation to the ubiquitous ways in which 'men run the world' through a system designed, administered, and propagated for the maintenance of their power. More elusively, 'freedom' may also need to be protected from the established institutions, ideologies and languages that claim to represent women's rights in opposition to identifiable forms of oppression.

So, on the one hand, Chandra identifies her struggle for 'freedom' specifically as a woman in the larger context of the women's movement both in India and the world. At the same time, she has resisted the articulation of this struggle through the academic and official languages of 'feminism' as propagated by women's studies groups and established feminist forums.[1] While identifying closely, even fiercely with feminist concerns, she has also upheld her right as an artist to explore other, more textured and ambivalent 'languages', in order to be true to herself and her sense of history. It is in affirming these 'languages', which are the focus of attention in this chapter, that she has occasionally run into problems with some of her closest friends who happen to be feminists in their own right.

As she herself puts it with her customary candour:

> I have always felt very close to the women's movement in India, but my interaction with feminist groups has been limited. My area is 'culture' in which the least work is being done by feminists. On the one hand, they have mystified me; on the other

hand, they have not understood my concepts of women.

In the course of contextualising Chandra's relationship to 'feminism' in the Indian context, it would be only appropriate to recapitulate some of the important choices in her life that have been discussed so far both in relation to her life and work.

Long before 'feminism' was instituted in India in the late seventies through the emergence of women's groups, Chandra had already advocated certain principles and values that could be considered 'feminist' or 'protofeminist'. By the early fifties, she had left home, dropped her family name, explored relationships with men on her terms, and consciously resisted the pressures of marriage and child-bearing. In terms of dance, she had rejected 'careerism' and the larger 'patronage' provided by men. Instead, she chose to work on herself by pursuing all kinds of creative activities including design, writing, painting. Through all her 'experiments on self', she continued to live alone, embracing the status of the 'single woman.'

Later, when she chose to share her life with her live-in companion, Sadanand, in a mutually defined relationship, she began to explore 'politics' in the alternative sector. Even while resisting the Emergency, she did not affiliate herself to any political party. In 1982, she was charged with sedition along with Sadanand, which indicates that her seemingly 'amateur' and 'naive' politics was sufficiently subversive for the State to intervene decisively in her life. She fought the case, won, and returned to dance to which she has increasingly devoted most of her time and energy, while continuing to be linked to all kinds of social activities including 'feminist' explorations of myth, history, and the body.

In this short encapsulation of her life and work, one obvious motif is that of the 'rebel' resisting the categories generally thrust on women — 'daughter', 'wife', mother'. Even as an 'artist', Chandra is not conventional. It would be a mistake to associate her with those dancers, for example, who have completely 'lived for their art' and in the process imprisoned themselves in illusory worlds. If anything, Chandra would take pride in saying that she has lived primarily 'for herself', while attempting to intervene in compelling social matters relating to human rights, ecology, and any kind of regimentation, threatening the possibilities of 'freedom'. While drawing her creative sustenance from dance, she has cheerfully interrupted her 'creativity' by getting involved in quasi-political activities or just by '*doing* nothing.' The fact that she has been able to afford such a life could be subject to a certain cynicism, but the fact is that Chandra has used her financial resources strategically and almost entirely to facilitate creative work which she has shared with diverse individuals and groups over the years.

Chandra's seeming 'freedom', however, has not been without its limits and restraints. 'It always comes with a price' as she so often laments. To be 'free', Chandra has learned the necessity of confronting certain laws that have been determined by the very system in which we are placed. There can be no absolute state of 'pure freedom': it is always in the process of being circumscribed by a larger network of forces that question its right to exist. But — and this is the important intervention — the larger constraints on freedom cannot make us disbelieve in the possibilities of its realisation. And thus, one is always in the process of negotiating one's freedom, as Chandra would put it, 'by never taking it for granted.'

'Freeing Myself From the Wall': Request Concert

It is ironic, yet telling that I got to know Chandra when I and a German colleague in the theatre, Manuel Lutgenhorst, approached her to act in a one-woman wordless monodrama called *Request Concert* by Franz Xaver Kroetz, a play that almost negates the possibility of freedom in a woman's life. The negation, of course, is not meant to valorise a state of oppression but to provide a critique of the very absence of resistance in an increasingly mechanised world. Since I have written extensively about the production elsewhere,[2] I will focus here primarily on the problem of 'freedom' and its representation in a radical interpretation of Kroetz's text which was danced (rather than acted) in a minimalist adaptation of Bharatanatyam and modern dance.

Request Concert was part of a larger intercultural theatre project in which Kroetz's play was adapted in different Asian cities including Calcutta, Bombay, Madras, Jakarta, Tokyo, where individual actresses from these cities also functioned as the co-directors for their respective productions. Manuel and I were the co-ordinators of the entire project. The purpose was to situate the text within the particular *context* of particular cities, adapting the everyday routine of the woman's life depicted in the German text according to the specific social, political, and economic conditions of different Asian cities. In Madras, the project was further enriched through Chandra's decision to *dance* the predominantly 'realist' text, so that Kroetz was confronted (and subverted) not only through the adaptation but the performative idiom itself.

Suffice it to say for the purpose of this discussion that Kroetz's monodrama is made up of a series of 'ordinary' gestures and actions, bordering on total monotony and banality. The non-eventful 'action' of the play is made up of gestures relating to eating, drinking, sleeping, dressing, undressing, stitching, listening to the news on television, and most of all, listening to a radio programme called 'Request Concert', which has its equivalents in almost any part of the world. The sheer mechanisation of the woman's routine and the subsequent alienation from her actions and gestures were represented by Chandra through a most rigorous adaptation of the existing *hastas, mudras,* and walks of Bharatanatyam. For example, when she was eating, she would splay her fingers with one hand to suggest a food container and lift the other hand with mechanical eating gestures, while her face would remain almost abnormally blank and vacant. It would seem as if she was not participating in the act of eating at all.

This kind of *sattvika abhinaya* indicates that there is a flexibility within the idiom of Bharatanatyam which can register contemporary states of mind like alienation. One should also acknowledge that this *abhinaya* was possible only because Chandra had the consciousness to confront the basic vocabulary and 'grammar' of her dance tradition. Economising her gestures almost to the point of erasure, Chandra consciously worked against virtuosity to create an elimination of any decorative or excessively nuanced *abhinaya* on her part so that when she first listened to the radio, she did so like a *nayika* listening to the distant strains of Krishna's flute. But in the very next rehearsal, all the conventions of listening were 'minimalised' so that all one saw was a mannequin-like woman, her arms stiffened by her sides, swaying her shoulders ever so slightly from side to side to Tamil film music.

Significantly, while remaining 'true' to the relentless routine of gestures prescribed by Kroetz, Chandra would occasionally add some colour in her performance, even in the most dreary routines. There was also an extended fantasy sequence in which the radio programme was temporarily silenced to reveal a woman in her own dreamworld. This would be conveyed in total solitude in which the woman seemed to be reaching out to the elements till very gradually the advertisement jingles on the radio would bring her back to 'reality' — the banalities of kitsch, consumerism, advertising, and the market.

This 'fantasy' was part of Chandra's need to puncture Kroetz's text with more feeling for the woman. The real subversion came towards the end when Chandra negated the woman's suicide which comes as a totally unexpected conclusion to Kroetz's text. After preparing for the next day's work and going to bed, Kroetz's character gets up and takes her life. This is done in a very matter-of-fact way which adds to the horror of the situation. As she swallows sleeping pills with small sips of wine — an ironic touch of celebration — she accidently drops some wine on the table whereupon she promptly wipes it with the sleeve of her nightgown. This is the one 'untidy' gesture in the course of the entire play where the woman unconsciously breaks her routine. Then, in the final moments of the play, she sits at the table, and gradually, there is 'a look of interest in her face.'

While this ending received very strong interpretations in the more realistic productions of *Request Concert* in Calcutta and Bombay, it was totally altered in the Madras production with Chandra opting for a very heightened representation of the woman's inner suffering. This was represented through a slow and tortured roll on the ground with the hands flailing outwards, which would occasionally culminate in freezes where the body would be locked into disembodied shapes. These spasms of movement, which almost resembled death-throes, would continue till Chandra would gradually rise from the ground with her back to the audience and press herself against the back wall of the theatre. Against this expanse, she would rise on her toes stretching her hands upwards so that it would almost seem as if she had hanged herself. Then, very gradually, she would turn and gradually 'free herself from the wall', raising her hands upwards in a tentative gesture of liberation.

When I first saw Chandra perform the sequence, I was stunned by its power, but I was also compelled to ask: 'Are you committing suicide?' To which she responded promptly: 'Of course not. All I want to do is to free myself from the wall.' What she chose to play was not the suicide itself, which Kroetz himself had associated somewhat contemptuously in his play with the 'unfulfilled expectations, endless hopes, and petty dreams' of people who are unable to free themselves from 'the slavery of production.' Where Chandra found more affinity in Kroetz's position was in his hypothesis that 'If the explosive energy of this massive exploitation and oppression were not so sadly turned against the oppressed and exploited, we would have a revolutionary situation.' In other words, if the people who commit suicide could only direct their energy not against themselves, but against the society that is perpetuated through their death, then the world could change. Or, if not change, then at least its complacencies and mechanisms could be disturbed.

Kroetz's statement on the possibilities of resistance made immediate sense to Chandra. 'That's what I am dancing', she said, 'not the suicide itself.' What concerned her was the representation of a process wherein a woman is completely immobilised by the pressures of her existence, then freed from the wall (her eternal prison) through an inner energy and volition that suggests a new growth, a renewal of spirit.

One challenge in the production was to find the 'joinery' between expressing the sheer torture of the possibility of suicide, which was represented through Chandra's floor movement, and the affirmation of life conveyed in the final gesture of the production. What moved the spectators, and women in particular, was Chandra's total absorption in her representation of the death-in-life of the woman which was sustained till she 'freed' herself from the wall. If this final choice registered powerfully, and not just didactically, it was because it had been fully *lived*.

In this context, it becomes clear that what makes Chandra exemplary among feminist performers in India today is that she totally internalises the oppression of women before subverting it through her own energy and consciousness. Unable to separate her art from politics, she cannot justify an agit-prop representation of any problem, however critical, if the enactment has not been interiorised. Sincerity, for her, is not enough. A woman who wants to represent another woman's suffering has to take on that suffering. She cannot simply depict it from the neck upwards, as in television or a poster play. Her commitment, therefore, cannot be assumed through the mere upholding of an ideology. It has to be physicalised through the 'being' of the performance itself.

'One More News'

Only after the production was over did I realise the depth at which Chandra had contemplated the reality of suicide afflicting Indian women through yet another of her creative endeavours. Early in the rehearsal period she had mentioned that Harindranath Chattopadhyay had written a poem about a woman's suicide. This poem provided the text for Chandra's book *One More News,* which is a juxtaposition of images and words concluding with a statement about the futility of suicide. Only in retrospect did I realise its close affinities to *Request Concert* despite its exploration of an altogether different 'language'. It is part of Chandra's strength as an artist that she is able to view the same problem from multiple perspectives in different disciplines.

The stimulus for *One More News* came from a caption in a newspaper: WOMAN THROWS HERSELF IN WELL. Quotidian, almost dismissable. However, it made Chandra *think* about who that woman could be in the first place:

> I kept staring at the report. I visualised her. I could see her. She was real. I could see her, so totally still and silent. I could see her move, trance-like, dance-like. She related to nothing around her except space. A tense space that moved. In and out. Through her eyes. I saw the look in her eyes as she moved the space.[3]

This initial 'encounter' with the woman convinced Chandra that newspapers 'devalue life' by 'taking death for granted'. Reportage merely dehumanises in its attempt to be socially relevant. After sharing her thoughts with Harindranath — and this surely goes back at least forty years in time — he responded to the situation with a poem in Hindi that attempted to reclaim 'lost feeling.'

Over the years, Chandra has 'lived' with this poem which has been shared with other women in workshops, where it has been set to music and dramatised for women-audiences.[4] 'Each medium', as Chandra reflects, 'was explored to extend the impact of the content, to create an experience, to personalise involvement, to humanise the response.'

Without resorting to a 'programmatic art' which she loathes — solarised photographs attempting to be 'objective' and 'real' — Chandra settled for a passionate use of colour, graphics, and images to create her 'idiom' for the woman in *One More News*. It is a bold interpretation that consciously counters the stereotypes of women as victims.

Beginning on a lyrical note — the 'sound of the moon' — the opening images of *One More News* reveal the deep indigo of the sky emblazoned with the golden disc of the moon, which in turn becomes orange and red as the sky brightens to a sunflower yellow. Then, in an abrupt cut, we see the disembodied image of a woman's feet suspended in space. Later, she is seen at closer quarters, veiled, her head lowered, almost pensive, one hand touching the end of her sari, the other by her side. It is a pencil sketch, nothing dramatic, rendered with a simple flow of lines. As the images become increasingly stark, 'silence is shattered' with the moon becoming more prominent, till it is fully red in a close-up, almost like a bloodied womb, with the barest lines of the woman's body scrawled underneath.

As the anger in the poem takes over with 'a cry resounding in a world gone deaf', Chandra breaks the early patterns of the imagery by consciously inserting the colours of the national flag — saffron, white, green — but in reverse order with the scrawled inscription of the woman's body replacing the *chakra*. It is a blatantly subversive use of 'national' colours which are juxtaposed in different perspectives — vertically, horizontally, at time left almost disturbingly unchanged. In the final image, which is not climactic but merely a continuation of the earlier images, we see pencil sketches of women's heads with prominent eyes evoking a 'world gone blind' in which the 'cry' heard earlier continues to resound.

Undeniably, it is a very difficult and complex matter to create images around a women's suicide, particularly in the Indian context today when suicides continue to be legitimised, silenced, and even deified in certain parts of the country where there has been a resurgence of *sati*. To respond 'artistically' to such a disturbing reality is at once fraught with contradictions and tensions, but for Chandra the only valid response to such a reality in artistic terms demands a fully committed creativity, not merely an activist's fervour. It is in defence of this 'creativity', that Chandra has sometimes chided feminists for their seeming indifference to the textures, colours and materials through which statements in art have to be shaped. Not to understand the significance of these seemingly 'formal' matters is to trivialise the content of social realities. It is also a way of subscribing to the existing images of women as inscribed in patriarchal 'political' idioms which are so often echoed in the crude posters advertising women's rallies and meetings.

Whether or not one responds to the 'artistry' of *One More News*, one cannot deny that it exists without dehumanising the woman. The verbal statements at the beginning and end of the book are also written in a style which counters the statistical dryness of a 'suicide report' where women are completely dehumanised through the rigour of official discourse. Chandra may not 'humanise' the woman in the form of a 'character', but she makes us feel something about her condition. Most daringly, she does not deny the woman (or herself) the possibility of sensuality, juxtaposing the spectrum of colours associated with her presence with the more official colours of nationalism.

To avoid the possibility of the images being 'misread', Chandra adds a statement in which her position on suicide is clearly spelled out:

> If women become aware that their dying will not change other women's destinies but, on the other hand, will reinforce their oppression, will they not opt, instead of death, for life, however difficult, rough, harsh, cruel.
>
> Would they not give their energy to change rather than to the maintenance of oppression, of status quo? Would they not give their energy to their sisters, rather than to their oppressors?[5]

Without subscribing to any of the patriarchal assumptions that attempt to relate suicide to a wóman's innate limitations or inability to cope, Chandra views it as the very means by which patriarchy can be reinforced. Yet, there is no accusation of those 'sisters' who have yet to realise the larger implications of suicide; there is simply a question suggesting an alternative use of 'energy' — that 'explosive energy' examined earlier in *Request Concert* which, if turned outwards against the oppressors rather than directed inwards towards one's self, has the possibility of facilitating a process of liberation for society at large.

Fire, Counter-Fire

If *One More News* is almost self-consciously 'vivid' in its representation of a woman suicide, *Fire, Counter-Fire* offers a very different visual language on the politics of ecology. Structured around a series of black-and-white drawings in the form of a book with a lyrical text counterpointing each image on a separate page, the statement is designed to instil a more acute consciousness of the environment.

In its economy and total lack of ostentation, *Fire, Counter-Fire* exemplifies a particularly rare kind of publication in the Indian context in which the author attempts to be the producer of her own work. Countering the dominant trend among alternative groups to get their literature published through the established publishing houses or, at the other extreme, through cheap monographs, frequently cyclostyled with a total absence of design, Chandra (in collaboration with Dashrath and Sadanand) has attempted to find a creative counter by designing her books like handicrafts.

To sustain this activity has not been simple because the entire production process is personalised with Chandra participating in the actual technology of printing the book in low-cost circumstances. Significantly, it is worth pointing out that despite the total lack of 'marketing', a book like *Fire, Counter-Fire* (which had an initial print-run in 1983 of 1,000 copies) has sold out. Here again, Chandra has devised her own 'economics' to sell the book by adopting what she calls a 'triple-price' policy — one for rich donors, another for book-stores, and yet another for friends who are sold the book at the production cost, if not less. In this assertively informal, if not amateur way of producing and distributing her work, Chandra has attempted to be true to the very nature of her creativity.

Fire, Counter-Fire can be viewed as a lyrical statement on the history of the 'environment' over a passage of time.

In a fictional mode, the narrative traverses at least three cycles of time. Through a flow of images and words, we are taken back to a point in time when 'dreams were the essence of life' and 'male and female were harmonious and together'. Without elaborating, the text implies that there was too much 'indulgence' in 'moon-worship', which had kept the earth 'cool and watery'. This resulted in the earth itself becoming 'drenched' through a deluge of 'primordial waters'.

As life is renewed once again after the flood, the order of the universe is reversed with people worshipping fire instead of water, sun instead of moon, men instead of women, work instead of leisure. This conscious affirmation of a 'man's world' results in increasing 'enslavement' and a goal-oriented society. 'Fire-power', which is now the governing principle of life, results in an increasing control over the 'nature', 'bodies' and 'minds' of people. The earth is gradually poisoned, rivers stop flowing, clogged with waste matter. Skyscrapers, 'cement-concrete', and robots replace trees, forests, and human beings respectively. With the proliferation of 'guns, gases, rockets, missiles, bombs', nations are at war. Men and women are also at war with one another. Despite the feeble interventions and warnings of a few people, the environment continues to be destroyed. It is in danger of a 'heat death'.

In the brief conclusion to the narrative, we enter the realm of *possibility*, both at the level of action and consciousness, poetry and politics:

>now is the time to pacify our earth
>now is the time to invoke female power, the
>primal energy, the shakti
>now is the time to fight fire with counter-fire,
>outer with the inner

Taken out of the visual context of the book, these words are almost flagrantly euphoric but the entire experience of the book offers a refreshing perspective on ecology, countering the turgid reportage it has received in the media. The

Chipko movement in particular has been trivialised in the Indian context, inspiring some of the worst dance-dramas and children's productions that I have seen in recent times. Where Chandra scores over other artists 'cashing in' on the environment is through the originality of her creative response and the very 'smallness' of her vision. She also has a way of transforming fact into fiction so that her statement acquires the immediacy of 'another language', which is intrinsically creative.

Her evocation of *shakti*, for example, is represented through a most non-Hindu-like persona: a slight woman, almost without any distinguishable features, but with the barest trace of a smile, holding a crescent-like sword in one hand and a branch of leaves in the other. This is one of Chandra's most graceful visuals of a woman, so evanescent in effect, that the sketch totally counters the more elaborate and fearsome images of deities and figures associated with *Shakti*. Indeed, it is kind of *chutzpah* on Chandra's part to visualise *Shakti* in such a way, standing sideways with a smile, wielding the sword with as much grace as she holds the branch of leaves.

Even a cursory look at *Fire, Counter Fire* reveals a woman at play. Chandra is obviously addressing 'serious' issues but her style is light and fanciful. To demand a more elaborate and technically proficient rendition of the theme would be to deny the essential directness of the work, which is intrinsically part of its strength. *One More News* and *Fire, Counter-Fire* may not be 'great works of art' or 'profound statements' on the subjects of suicide and ecology, but perhaps, they are not meant to be viewed in such categories in the first place. What makes them so distinctive in the Indian context are their links to a tradition of hand-made books and chapbooks which have played a very important role in the propagation of 'alternative' countercultural idioms since the sixties.

In their own ways, these books exemplify that age-old maxim in which Chandra continues to derive faith: 'Small is Beautiful'. At one level this could be dismissed as a remnant of the sixties, but in an age of computerised technology, it is still reassuring and oddly moving to know that the production of books can be humanised through involvement, fantasy and a sense of play. It is in this spirit that I believe Chandra's images of ecology can be most meaningfully viewed.

Posters For the Women's Movement

One of Chandra's earliest contributions to the women's movement was a series of posters. For a long time, she was, perhaps, the only woman graphics artist whose images registered with a strong stamp of her individuality. One could recognise a 'Chandralekha poster' almost anywhere. Earlier in the book we have discussed Chandra's incorporation of dance images into posters focusing on concepts of time, distance, *shakti, purna*, friendship. Apart from two posters for Air India, all the other posters were designed with particular art forums in mind. As time passed, Chandra found herself focusing most of her energies on the diverse activities generated around Skills, which had organised citizen's forums and development activities through poster workshops.[7] By this time the women's movement had become an integral part of her consciousness.

By 1974 the Chipko movement had already started though it was not initially identified with the women's movement. Simultaneously, Chandra was designing her own hand-made books on plants and seeds and designing jackets covers for books connected with the environmental movement. Already by the mid-seventies there was a need for symbols that could represent the numerous organisations for women that began to be registered around this time. It was in 1978 that Chandra found herself more directly involved with the women's movement when a group called Samata decided to publish a women's magazine called *Manushi*, which is now, of course, almost synonymous with the women's movement in India. Chandra's image for the cover of the opening issue of *Manushi* was rejected, which highlighted some of the differences between Chandra's concepts of women and the more directly activist position of Indian feminists.

Chandra had chosen the emblem of the inverted triangle, which is at once a traditional icon of 'the female creative principle', and more ironically, the government logo for family planning. Chandra's intention in using the image was to 'reclaim' the icon from its appropriation by the government and reinvest it with new energy and belief in the primacy of women's creativity. Her argument, however, was not convincing to most women, who felt that the time had come to register a more clear-cut militancy. Chandra, on the other hand, contended that most Indian feminists have no cultural base. Indeed, she continues to complain that, 'They have not done their homework on our cultural sources. You can't turn to the suffragettes for inspiration.' Significantly, the opening image of *Manushi* was an etching by Ira Roy showing a cluster of women with clenched fists. While this image for Chandra was a mere cliché of protest cast in a 'male' idiom, many Indian feminists thought that it was an appropriate symbol in the late seventies to register the women's movement in India.

It is at this point that we have to ask ourselves what an alternative image of women's protest could be. One gets a valuable clue from the feminist film director, Chantal Ackermann, who in a brilliant illumination on the subject once said:

> If women imitate men's battles they will become weaker and weaker. They must find new forms of struggle. This became evident in Hendave where women demonstrated against the death sentence in Spain. Some women shouted and clenched their fists, while other just hummed. They went 'mmmmmm' with their lips pressed together, and moved forward in a row. That is a new way of demonstrating which can be a hundred times stronger than fists... In film and in the arts we must also find a language which is appropriate to us, one which is neither black and white.[8]

This statement, I think, is very close to Chandra's line of thinking and general antipathy to any kind of 'fist' imagery. Even in the boldest of her images there is invariably a touch of irony, for instance, in her use of a multi-handed female deity who holds on to various household items representing the burden of domesticity, as well as a policeman's head.

This image was initially criticised for being 'anti-man' and 'too Hindu' in its visual orientation. The fact that the traditional perspective of the deity was being thoroughly subverted through the insertion of contemporary social elements was not sufficiently taken into account by feminist critics. Increasingly, there has been a resistance to the use of any icon or symbol with a recognisable 'Hindu' aura. At one level, the argument is valid in so far as Hindu icons have been appropriated decisively and dangerously by fundamentalist and communalist organisations. Chandra's argument would be that one needs to counter these appropriations through more strategic uses of religious icons not to promote religious beliefs but to assert contemporary statements about identity and resistance.

On the one hand, her secular position is undeniable but it is textured and inflected through the mediation of cultural sources, which many of her critics would term 'Hindu.' Thus, there is increasing discomfort with the 'contemporary' use of an image like *Agni-Pariksha* (a test of fire) to show a woman coming through a process of trial and suffering. For most Indian feminists, this is too close to the violent uses of fire in our society, most graphically in the recent spate of bride-burnings. Such are the sensitivities to these dual associations of images that at the National Women's Conference in Calicut, some women objected to the torch-light demonstration on the grounds that 'fire is not just a purifying element; it is also the cause of murder and destruction.'[9] From this position, it would seem that most feminists in India are no longer content to receive merely the affirmation of a particular image without a critique of its construction. And Chandra's images are almost unquestioningly affirmative without seeming to problematise their content.

For an image to be 'ideologically appropriate' is one thing, but for this image to be actually created and shaped is another matter. The 'language' of any artist is steeped in particular cultural formations. Paradoxically, one's resistance to these formations may have to be expressed through the very symbols by which they are known to us. Chandra, for example, may not be religious, but the power of Kali as an image is undeniable to her. To reject the validity of this source of inspiration could only result in the censorship of her desire and capacity to fantasise and transform her creative sources. Indeed, can one collectivise symbols of liberation on the basis of 'uniform codes'? Who determines these codes in the first place? And on what criteria?

One also needs to probe the assumptions underlying the criteria of cultural differentiation. If it has been said, for instance, that Chandra's images are 'too Hindu', then one can only assume that the person making such a charge knows (approximately) what 'Hindu' is. More problematically, the criticism assumes a knowledge of what 'Hindu' *is not*. Perhaps, these distinctions which exist politically and increasingly in a communal context are not so clear-cut in the more cultural aspects of human interaction, public life, and entertainment. For instance, there could be areas in which the so-called 'Hindu' and 'non-Hindu' elements can be fully implicated, if not blended in particular representations. Much more discrimination and self-reflexivity is needed before one brands anyone's work as 'too Hindu' or 'Muslim' or 'secular' or whatever.

Needless to say, it is very easy to say what women's images should clearly avoid. As Vibhuti Patel lists some of the most offensive details that flood the worlds of advertising and film: 'Gooey eyes, 36/24/36, statistics of victimisation, over-solicitious mothering, subliminal signs revealing that a woman is submissive, or worse still, asking to be raped.'[10] While these images are clearly to be opposed, one challenge is to find ways of reinstating the sensuality of women that counters the increasingly pornographic use of the 'female body.' Anti-pornography need not be anti-sensual.

In this respect, Chandra has probably explored sensuality more than any other woman artist in India, more in her dance work than in her posters, which are, nonetheless, distinguished by their vibrant colours and textures. One of her images for the *Stree* exhibition, for example, depicts Ganga riding on the body of a fish in an aquamarine glow framed by the dominant red of the poster. But here again, the criticism has been 'it's too Hindu.'

At such moments, Chandra simply throws up her hands in mock despair and points to the *bindi* on her forehead (which is simply inextricable from her appearance), the colours of her sari (which are invariably black, red, deep yellow), and affirms that her name is Chandra, *not Georgina*. Inevitably, such self-affirmations are invariably followed by peals of laughter: the branding of 'Hindu' is at once too narrow and, at a certain level, redundant in her search for creativity as a contemporary Indian woman.

Stree

The 'Hindu controversy' once again resurfaced in a very different context during Chandra's exhibition of *Stree* which was held at Krimsky Hall in Moscow as part of the Festival of India in the Soviet Union. Here there were two aspects relating to the use of 'Hindu' material in the exhibition which were criticised: one came from a section of feminists who believed that there was insufficient representation of non-Hindu communities and religious traditions in India. The other came from the Government of India itself which prohibited the screening of Aravindan's film *Sahaja* based on the concept of *ardha-narishwara* which Chandra had conceptualised within the larger framework of the exhibition. The film was eliminated from the exhibition following the much-publicised comment by the head of the Indian Consulate, Mr. T.N. Kaul, who believed that the representation of god as half-man and half-woman could only besmirch the image of India (and, I suspect, Indian men) abroad: '*Hum to poore mard hain*' was his jocular defence.

Before entering the details of this political controversy, it will be necessary to provide some general background to this unusually creative and intelligent exhibition on Indian women which has yet to be seen in India. Conceptualised by Chandra, the exhibition, nonetheless, drew on a great deal of support from diverse groups of women. At first when Chandra had approached some of the leading feminist groups and research centres, her decision to work with the government was viewed with scepticism and even suspicion. Some groups decided that they would have nothing to do with the exhibition. Others were more divided because, on the one hand, they respected and trusted Chandra, but they also felt that her credibility was being used by the government. Finally, it was left to individual women to decide whether or not to participate in the forum as contributors and collaborators.

One such woman was the feminist activist, Vibhuti Patel, who is closely connected with the Women's Centre in Bombay. She had come to know Chandra in 1980 when both of them had attended the Perspective for the Women's Liberation Movement in India organised by the Forum Against the Oppression of Women in Bombay. Two years later, they met again at the Kriti workshop held in New Delhi which was a multi-class, multi-lingual, multi-cultural meeting of diverse women from almost fourteen states.

What impressed Vibhuti most about Chandra in these early encounters was not so much her dance or her posters (which did strike her as being somewhat 'too Hindu'), but her grit as a woman. She mentions one specific detail: 'While most of my middle-class friends fled when they saw the cramped living conditions and the filthy toilets, Chandra stayed on in the camp centre.'[11] Continuing to reflect more generally about the class-conditioning of metropolitan Indian feminists, Vibhuti adds:

> All of us who come from the Left are anti-caste. We are strong advocates of the 'toiling masses'. But I realise now that this is somewhat abstract. When it actually comes to 'live contact' with people — I mean the sweat, blood, and shit — then one's repulsion to that reality surfaces. After living with

Chandra at these workshops, I realised that she does not have that repulsion. Without using the jargon of de-classing, I found that she had de-classed herself.

Undeniably, this is a very real tribute to Chandra as a woman which becomes all the more meaningful because it comes from a feminist who openly acknowledges her general distrust of artists. Contradicting the mannerisms and hypersensitivity that one associates with most dancers, Chandra was refreshingly different in her interaction with diverse groups of women.

The Kriti workshop was also important because it enabled Chandra to discover Vibhuti's own creativity in conducting singing sessions with the women participants. Vibhuti found that many women could not get involved in a number of the activities on account of the language-barrier, or their general lack of interest in activities like photography, which they would not have been able to sustain in their own homes due to the lack of resources. To involve these women, Vibhuti conducted a folk-song workshop in which she could justifiably resort to the 'oral method' of communication as she taught a wide variety of songs to women from at least six language groups.

Chandra had not forgotten this experience. When the *Stree* exhibition was being organised, she promptly invited Vibhuti to conduct a similar workshop with Russian participants in the course of the exhibition itself. This was part of Chandra's ingenious plan to incorporate an interactive element within the exhibition, so that along with the visuals, paintings, sculpture, artefacts, the spectators also had an opportunity to participate in one of at least six workshops, which were conducted simultaneously in Krimsky Hall itself.

The workshops included *veena*, Bharatanatyam, *kolam* (floor-painting), which were conducted by Vidya, Sujata and Geetha, all personally known to Chandra. In addition, a woman called Rubab-bai applied *mehendi* on the hands of literally hundreds of spectators, including a Red Guard in whose exposure to Indian femininity Chandra took personal interest. There was also Toofan Rafai, the only male par ticipant in the workshop, who demonstrated his considerable skills in vegetable dyeing and block-printing. Vibhuti, of course, conducted her song workshop which was attended by 93 students who met in three different groups at three different times during the day.

In the course of a month, these predominantly monolingual Russian participants had learned folk songs, feminist songs, children's songs, and lullabies, in more Indian languages than the average Indian is capable of knowing. Such was the bonhomie of these workshops that on the concluding day of the exhibition, there was a mingling of all participants along with spectators and security women who danced and ran through the exhibition hall in a 'human chain' led by Chandra, generating tremendous energy and a most fantastic feeling of 'community'.

This celebration, however, was cathartic in more ways than one because it followed some acute tensions, if not an open confrontation with the representatives of the Government of India in the Soviet Union. In this confrontation, Chandra received the support of all the participants in the exhibition along with feminist groups in India. The basic problem was that the Government wanted to substitute the film on *ardha-narishwara* with a propagandist film on Indira Gandhi. At one level, this was totally inappropriate to the general scheme of the exhibition in which Aravindan's film had been conceived and located by Chandra in a very specific way. As the chief researcher of the exhibition, Kamala Ganesh, points out:

> The film has to be seen in the larger context of the exhibition. This relationship between concept and context is something that Chandra is keenly aware of, and the bureaucrats were not. She had envisioned not just the theme of the film, but its actual location in the exhibition, at what point it should be seen as part of a cumulative experience. Once again, it is like choreography, it's like waiting for *Naravahana* in *Angika*. Something would be unavoidably affected through its exclusion.[12]

Apart from its total insensitivity to the larger 'choreography' of the exhibition, the Government wanted to establish Mrs. Gandhi's centrality within the larger context of Indian women. 'From the beginning', as Chandra explains her position, 'I made it clear that this was not going to be an exhibition about Mrs. G. The focus would be on showing that the greatest achievement for most Indian women lies in the survival itself.' As an 'achiever' in the political sphere, Mrs. Gandhi had been duly acknowledged in one of the sections of the exhibition, but this was not enough for the politicians who were clearly disturbed by the representation of women's struggle in the exhibition. Thus, they were piqued by a photograph depicting a woman pulling a hand cart with her son and husband seated on it.[13] This obviously revealed Indian patriarchy in its true colours. They also objected to another photograph showing a woman and her child standing near a family planning van. This was viewed as anti-family planning.

In addition, the focus on daily tasks, such as husking, weaving, smearing cow dung, sewing, combing hair, was regarded as far too 'unglamorous', if not 'common'. Instead Chandra and her associates were often bombarded with suggestions such as: 'Why don't you show bridal costumes from different parts of India?' This was a bit like the kind of 'advice' that Chandra would receive from ministers during the inauguration of the Festival: 'Why don't you dress the participants in the colours of the national flag?' To all these philistine suggestions received during *Stree*, the bureaucrats had to be told that the exhibition was not about costumes but about women.

Ethnicity was another priority underlying their suggestions, contributing to the general 'touristic' image of India that they wished to reaffirm along with the most familiar icons of 'Indian culture' — Nehru, Indira Gandhi, Rajiv Gandhi, and of course, Raj Kapoor thrown in for good measure. What they had failed to anticipate was that an exhibition on 'Indian women' automatically eliminated most of these icons, so it was Mrs. Gandhi who was the obvious focus of their political zeal.

At the heart of Chandra's concept for *Stree* was a belief in a certain 'continuity' provided through the creativity of women which has persisted through any number of trials, struggles, and histories of oppression. Instead of focusing on the obvious evils of patriarchy, Chandra chose to emphasise the numerous ways in which women have been able to resist and survive at a micro-level. This creativity is not to be found only in the obvious areas of dance, singing, and painting (all of which were amply represented in the exhibition). It is also evident, yet unacknowledged, in the everyday activities of most Indian women beginning with the 'art of the threshold',[14] as they start the day, by decorating the ground outside their house with a drawing. This is followed by numerous household chores in which women have learned 'to make a little go a long way' through their subtle skills of seasoning the food, caring for children, and 'budgeting, conserving, coordinating, integrating.' Sadly, this very creativity which facilitates 'comfort and well-being for all' is what 'confines women within four walls', 'localising her, reinforcing her backwardness, marginalising her in a male-dominated world.'

Even so, through the daily grind of life, this creativity persists. Envisioning it through a most suggestive image, Chandra reminds us of the delicacy with which Assamese women remove the end of a silk thread from a cocoon. It is almost as if their finger-tips have eyes. Reflecting on this image in a larger, metaphorical framework, Chandra believes that Indian women need to 'draw out that silken thread from the cocoon of their lives', and thereby reinforce their connections to life-sustaining forces that have been sustained through concepts like *prakriti*.

Conceived as 'the undifferentiated nature', *prakriti* is a holistic concept that is invested with multiple meanings — philosophical, mystical, magical, ritualistic.[15] To deny these dimensions of life in favour of a 'purely historical' approach towards understanding women's problems is both evasive and limiting for Chandra. There is a 'poetry' in these concepts that cuts across regional and communal barriers. In this context, Chandra has consciously opposed the official and academic tendency to 'regionalise' Indian culture, and thereby, divide the country into zones and states, with fixed percentages allotted for the representation of particular communities on a quantitative basis. *Stree* rejected what Kamala Ganesh has described as this 'specious kind of mathematical equality' in determining the cultures of people.

Instead it offered a more creative and inclusive envisioning and recording of women's lives in India that was structured around dynamic concepts rather than streamlined within the strictures of a programme. If terms like *'prakriti'* and *'Kali'* were used in the exhibition, it was not to affirm a 'Hindu' ethos but to structure a particular continuum of experiences in which contemporary realities could be juxtaposed along with traditional concepts, icons, and symbols. Thus, within the context of the *Stree* exhibition, Kali is not just a goddess, but a symbol of resistance represented through a collage of photographs and reports detailing various kinds of feminist activity, interspersed with traditional iconography. Not to confront how Chandra *uses* the so-called 'Hindu' material is to minimise the importance of her intervention.

As Kamala Ganesh so pertinently points out as a scholar and feminist in her own right:

> The way Chandra uses traditional symbols is far from 'Hindu'. For example, the images of Tantra are powerful in their own right, but used decoratively, they can be harmful. This is where Chandra's intervention matters because she is able to place these seemingly esoteric sources in a contemporary context. It is not just the inclusion of the sources, but the way it is included that matters.
>
> Moreover, Chandra's very grasp over form enables her to free these images from their religiosity and endow them with a power latent in them but which is fully magnified in performance. So the *Naravahana*, at one level, evokes Durga and other mother goddesses, but it is also a statement in its

own right about feminine power, femininity as an elemental principle, primal to creation.[16]

This statement is valuable not least because it implicitly endorses that the 'meaning' of any image in a creative context lies in its 'use.' And the 'use' of Hindu sources in *Stree* was far from sectarian or even religious. Rather, it was shaped by a contemporary sensibility, predominantly 'secular' in its values and commitments, yet open to the ambivalences, concepts, and energies of Hindu myths without being needlessly defensive or apprehensive about being inspired by them. Ultimately, it is the conviction of the overall concept of *Stree* that registers, combining intelligence and sensuality, militancy and grace, rigour and a sense of fun, all these levels contributing towards a tribute to the struggle and survival of Indian women.

Sahaja

Having provided an overall context for *Stree,* it is now possible to situate Aravindan's film *Sahaja* which was so callously rejected by the government. It is only obvious that Chandra's impulse in exploring the concept of *ardha-narishwara* was far from 'religious.' The concept of God as half-man, half-woman offered her a point of departure for envisioning the possibilities of male/female coexistence at a time when the polarisation of the sexes has deepened in the world.

Ardha-narishwara is nothing short of a radical concept of gender that cuts across fixed notions of biology and sexuality. As interpreted by Chandra through Aravindan's *Sahaja,* it is less a state of androgyny than a process of 'becoming woman.' This process is viewed and experienced through dance performances in which we see men becoming women — Radha, Bhagwati, Surpanakha, Satyabhama. Countering the fairly widespread feminist assumption that these performances are male appropriations of 'female identity',[17] Chandra says:

What we see in these depictions of *ardha-narish-*

wara is more than an art form. What we witness is a genuine anguish for becoming. When women play women, there is at a certain level a representation of truisms, even a surrender to naturalism. When a man is shown becoming a woman, we are made to see the process of 'becoming' more vividly.

'But what about women becoming men?' I question hypothetically. Chandra laughs out loud at the question: 'There is no question of women becoming men — that would be a denial of creativity. All men can do is to aspire to the state of becoming women. We are talking of primacy, not equality.

In this interpretation, it becomes obvious that Chandra posits the 'female principle' as primary to creation, and in the process, lays herself open to criticism that she is 'essentialising' femininity. However, one should also point out this 'principle' cannot be assumed by women on purely biological grounds, for they, too, need not necessarily be in touch with their femininity. 'Hypothetically, conceptually,' as Chandra clarifies her position, 'women are closer to *prakriti*, but this need not be the case in reality. They, too, have to address the split within themselves.'

Ultimately, regardless of one's particular sex, the movement being addressed in Chandra's particular conception of *ardha-narishwara* is towards wanting to unite and become one with ourselves. In such a process of 'becoming', the male/female division dissolves into a yearning or submission. Whereas in metaphysical texts, this could be seen as the mergence of spirit and matter with the Absolute, Chandra would not take the concept into such metaphysical dimensions. Instead, she would prefer to leave it in a processual condition, always in the state of becoming, of moving towards one's self, which is one of the most potent (and ambivalent) ways of transcending the strictures of gender in a patriarchal society.

Undeniably, there is much that can be debated about Chandra's position relating to *ardha-narishwara* and its seeming conflation with the doctrine of Sahaja, which seems to have originated with the Tantrik Buddhists, according to Ananda Coomaraswamy, in which 'the adoration of young and beautiful girls was made the path of spiritual evolution and ultimate emancipation.'[18] What is memorable about Aravindan's film is not so much its historical perspective on *Sahaja* as its sensuous evocation of the process of entering a state of femininity through performance. Here the male presence and the female persona are constantly intercutting and dissolving into each other as we see some of the greatest dancers in the Indian classical tradition including Guru Kelucharan Mahapatra, Guru Vedantam Satyanarayana Sarma, Guru Kodamalur Karunakaran Nair, along with Gotipua dancers from Orissa and ritual performers of Theyyam *become* women within the specificities of their dance idioms.

While the focus in all these idioms is on the creation of curves and the maintenance of flow, there are subtle cuts within the performances which are initiated through the mediation of cinema. For example, the same performer could be shown performing the same dance at first without his *aharya* (costume), only in his *dhoti* and bare-chested, which could suddenly be followed by him fully attired in feminine garb. Ironically, his femininity could be more pronounced when we see him 'more as a man' (himself?) than when we actually see him encoded within the conventional dress of a 'woman.'

The split between the performer's self and the female role is further intensified through the soundtrack in which, at certain points, we could hear the performer singing while dancing, which could be followed in a later sequence with the performer dancing but with his voice pre-recorded. So through these differentiations between 'voice' and 'body', 'pre-recorded time' and 'real time', 'dance' and 'cinema', we are compelled to experience a series of disjunctions that amplify the larger dichotomy of man/woman in the language of cinema.

Perhaps, the most memorable sequences in *Sahaja* are those in which the coalescence of male and female energies is metamorphosed in the more abstract terms of 'self' and 'nature'. Here again, it is the concreteness of the performance language that suggests the transition from one state of being into another. In the opening sequence of the film, for instance, which is shot in an open field with the lush green foliage of Kerala, we see a Theyyam artist preparing himself for his performance. As bird sounds fill the air, he is transformed before our eyes. In the background, we see his skirt being made out of bamboo pieces. As the face of the performer gradually becomes a red mask, the artist seems to enter a state of *dhyana* (meditation) Gradually, pieces of his *aharya* (costume) are literally hooked and added to his body — shoulder pieces, anklets, 'breastplate,' but he is still male. Only when he looks at himself in the mirror, only at that moment does he confront the other in his transformed self and enters the state of femininity.

An even more cosmic evocation of the celebration of the five elements is conveyed through two *bhaktas* from Orissa who balance earthen pots of water on their heads, suggesting fertility, vegetation, and growth. Later, they are shown dancing on stilts, which automatically endows them with an air-borne quality. Still later, fire is blown into the air. As the movements continue to be vigorous, drops of water are splashed in the air from the pots so that the dancers do not merely appear to be *patras* (vehicles) celebrating the elements of nature, they *become* nature. Prakriti is *embodied* in performance. It is through the 'rough magic' of ritualistic dance that *Sahaja* celebrates its immediacy.

The tragedy, of course, is that this 'immediacy' was lost on our politicians and bureaucrats who attempted at first to suggest that the film was much too obscure for Russian audiences. At least this was a 'diplomatic' response. The really crude reason mentioned earlier in the chapter that merely substantiated the patriarchal norms of the Indian cultural establishment came from our ambassador in the Soviet Union in his now 'famous' words: *Hum to poore mard hain*. This kind of crass assertion of masculinity reminiscent of Hindi films, is not just offensive in its own right, it reveals a deep ignorance of the basic sources of energy that animate concepts like *ardha-narishwara*.

On a more positive note, one should acknowledge that Mr. Kaul's response received wide publicity in the Indian press, and for the most part, the public reaction was very critical of the government's role *vis-à-vis* the censorship of the film. This contrasted sharply with the bad press that Chandra had received for the opening ceremony of the festival. Now she found herself supported by a wide range of artists and activists. She received letters from the far corners of India from people expressing their distress and sorrow that 'Indian culture' should be so grossly misunderstood. Most moving of all was an anguished phone call that she received from Kamaladevi Chattopadhyay who was compelled to ask: 'Is this what we have fought for all our lives?'

In retrospect, one of the saddest things of all is that Aravindan himself has passed away and the film has been screened only in a few film forums. *Stree* itself was not brought to India, so all the research and months of work that so many women had put into the exhibition have not been shared with feminist groups and general audiences in India, apart from a few video presentations and discussions.

What *Stree* did generate was a great deal of controversy regarding the role of the State in relation to the creative autonomy of the artist. Almost clumsily, the government officials had imagined that they could assert their own choices and thereby affirm their political biases. What they had not anticipated was Chandra's resistance. As pressure mounted from the government for the screening of the documentary on Indira Gandhi, Chandra planned her own course of action.

After much intense discussion with the women participants and Sadanand, whom she would call almost every night for his long-distance advice, she decided to register her protest by simply stopping the workshops for a short time. Almost everyone went on 'sick leave' with complaints of chest pain or exhaustion. In Chandra's case, this was certainly true because by then her health had broken down. She continued to fight in her own way, challenging the highhandedness and occasional threats from the bureaucracy with her own temperament. Eventually, on the last day, she lifted the boycott on the workshops (many of which had continued unofficially) and brought all the participants together in the final celebration as they ran through the exhibition in Krimsky Hall which, for many of them, had become a 'second home.'

Contrary to what some of her critics had predicted, Chandra did not jeopardise Indo-Soviet relationships. On the contrary, in her own way, she may even have deepened them through any number of creative encounters and relationships. Not only was the exhibition viewed by more than 75,000 people at the end of three weeks (a fact that even the bureaucrats could not deny), the most unusual feature was that many people kept returning to it to take notes, copy designs, or participate in the workshops. This exhibition really *humanised* the very concept of exhibitions, transforming the norms of a static spectacle into a living encounter with women's history and creativity.

Judging from the numerous statements made by spectators in the 'Comments Books', one can sense that *Stree* had really reached out to the hearts and minds of Muscovites. As Kamala Ganesh reports:

> Deep emotion had been stirred by this 'sunlit exhibition'. Those who had 'forgotten what it is to be a woman' in the pursuit of 'more, better, quicker', began to 'look at ourselves with different eyes'; 'all the fight and blood on the panels, they allowed us to understand that under any circumstance we can fight if we have the goal.'[19]

Perhaps, tellingly, one of the surest signs that the message of *Stree* had got across to the participants, came from a man, who had signed up for the *veena* workshop. This is what he learned:

> *Veena* is a tender instrument. It is not possible to play it unless you feel you are a bit closer to becoming a woman.[20]

'Becoming a woman': this, in essence, is what *Stree: Women in India* had the courage to question along with its affirmation of women's struggle in the larger context of survival and resistance. Having provided a framework for this process of 'becoming' through the various idioms explored in this chapter, including theatre, poster design, ecology and cinema, we can turn now to Chandra's most heightened statement in dance about the empowerment and enslavement of women — *Sri*.

||| स्त्री |||

e is radiant like the rising sun || Her
auty lights up the world || she wears
n &, moon as her jewels || Her eyes are
e fish & lotus & darting deer ||

face is fragrant like chambaka
her hair like incense || she has
acities || she is active || she is
are || she is fearless || she is free ||

54

55

56

57

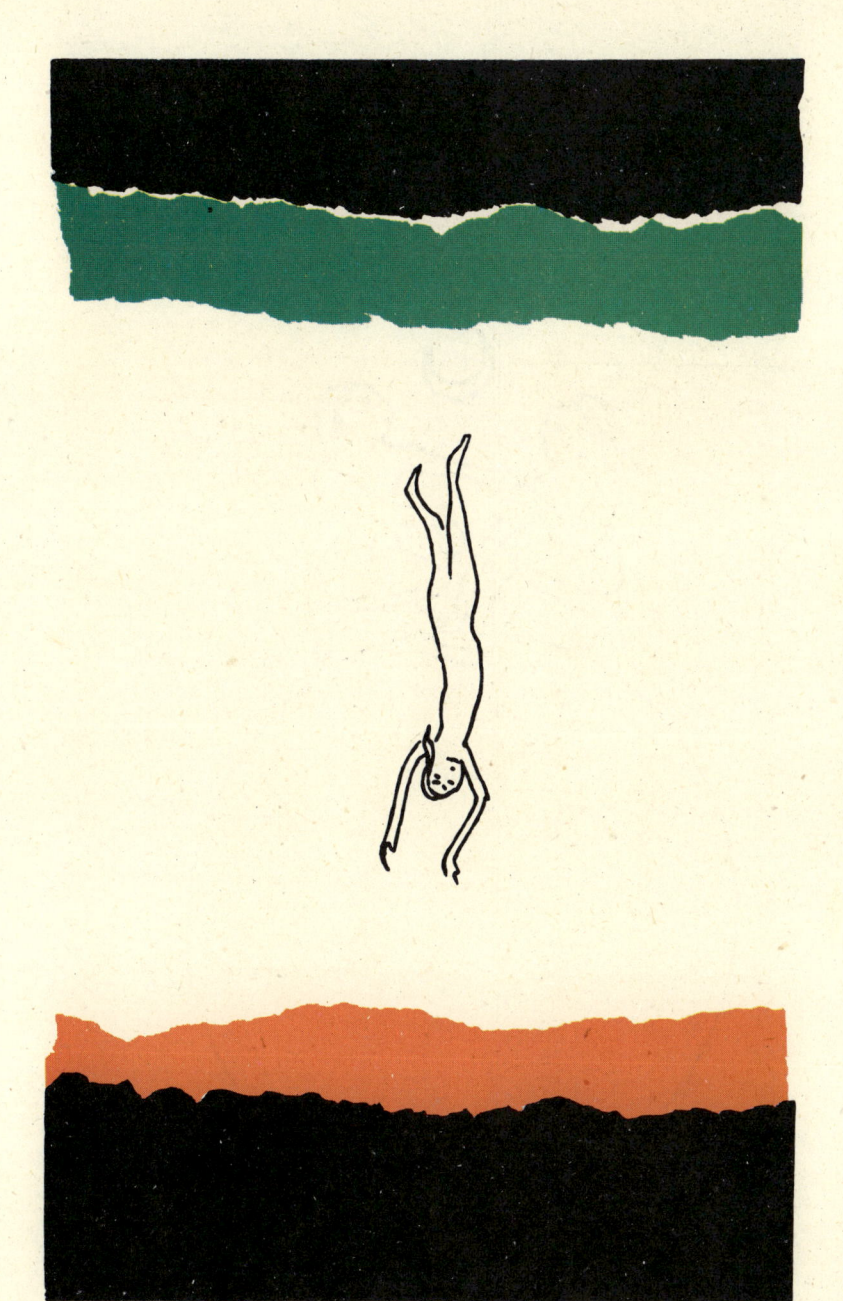

58

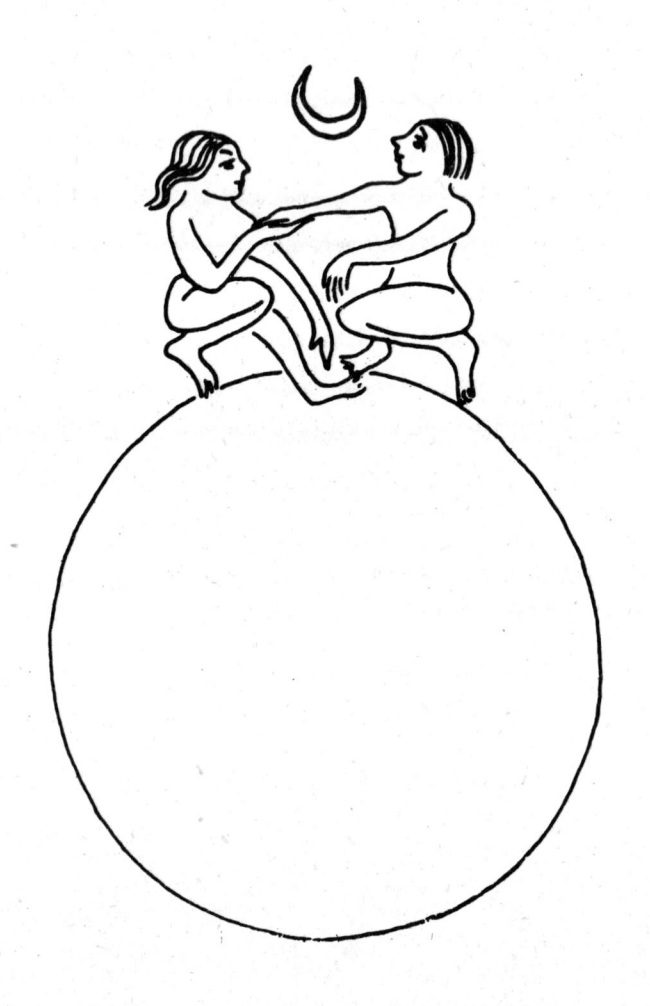

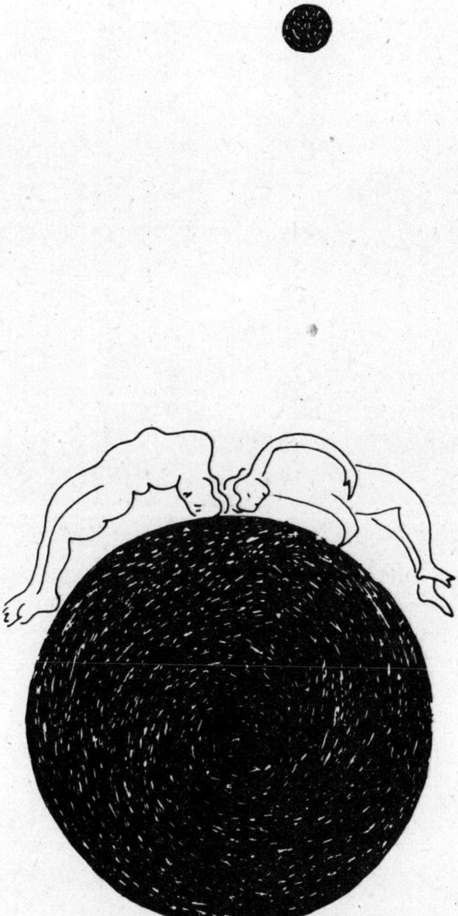

12

Sri

Though Chandra's self-representation may be problematic to many feminists, her resistance to patriarchy cannot be denied. Only she continues to express it in her own language which is neither academic nor 'theoretically consistent.' When Chandra talks about the 'cleverly designed institution' of patriarchy, she responds to it very graphically. She sees it operating with at least two voices: 'While one voice says, "She is beautiful, rare, strong in limbs", the other voice says, "Don't let her go. Use her." ' The apparent appreciation of a woman is invariably a pretext to keep her bound within patriarchal norms.

Though Chandra has fought these norms in different ways, both in her life and work, ultimately it is through the 'language' of dance that she has been able to express her resistance most vividly. In this context, her most textured statement on women can be witnessed in one of her most recent productions, *Sri,* which reveals a certain breakthrough in choreography that testifies to Chandra's own 'journey' as a woman from the time she staged *Devadasi* in 1960.

The very title of the work — 'Sri' — suggests a certain inclusiveness of meanings, at once open and auspicious, synonymous with the goddesses Lakshmi and Devi, but also connected to a wider spectrum of earth energies and fertility symbols. *Sri* could be described as Chandra's most mature attempt as a choreographer to trace different layers of significance in dominant concepts of Indian women. It is not a programmatic work, an explicit denunciation of women's oppression. If anything, this reality of 'oppression' could be regarded as the base of the conception, the ground on which Chandra weaves the most intelligent and non-decorative patterns of movement relating to the process of women's consciousness. In the final episode, in particular, of this three-part work which includes a prologue and epilogue, we are made to confront a continuous dynamic of fears, hesitations, gropings, groupings, breaks, re-assemblings, all these elements moving towards the affirmation of a collective feminine strength composed of individual energies.

a) *Pre-History*

Unlike *Lilavati,* which is danced almost exclusively in Bharatanatyam, and *Prana* which juxtaposes Bharatanatyam with Yoga, *Sri* is closer to *Angika* in its exploration of dance and martial arts. Indeed, the opening section of the production following the prologue (to be discussed later) relies almost entirely on martial walks, movements, and postures, only marginally modified with the tonalities of dance. Using an entirely female cast, Chandra provides some flashes of insight into the pre-history of women, a vibrant matriarchy in which women are viewed in a state of resplendent grace and strength.

Without attempting to tell a story, the configurations of movement on stage unconsciously stimulate narratives of women moving singly, in pairs, and in clusters, against the background of a primordial world.

We first see these women as *matrikas,* matriarchal figures, each in her own space, rooted to earth in seated postures, their brooding eyes seeming to look beyond time. With an almost invisible movement punctuated by the sound of two stones backstage, they rise from the ground filling the space with the strength of their bodies amplified by the slow dilation of the hands with outstretched fingers. Each of the women rises with her own consciousness of power, creating a distinct hieratic posture with the stillness of her body and the gesture of her hands.

Then, in one explosive moment, the women jump around in unison and with their backs to the audience, legs outstretched to the utmost limits, they slide their feet on the ground to the very back of the stage. Once again, there is an abrupt switch of movement, as the dancers swivel around to form a horizontal line in which they begin a half-squatting, martial walk, with the feet sliding against the ground with the body held erect, the buttocks sticking out. This walk constitutes the visual signature for the opening of *Sri*. Sustained with total rigour and concentration, the 'drama' arises from the asymmetric arrangement of the bodies on stage occasionally accentuated through the juxtaposition of a group of women moving in one direction with a lone woman moving in the opposite direction.

The other strong contribution to the visual dynamics of the scene comes from two dancers who face each other like warriors, earth-bound and resilient in their militant standing postures. With a measured rotation and swing of their hands, they strike their palms, flesh hitting flesh with a very audible sound. This gesture is repeated over and over again, contributing to a momentum that is heightened through the dynamic stillness of the women. Later, there is a sequence of movements in which the bodies of the women seem to be interlocked with their palms pressed against each other. Both the women have to stretch their bodies in order to convey the full intensity of their interaction.

This movement, which was inspired by a small prehistoric sculpture depicting two women wrestlers, is repeated by the dancers in opposite directions with a measured stealth that adds to the overall sensuousness of the movement. Indeed, what is distinctive about the entire sequence is Chandra's ability to represent the militancy of women without denying them their sensuality. Thus, the evocation of feminine power goes beyond the usual notions of 'confrontation' and 'battle.' The women seem to be using their force not *against* each other, but almost *with* each other, celebrating their mutual strength without surrendering their self-sufficiency.

As abruptly as the women get into a martial clinch, they also separate, breaking the dimensions of movement on stage by moving forwards while the rest of the group suddenly re-appears in a straight line backwards. Or else, the two dancers get re-absorbed into the larger group, or one dancer gets re-absorbed while the other continues to go her own way. Variations on the martial walk are accentuated through kicks, squats, and eventually, jumps which culminate in splits. Since there is no music apart from the two stones being hit against one another, every movement on stage resonates with a strong tonality.

In the final moments, two groups of dancers move towards one another on the diagonal with vigorous thumping movements of the leg culminating in a jump and split. They then exit backwards with the same impetuous movement leaving the stage barely for a moment, whereupon the two dancers who had faced each other earlier re-appear and face each other on a diagonal, their legs in a split position, their eyes locked in a fierce, yet intimate sisterhood.

b) *The Feminine Principle*

After this stark ending, which is cut abruptly, there is a transition into a different plane of experience as the 'feminine principle' is integrated through the mediation of Tantra. Here, the focus is on abstracting femininity through the distillation of form: an inverted triangle evoked through the placement of three dancers lying on the floor, their knees bunched together. To the oscillation of two strings on the *tanpura,* suggesting the interplay of 'male' and 'female' energies, the dancers slowly part their legs which open like the petals of a flower. In their midst is the still figure of a man, his back suggesting the *lingam* in a state of repose.

When asked to comment on the central motif of the choreography, Chandra unhesitatingly says: 'Pulsating vulva.' The movement itself is less torrid than her language, as the dancers suggest the dilation of the *yoni* through the slow, measured movements of their parted legs. Punctuating this movement is the elevation of the bodies of the dancers in a flexible back-bend which coincides with the vertical undulation of the man's back in the centre, so that an interplay of energies is evoked between the centre and the periphery.

What emerges in this ritualised choreography is the creation of an 'intermediary space' within the triangle, which is activated through the oscillation between negative and positive points of energy concretised through the two notes on the *tanpura*. Out of this 'space' emerges the archetypal figures of Purusha and Prakriti which are juxtaposed against each other. In a distilled exchange of movements, the two dancers survey each other, holding the earth as it were with their half-squatting *mandalas,* which are broken with abrupt movements towards each other on the diagonal. Despite their close proximity, there is a total absence of the flirtatious male/female interplay of energies explored in the duet episode of *Lilavati.* In *Sri,* the figures of the two dancers are not quite 'human' as they solemnly regard each other, pounding the earth with the insistent rhythm of their feet in one still position.

Interrupting this evocation of the archetypal equality between man and woman is a most unexpected gesture: the man bends down almost deferentially and holds the right toe of the woman, drawing her foot forwards. The gesture is so 'real' in its immediacy that one is compelled to recall Brecht's famous reflection on the efficacy of 'making the familiar unfamiliar.' What follows, however, is most disturbingly familiar as the man proceeds to lead the woman with measured steps. No longer deferential, he asserts his masculinity, his body dilating with power on stage, as the woman follows behind him, her head bent, almost cowering, yoked to his being. In their seven steps, the Hindu marriage ritual is encapsulated in which the man leads his spouse around the fire.

As an archetypal couple, they move towards the audience with almost eerie stealth as they are joined by the other women in the company, their heads lowered, their hands outstretched in a tentative gesture of submission. It is on this image of man leading woman that the second part of *Sri* ends as we move from the 'intermediary space' inhabited by Purusha/Prakriti to the history of our times.

c) *Towards Empowerment*

It is in the third part of *Sri* that Chandra's statement comes through with a most original and substantial piece of choreography set to an orchestrated score composed by the violin maestro, Sri V.V. Subrahmaniam. This is the closest that Chandra has come to exploring the 'real' in dance. While *Request Concert* was inspired by a 'realistic' text, the third part of *Sri* is Chandra's own response to the lives of contemporary Indian women unmediated by any text or submission to any set of rules determined by a particular dance tradition. Though Chandra incorporates some *charis* and *jathis* from Bharatanatyam in this sequence, they are constantly juxtaposed, if not 'broken' by 'real' actions and gestures. Here, in her exploration of dance language, Chandra is more 'free' than she has ever been in her play with forms and ideas, which almost collide into each other before cohering with an altogether unusual intensity.

One of the sources of 'liberation' in the piece can be related to the total absence of *nattuvangam* or dance direction. Now this can be misinterpreted, for Chandra herself has explored the 'freedom' of the Bharatanatyam idiom within the patterns of the *sollukattus* (rhythmic syllables) voiced by the *nattuvanar*. These patterns can accentuate, counterpoint, challenge, and even protect the dancer as the *nattuvanar* himself radiates a reassuring, yet authoritarian presence. While accepting the power of this traditional role, there has been an increasing resistance within Chandra over the years towards the ritualistic 'control' provided by the *nattuvanar* — a fact that was ironically resonant in her representation of the woman in *Request Concert,* who is imprisoned (as a character) within the mechanisms of her routine and (as a performer) within the measured time-beat of the *nattuvanar.*

In *Sri* Chandra has finally made some kind of a breakthrough in her choice of music through a most inspired collaboration with Sri V.V. Subrahmaniam, whose score with four violins, *mridangam,* sitar, and occasional *taalam* is a breakthrough in its own right initiating a new kind of relationship between the worlds of classical music and dance. Strikingly, however, the music itself is inscribed within the overall concept of the choreography through a consciously ironic introduction: the sound of a man's voice that embodies the very essence of patriarchal power in a 30-second improvisation of pure notes by master singer, Sri

G.S. Mani. The very power of this 'voice' is what Chandra's choreography is pitted against. It provides her with the stimulus for the rage contained within her work.

From the beginning, the tensions of the piece are palpable as the dancers cluster at the far end of the stage and drag their feet on the ground, their bodies bent in a humiliated mass of suffering. This 'drag walk' which continues for five minutes proves to be agonising for the dancers. By the end of the sequence they really feel that their backs have been 'broken'. When Chandra choreographed this section of *Sri* for Shobna Jeya Singh's dancers in London, this walk was described as a 'killer.' And indeed, it is so sparse and unremittingly cruel in the pressure that it places on the back, that there is some truth in the description.

Chandra herself has spent hours exploring the walk, which was one of her earliest images for the piece. At odd hours she would get up at night and try out the walk to Sadanand's utter bemusement. As Chandra says:

> I had to find out: what is the meaning of drag? If the women are going to drag out their existence, then I had to discover within my own body how exactly the movement would work.
>
> Ultimately, you have to find out what it feels in terms of dance language. You want to say everything within the dance idiom, dance time. Even if you are dragging yourself, the body cannot be loose. The spine should reach for itself continuously. There can be no faking about the extremities of the spine. If you want to say that your backs are broken, it is the vigour of the spine that conveys the message.

'Spine' becomes the metaphor for the women's search for freedom in *Sri*. Almost all the movements are related to it either to show the 'enslavement' of the body or the beginnings of self-discovery and resistance. As the dancers gradually straighten their backs after the drag walk, after moving backwards in two groups, revealing a void in the centre — an empty space that somehow suggests the terror of the unknown — they look over their shoulders. This is the first time that we see their faces, which reveal a sense of being pursued by unseen assailants. As the eyes move in one direction towards the audience, the bodies move in the opposite direction, creating a sense of dislocation in movement.

This is followed by the 'flop' as one by one, at different moments, almost randomly, the dancers throw their bodies forwards and then, very laboriously, pick themselves up only to flop again. Reminiscent of the 'contractions' associated with Martha Graham's school of dance, the 'flop' accentuates the earlier motif of 'broken backs.' Indeed, at no other point in her career has Chandra explored this kind of 'realism' on stage, where the movement is clearly associated with a particular state of being, and in the process, almost literalised.

In the next sequence, the women are shown sweeping the floor, their bodies rotating in a harmonious, yet anonymous coexistence. With it Chandra captures the profound humiliation of labour that has yet to be acknowledged as work, and which has reduced women to the condition of slaves. Along with the acknowledgement of this degraded status, there is also a refusal on Chandra's part to deny the dignity of the body. Therein lies the subtlety and depth of her statement.

What is significant to point out, however, is that Chandra does risk a new vulnerability through an insertion of melodrama, which functions like a quotation. In this context, one of the dancers actually mimes receiving a blow. As she lies prone on the floor, the other women watch impassively, their bodies shrinking with fear and the inability to strike back. In the meantime, the figure of a man emerges from behind the group for a few seconds before dissolving into another cycle of the group dynamics. 'Man' is not singled out as 'attacker' but the suggestion is there before the women gradually move towards their first 'formation' by trying to find their centre of gravity through a series of imbalanced movements as they sway from one side to another till they almost fall. This is followed by another exploration of their verticality in which they move up and down in the same spot, always in relation to the other dancers, so that there is a 'relativity' of positions. From these transitional movements, the dancers establish their first grouping through the ordering principles of dance.

Such is the complexity of Chandra's thinking of concepts through dance (which is different from mere conceptualisation) that she never allows the formations to emerge in a linear manner. On the contrary, she constantly breaks the formations through scattered walks, which the dancers have yet to render meaningfully. It is so easy for a 'scattered' walk to appear delicate, or at best diffident, in the rarefied world of our dance culture.

Chandra intends the walk to suggest a total loss of bearings. This may be the first time that she has consciously inserted rhythms and movements that contradict the language of Bharatanatyam, though she has had to make some compromises because the dancers are yet not able to handle the disjunctions between 'real' and 'dance' walks. So the 'scattered' walk is also a Bharatanatyam walk but it is so 'random', almost unchoreographed, that it gives the impression of women searching for themselves on a street. To the extent that Chandra is capable of rupturing her own idiom of dance, *Sri* may be the most 'contemporary' of her works, the one that might be remembered not only for its bold rearrangement of traditional idioms but for the actual emergence of a new language in Indian dance.

One particularly significant breakthrough lies in the way Chandra has been able to realise the contradictions underlying the process of women's liberation within the bodies of her dancers. Just as the spine has to be asserted even when it is being 'broken', so also the dancers have to 'fight back' the momentum of movement as they seem to be pushed against the wall. For every movement forwards, there is always the possibility of being thrown back. This basic lesson of any social transformation is embodied in the choreography.

As the piece progresses with a greater, and more intricate incorporation of dance, the fragmentation continues, with the dancers repeatedly interrupting their *charis* and *jathis* with the 'scattered' walks described earlier. Technically, the challenge for the dancers is to 'spill' their energies in an almost improvised manner to all corners of the stage to suggest their disorientation, and then, on cue, consolidate their energies through a particular formation. This rupturing and coordinating of energies demands the most acute concentration and tuning, so that this is one piece in which the dancers in Chandra's group do not merely 'dance' by going through the movements which have been previously worked out. In the actual act of performing *Sri*, they are almost compelled to fight for their directions and to *live* the very uncertainty of the process being dramatised.

As *Sri* moves towards its coda, the dancers form a vertical line centre-stage, and then proceed to perform the Dashabhuja sequence in which Sri is embodied through a ten-armed figure which could be Durga or the 'future woman' who is simultaneously auspicious, bold, sensuous, and supremely self-possessed. The structure of this sequence is created through the seemingly disembodied use of multiple hands. Only the dancer's face in front of the line is seen as she holds her hands in the *abhaya mudra* or gesture of reassurance. All the other dancers are concealed behind her apart from their hands which protrude in different directions wielding weapons. Finally, the total image is created through a cluster of hands that seem to emerge from one body, an image that never fails to thrill the audience with its immediacy.

If this is 'too Hindu' for some tastes, one should remember that *Sri* does not close on this image, which is dismantled as the dancers leap in the air one by one, with their arms stretched outwards, thumbs raised, to hold a perfect *mandala* with their bodies. In this mass of *mandalas*, the dancers then proceed to move forwards, sliding their feet on the ground, while maintaining a total centrality with their bodies. And on this surge of movement, embodying the assertion of women's empowerment, *Sri* comes to an end.

One could argue that there is always a risk in ending any performance with a 'thrilling climax'. But in *Sri* which has persistently denied the possibility of any climax through its abrupt endings, ruptures within sequences, and disorientations coexisting with the 'search for spine', the climax is almost necessary to hold the piece together and end it with a powerful, multifaceted image.

Conceptually, this ending can be questioned by those who would prefer a more abrupt conclusion that would leave the question of 'empowerment' more open. Other spectators would possibly opt for an image outside Hindu iconography. Once again, it needs to be pointed out that the very formation of the *dashabhuja* in Chandra's dance-language (and the movement that follows it) works against religiosity. Certainly, it is 'auspicious', but as Chandra would say, 'Why deny that dimension to women?' In purely theatrical terms, the ending is a most forceful way of countering both the agit-prop representations of women's 'liberation' and the more sentimentalised evocations of the 'oppressed woman' which pervade our mass culture. In the final surge of movement as the women advance forwards, the choreography suggests the potential energy of Indian women in facilitating a process of social transformation and change.

Beginning With Sakambhari

For a long time, *Sri* was incomplete in the absence of a prologue that Chandra had choreographed for herself. This short, minimalist abstraction of the earth goddess, Sakambhari, or the 'herb-nourishing one' could be one of Chandra's most daring experiments on herself as a dancer. It is a piece that is performed entirely with the legs, which are suspended in the air with the body placed on the ground. As everything remains still, only the legs create a profound gamut of feelings which are sculpted in the air with a most forceful sensuality and power.

Like *Naravahana* or the *Purusha-Prakriti* principle explored in her earlier productions, the image of Sakambhari

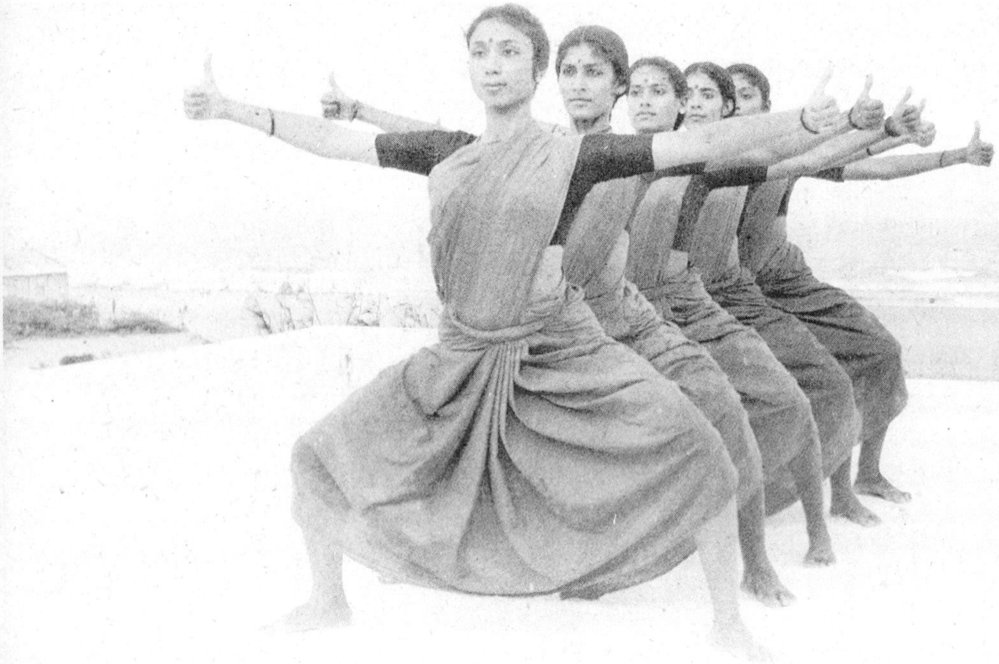

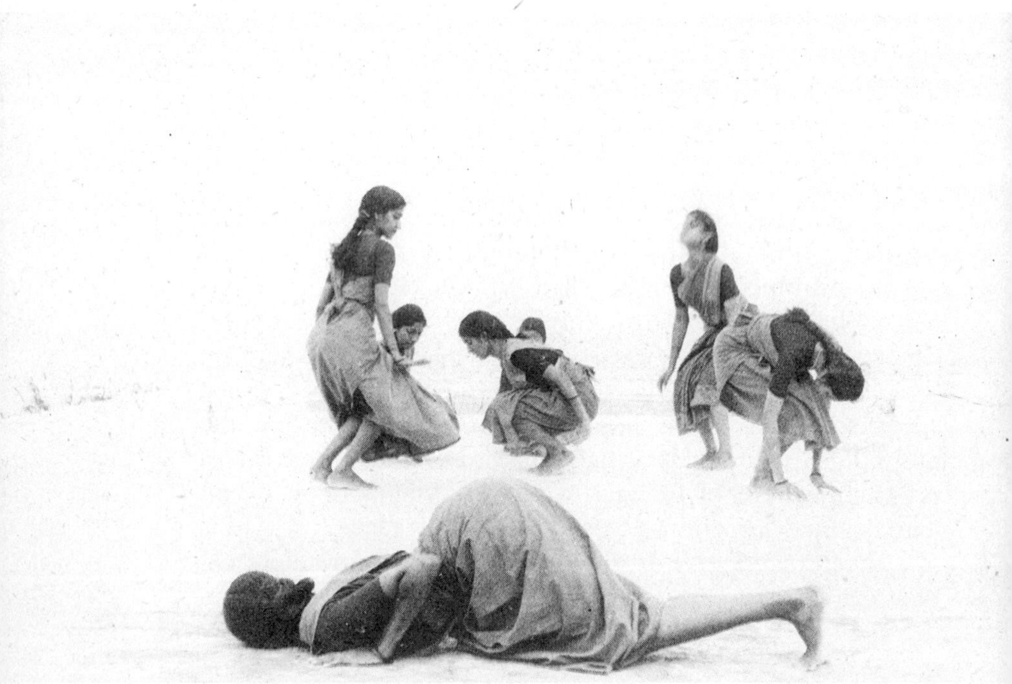

68

69

has 'slumbered' in the depths of Chandra's consciousness for a long time, intimately connected with her general fascination for female deities and mother goddesses. Unlike academic feminists and anthropologists who have turned to 'mother goddesses' with something of a vengeance in recent years, attempting to read theories and genealogies through them, Chandra's interest in these primordial figures is more instinctive, and to use her favourite word, 'visual'. For her it is the possibility of envisioning the entire world with life-sustaining vegetables and trees sprouting from the legs of Sakambhari that moves her tremendously.

At one level, she is drawn to the fecundity principle in figures like Sakambhari that transcends the notion of 'reproduction' in a purely biological sense. In this goddess, Chandra is able to embody her most potent fantasies connecting the human and plant world. Then, also, the fact that Sakambhari does not have to be activated by an outer force, but is creative in her own right, testifies to the fact that 'everything that lived and moved was born of her body'.[2] In this overwhelmingly 'natural' goddess, there is a source of potent energies nourishing soil, water, air, light. Sakambhari encompasses all these 'spaces', her *yoni* wide open to the splendour of her own creation.

Once again, it is not just Chandra's 'instinct' that enables her to crystallise figures like Sakambhari, but her most immaculate sense of form, the movements which cohere with an inner logic. Once again, as in many of Chandra's previous pieces, the 'take-off point' is an image of a Harappan seal which has been internalised and abstracted to the point that it acquires an almost disembodied dynamism in performance. Almost entirely still in the face and hands, the body alone is animated through the legs which create molten patterns of energy in space evoking a process of 'becoming'.

In the course of this strangely hypnotic experience in which the legs acquire a life of their own, we are alerted to the most subtle modulations of emotion through the different placements, rhythms, and distinct energies of the individual legs. Never symmetrical, they almost seem to counter each other, one stretched, the other bent; one moving upwards, the other drawing inwards; one seemingly 'male', the other 'female'. The recurring motif in this fluid piece, which seems to have no fixed divisions, is the 'opening of the *yoni*' through outstretched legs. Here it is not just the outer boundaries provided by the legs that register with visual immediacy, but the space in between, a cavern of darkness that is at once still and shifting.

At one point, both the legs are lowered onto the forehead, evoking a deep sense of anguish. It is almost as if the legs are crying. They *become* cries. It is a most extraordinary embodiment of vulnerability.

Then, with the knees pressed against each other, the legs are turned from side to side almost like a mobile sculpture. This is once again followed by the parting of the legs, the opening and closing of the yoni. This is not just a technical movement as Chandra emphasises. An entire psychophysical process goes into the shaping of the image that is, at one level, primeval, and yet alive in the moment of performance. The dancer has to be able to internalise this span of time in order to suggest the image convincingly, and not just decoratively, which could only result in a somewhat embarrassing voyeurism.

Other feelings are evoked through the forward thrust of the legs, which conveys a sense of supplication. This is contrasted with the more lyrical interlocking of the legs so that the feet (which register for the first time independently of the legs) appear like the heads of cranes. Once again, the image is not illustrative but evocative, suggestive of an entire world of nature that emerges from rhythms of the body itself.

Finally, the iconographic form created through the outstretched legs is reasserted, the legs parted wide and almost stiffened so that they acquire a very strong musculature. It is almost like a state of 'readiness', the body totally poised for the 'moment of birth'. At this point, the visual of a tree and the shadows of vegetation emerge very unobtrusively from her outstretched legs and then fill the entire space around her with their natural splendour. On this visual, which is still in the process of being explored, Sakambhari sits up from her lying position and watches the glory of own creation with rapt wonder.

Body As Preserver of History

Undeniably, any representation of Sakambhari through performance requires more than technique. It necessitates a particular tuning of consciousness into areas of pre-history which are rarely confronted among performers today. Unlike the more familiar gods and goddesses in the Hindu pantheon, whose exploits have been trivialised through endless repetitions of the same episodes, Sakambhari is a relatively unknown figure. Not only is she harder to visualise, she also embodies a different kind of being whose body is the centre of the universe. It goes without saying that Chandra would not have been able to embody such a being convincingly if she had not been acutely tuned to its larger metaphysical dimensions.

Affirming her creative affinities to the earth goddess, Chandra risks a certain ridicule from sceptics and rationalists by saying:

> I am not just a woman living today, but I am all women living from all time. I am that Harappan woman. The way I stand, I sit is because of the primitive accumulation within the body.

Defending herself against the charge of romanticising myths, Chandra in turn questions the limits of existing representations of history. Firmly convinced that history cannot be adequately understood on the basis of facts and artefacts, she adds that:

> Stones and terracotta figures will give you a glimpse of history, nothing more. But can we get a total statement which is not just bits and pieces of history? Artefacts are just that: bits and pieces relating to this or that millenium, ADs and BCs. But the continuity

is registered in the body, which can be regarded as the preserver of history.

Predictably, Chandra is opening herself to the very obvious criticism that history is made up of discontinuities which have been created through ceaseless fractures and ruptures in time. How can we deny that our past has not come down to us through fragments and stretches of oblivion? Chandra would acknowledge this historical process, but nonetheless, she would assert that it has not resulted in a total fragmentation of the body. Representing her position with a discrimination altogether rare among performers, she clarifies:

> What exists are stratifications of time and space in the body, layers of time and space as in stone. Obviously, there is a vast time-scale that has been internalised. This is a complex process: how the body incorporates different layers of time from the 'beginning' to the present day. It is more complex than the splitting of the atom.

Then, with a most telling use of an image, which reveals her capacity to 'teach' with a most informal wisdom, she substantiates how we are capable of assimilating different areas of time simultaneously in one moment:

> To analyse it one could say that 'I am standing at this point in time seeing light from some planet or star that existed 50,000 years ago, another star which existed 250,000 years ago, perhaps some other which could be one million years old'. I receive all these lights at this point in time simultaneously. The body is that point which receives and internalises all these connections. That is why to know Sakambhari is crucial to know who I am.

And conversely, one could say that it is possible for Chandra to 'know' Sakambhari only because she is so closely in touch with herself.

One need hardly add that such statements invariably risk criticism from historians and feminists who are increasingly sceptical about any language relying on 'continuities', 'centres', and relationships between body and cosmos. All these areas are open to the risks of 'essentialisation' and the 'mystification of the feminine' in which one's position *vis-à-vis* ambivalent, and perhaps inexplicable areas of consciousness is insufficiently problematised within the rigours of a more substantiated historical inquiry.

In this context, one should point out that while Chandra would regard mysticism as a means of numbing a woman's capacity to make choices and think freely, she would be far less reluctant to deny the value of the 'irrational' in life. As she articulates her position:

> The irrational is a loaded concept. It has so much sway over our behaviour, our demeanour, over the directions we take, over the tonalities of all these things. The irrational could be more important in some ways than the rational. How often does the mind tell us one thing, the body another. Sometimes against all our rational judgement, our instincts lead us to a particular path.

Emphasising that the 'irrational' should not be mixed up with 'superstition' (a practice that she consciously resists), Chandra is more willing to view it in relation to a spectrum of inexplicable sensations. 'It is like light-perception, at a certain level', she says. 'Thank God we don't know how to measure it, unlike rationality which is always quantifiable, weighed, a mere yardstick understanding of the world. The irrational is more open, operating at multiple levels of infinitesimal perceptions. That is why it is rejected'.

In making such statements, Chandra is aware of being misunderstood. Nonetheless, she refuses to compromise her perceptions by accommodating them within the 'rational' categories of academia and, for that matter, certain schools of feminist theory which would regard any openness to the 'irrational' as a trap by which 'women play into the hands of men who will be better able to oppress them, to remove them from knowledge and power'.[3] Chandra would question the rationalist criteria by which 'knowledge' and 'power' have been hegemonised within the existing norms of patriarchal society. To counter these norms, she would uphold more 'deviant', 'playful', and 'fantastic' sources of knowledge that are not fully circumscribed within the dictates of Reason by which patriarchy is consolidated. 'Only when you search for rationality in the present system', as Chandra would assert, consciously echoing (and subverting) Simone de Beauvoir's famous words, 'that's when you construct a counter-penis'.

Holding on to her 'voice', Chandra acknowledges her close tuning to the simultaneity of time-perceptions which has enabled her to celebrate the 'continuity' of our cultural history. This celebration is evoked not within the categories of the 'pan-Indian tradition', which assumes a 'timeless' unity transcending all cultural difference, but more personally, through 'stratifications of time and space within the body', as Chandra perceives it.

Without succumbing to chauvinism, Chandra is nonetheless compelled to acknowledge the cultural specificity of her observations on 'continuity'. In this regard, she often recalls one of her travel experiences in the sixties when she was first alerted to the realities of 'cultural continuity' in India. This was when she was travelling through Egypt seeking out Pharonic art. She remembers being very moved by the physical shape and size and gestures of the human beings depicted in the Pharonic drawings and seeking an echo, a manifestation of it in real life on the street outside. But the more she wandered and observed, she found to her dismay that there was almost no trace of this art in the 'body-language' of the people around her. An entire period of history seemed to be erased. As she recalls:

> Everywhere I looked for these Pharonic forms — tight, flat-chested, slim — for a glimpse of continuity. But I found that Egypt is 'Middle East' today. I know

that is a harsh statement, likely to be misunderstood, but in my experience I found it to be true. It was a profound learning for me to realise the significant difference in our context where 'cultural continuities' can be actually seen and perceived.

Truly, one can say of Chandra that, for her, our 'tradition' is not just a repository of forms and concepts to which we have to 'return' to find our 'roots'. 'Tradition' *lives* in our everyday lives in India, despite the commodification and systematic destruction of our cultural sources. Perhaps, most of all for Chandra, it is in our bodies that the energies of our 'tradition' are most meaningfully incarnated. In the sun, moon, and stars that reside invisibly (and unconsciously) in our beings, there are lessons to be learned not only about the cosmic origins of art but of their ceaseless transformations into life.

Against Motherhood

After Sakambhari, it is almost an anticlimax to reflect on Chandra's *bête noire:* child-bearing. But it also reaffirms the distinction that Chandra never fails to emphasise between 'creativity' and 'reproduction'. More often than not, these activities are conflated so that the significance of 'creativity' is almost negated. Indeed it is more than a truism to state that an Indian woman is not normally considered 'fulfilled' if she is not also a mother. Her most heightened 'creativity' is almost inextricably associated with her 'reproductive' capacities. The fact that from time immemorial these capacities have merely reduced her to the ignominious level of a 'field', a mere vehicle, in which man's precious 'seed' is the real source of creation, continues to be widely upheld.[4]

Perhaps there is no subject in the world that angers Chandra more than the much mythologised virtues of motherhood. Deeply and uncompromisingly, she distrusts the institution of marriage to which she ascribes all the major problems in the world including social injustice, political and economic exploitation, and the continued enslavement of women. Most of all she refuses to accept motherhood as a 'natural' urge, an intrinsic part of women's 'creativity'. Here ironically, Chandra turns the tables on those feminist critics who continue to read significance into motherhood while documenting the systematised horror of the institution and its accumulation of anti-woman prejudice from the times of *Manusmriti*.

From Sukumari Bhattacharya's learned research on motherhood in ancient India, for instance, we learn how little has really changed for most mothers in contemporary India.[5] The focus is still on bearing children, and a boy child in particular. A woman's health and feelings are almost of no concern to the immediate family. She is a 'passive recipient' with almost no say in the rearing of the child beyond a certain age. Her rights of inheritance are limited. In old age she is granted an honorific status in which the concern for her well-being is more ritualised than real. And so, the realities of motherhood continue...

Within the overall degradation of her life, the mother is almost the antithesis of the 'mother goddess', who is in Sukumari Bhattacharya's words, an 'absolutely free, autonomous agent' with supernatural powers that enable her to ward off evil forces and demons.[6] Mothers-in-law and husbands are of no concern to her. At a biological level, mother goddesses do not have to endure the actual process of carrying and delivering a child through nine months of pregnancy (which Chandra, for one, regards very categorically in terms of pain, a waste of time, and a disfigurement of the body).

On a more conceptual level, the mother goddess is in a position to 'meet her children on the plane of ideas and emotions', receiving their homage in a spirit of equanimity instead of being made to feel eternally gratefully for being looked after by the members of a patriarchal household. At a cosmic level, of course, the mother-goddesses reign supreme, intervening even in those areas which male gods are unable to control. Contrasted to this omnipotence, human mothers are almost destined to live under duress and a seemingly endless state of oppression. Tellingly, Sukumari Bhattacharya ends her comparison of mothers and mother-goddesses with the question: 'Can any human mother feel any empathy with such formidable figures? Or project herself into these goddesses?'

For Chandra, who resolutely denies the validity of 'motherhood' in the first place, the possibility of empathising with the state of the mother-goddess at the level of fantasy and creation is not just possible but necessary. Certainly, she would not accept the somewhat querulous tone assumed by Sukumari Bhattacharya who almost seems to grudge the 'total autonomy' of mother-goddesses, which is contrasted almost too categorically with the 'diametrically opposite' state of human mothers. In such a dichotomised view of women's empowerment and enslavement, there is no option but to accept the total defeat of human 'motherhood' which allows a woman 'some months of bliss' with the infant so long as it is totally dependent on her, only to find herself almost abandoned as the child grows up. And thereby, 'the glory of motherhood fades slowly but surely'.[7]

One would imagine that such a bleak perspective of motherhood would almost necessitate the denial, or else a positing of strong alternatives to this tyrannical institution. This is where most academics stop and Chandra begins. Since her reading of the *Manusmriti* at a young age and her own critical observations of married life, she had resolved not to get married. This could be dismissed as youthful defiance, but in Chandra's case, it was clearly followed up through her rejection of marriage which was more than compensated through her exploration of other relationships with men and women. Significantly, Chandra's 'theoretical' resistance to marriage developed only after she had resolved *not* to get married, whereas most critics of 'motherhood' invariably fail to follow up on their theory in their own life-choices. It is not that Chandra is derisive of 'theory', it is simply that she anticipates it by *living* in a particular way.

On the subject of child-bearing, Chandra's views are predictably forthright:

What matters to me is my purpose in life: how I realise myself in this world. Why should women have children to be 'realised'? Certainly, this is not the case for most men. Why then should women submit to a different expectation? There cannot be one law for the lion and another for the lamb.

Rejecting the dominant thrust of most laws, institutions, and religious dogmas towards the 'propagation of race', Chandra firmly declares that her purpose is not to 'propagate' but to 'find herself'. Dismissing the widespread suspicion that any search for self is intrinsically 'selfish', Chandra qualifies that her idea of the 'self' is not hermetic, enclosed in some ivory-tower of make-believe wisdom, within which so many artists imprison themselves without almost any contact with social, political, and human realities. This is not the case with Chandra who believes that the concept of 'self' cannot be static. It has to 'pulsate' (to use her word), reaching out to environment, nature, universe. In dance or the act of living, which is an 'art' in its own right, 'you are involved', as Chandra puts it, 'in humanising yourself, and the world around you'.

Tellingly, Chandra's possibilities of self-realisation (and resistance to marriage and child-bearing) have emerged out of her seeming valorisation of the body. What needs to be pointed out, however, is that her knowledge of the body is far less 'rhapsodic' than is commonly assumed, grounded as it is in a specific vocabulary of dance mediated through particular concepts like *mandala*. In addition, the body is the means by which Chandra has acquired a critical consciousness about women and their relationship to power structures in our society. It is not a source of wish-fulfilment, a mystical sanctuary from the realities of life.

Indeed, as Chandra would put it, one's very resistance to notions of biologism can be enhanced through one's understanding of the body, inspiring a woman to adopt a more critical attitude towards 'nature', which is not always beneficent or respectful of a woman's space or search for freedom. As Chandra puts it categorically: 'When women acquire the knowledge that to realise themselves they do not have to go through the biological process of reproduction, then only will they emerge as knowers of their body, socially as well as politically'. The assumption here is that the body does not have to be viewed as an impediment to knowledge. One's very sensuous relationship to it can facilitate one's resistance to its appropriations through 'nature' or 'mysticism'.

Such is Chandra's conviction about the need for women to pursue their self-realisation without facilitating the careers (or progeny) of men that she has been very vocal on the subject both in everyday life and in conferences as well. Thus, in her keynote address at a workshop on 'Constitution and Family Law' in Bombay, she proposed nothing less than a strike — a 'moratorium on production'.[8] In this 'global strike' involving women everywhere, the purpose would be to 'strike at the very heart of patriarchism and male-power, which has brought the world to a brink of disaster' through militarisation, nuclearisation, pollution, and commodification not just of goods but of women's bodies as well. Echoing Lysistrata, Chandra advocated that women should not 'produce till men stop their war-like ways and sanity is restored in the world'. Note: the boycott is of 'production', not sex or relationships with men, though here too Chandra acknowledges that 'nature can trick you against your will'.

Contextualising her anti-production proposal within the larger context of 'fantasy' — a faculty that most feminists seem to have abandoned in their dependency on 'historicity' — Chandra envisions the social and economic consequences of such a production strike:

> One by one industrial empires will collapse
> kiddie industries
> kiddie wears
> kiddie fashions
> nappies, cosmetics
> food, toy industries
> kiddie programmes on radio/t.v./films
> Disneylands

>   creches, kindergartens
>   schools,
>   hospitals
>   maternity homes
>   closures and collapses on all sides.[9]

If this sounds somewhat too 'fantastic', it is, perhaps, meant to be so. As always in Chandra's sense of humour, there is an edge of sanity. During the moratorium on child-production as she envisions it, women will at long last find time to 'explore areas of freedom and empowerment' and 'to reclaim lost and forgotten capacities, energies, powers'. That would be the ultimate purpose of the 'strike', the hidden agenda of Chandra's fantasy.

Most women, including feminists, have not been able to take Chandra seriously in this regard. Even those who had earlier resisted motherhood on ideological and economic grounds, and had later decided to have a child, feel that it is possible to be 'realised' as a woman and a mother at the same time. Some feminists would even claim that having a child has deepened the 'humanisation' of their immediate environment, which was previously a work-space bound by ideological constraints.[10] Yet others would claim categorically that Chandra has denied herself a unique experience, which might even have diminished her quest for creativity rather than protected or enhanced it.[11]

To all these women, Chandra extends her good wishes, but declares that 'speaking for herself', she has absolutely 'no regrets' remaining single and childless. Ruefully, however, she has had to see her own dancers getting married one after the other, a reality that she can do nothing about. 'People have to go their own way', as she often reminds herself. 'And no one is indispensable'. The search for self-sufficiency is almost inextricably linked to her continuing quest for freedom.

Dreaming of the Future

As Chandra struggles to keep her group together without any professional infrastructure, she is often asked by her growing number of admirers about the 'future' of her work. To which, Chandra reiterates her resistance to the institutionalisation of the arts. Just as she rejects the idea of 'continuity' through revivals of productions, she also disbelieves that her work needs to be perpetuated through a school. In this regard, she has emphatically rejected the role of the guru. As we have emphasised earlier, she relates to her dancers more like a choreographer and friend rather than a mother or guru. Indeed, Chandra's resistance to the formalisation of any relationship may have deepened over the years.

Convinced that the purpose of 'humanising one's environment' is a 'full-time job', Chandra acknowledges that it necessitates a constant struggle with one's self. 'You never arrive', as she states honestly, 'You are always seeking'. In this self-acknowledged role as 'seeker', it becomes almost presumptuous to 'eternalise' one's art through any institution. 'Look at Santiniketan', Chandra says. 'All those offices with clerks. That gloomy atmosphere. Where is Tagore? Where is his spirit?' And likewise with Kalakshetra, Chandra recalls one poignant meeting:

> I remember seeing Rukmini Devi with files around her. I asked her: 'Why are you doing this? Why don't you get someone else to do this work? You should be giving your vision to this place'. To which she responded: 'Who needs my vision?'

Chandra, however, is confident that even without the imagined 'future' provided through an institution, her work will remain in the consciousness of the numerous people whom she has come in contact with through her deeply creative and eventful life. 'You touch people wherever you are', says Chandra, and not just those in one's immediate work-context but unknown spectators and strangers as well. 'I *dare* the people I know to forget me', says Chandra disarmingly, knowing full well that she has been internalised in so many different ways.

At this point in time, one of her unrealised dreams is

to build an aerial theatre, suspended above the ground in her courtyard, so that the performances can be set against the horizon of the sea touching the sky. This is a vision that genuinely excites Chandra because she feels it could open up an altogether different dimension in the way we see human bodies. Our sense of scale could be radically altered in such a space. Whereas in the Mandala theatre, the beauty is that the human scale is not diminished, the 'Sky Theatre' (*Akashamandala*) could actually enhance the human body in an unprecedented way, revealing new possibilities in envisioning the ecology of dance.

Once again, the source of Chandra's dream does not come from any architectural theory but from life itself. She had once been immeasurably moved by the sight of hoarding painters on a bamboo scaffolding with their bodies silhouetted against the sky. Chandra admits that she had cried 'pure tears' when she saw this image in which the men seemed to be holding the sky with the grid of their bodies. Now she would like to transform this 'vision' into a space in which people would be compelled to see the world in a different light.

As Chandra ages in her life's journey, she becomes oddly more and more youthful, but there are lines on her face which she makes no attempt to hide. Once, a famous expatriate classical dancer attempted to pay her a compliment on meeting her after many years. 'You haven't changed at all', the dancer gushed. To which Chandra responded that she had changed considerably and was grateful for it.

Confronting the mystique and illusion of youth on another occasion, when she was invited to conduct a 'body workshop' with a group of women, Chandra sensed a sharp division between the women 'under 30', who imagined themselves to be young, and the 'over 30' group who were struggling to remain young. Chandra cut through this false division by indicating her own face and saying: 'Youth is not here'. Pointing to her spine, she added: 'It's *here*'. The rigid binary of youth and age can be confronted only when women learn, in Chandra's words, 'how to *be* and not just appear'.

Over the years, Chandra has learned to be herself and that is why she has no reason to fear the passage of time. She lives almost entirely in the present moment from which she draws her deepest lessons. Immediacy is her natural state. Many years ago, while being driven through a secluded part of Rajasthan, she saw a woman running against the sky, her red skirt sharply etched against the sand, billowing with the sheer flow of her movement. As Chandra drove past, she turned around to have a better look at this radiantly youthful woman only to realise that she was old and wrinkled and running against the sky.

'At that moment', Chandra says, 'I made a promise to myself that I would be like her'.

And it is on this promise that I would like to end this book without providing any false conclusion to a life that continues to surge ahead, still in the process of exploring new connections between life and art. Almost effortlessly, Chandra dances before my eyes across the face of the earth and disappears into the sky.

70

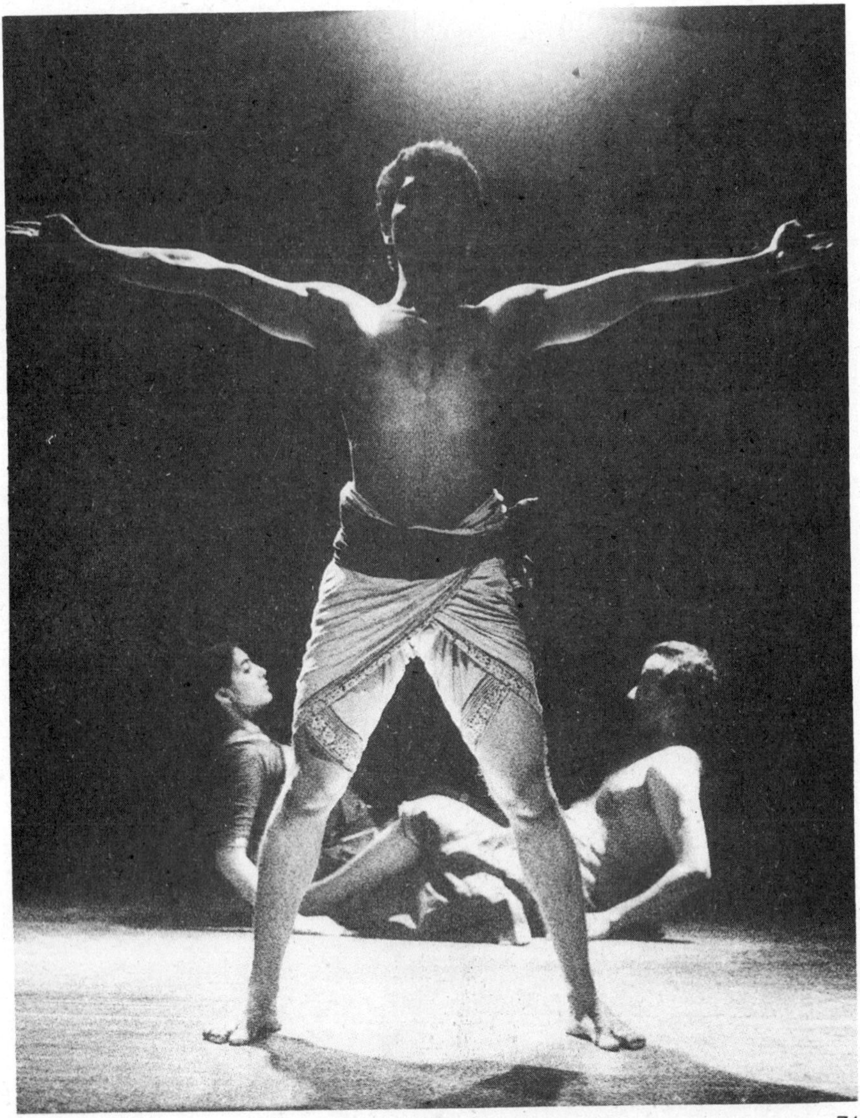

Postscript

In the final stages of its production, this book would be incomplete without a brief description of Chandra's latest production *Yantra*, which was staged in Calcutta, Madras, Bombay and Delhi in April 1994 as a tribute to Pina Bausch, whose *Nelken* (Carnations) was performed in the same cities. Once again, it was Max Mueller Bhavan that initiated this intercultural venture following up on its earlier East-West Dance Encounters in a search for dialogue cutting across cultures and disciplines of the body.

If the 'resources of hope' (to use Raymond Williams' resonant phrase) are still alive for artists as distinct as Chandra and Pina Bausch, contradicting the global despair shared by intellectuals worldwide as alternatives implode and collapse, it is because these resources are embedded in the relatively untapped potentialities of the body and the fictions emanating from it. Undeniably, the modes of perceiving these fictions are very different for Bausch and Chandra, contextualised as they are in distinct physical traditions and philosophies of the body. If Bausch's work is almost corrosively eclectic, drawing on expressionism, hyper-reality, absurdity and parody, Chandra's choreography continues to delve into the inner energies of Bharatanatyam interspersed with a minimalist abstraction of yogic principles of movement and martial arts.

Moreover, if the disjunctions are explicit in Bausch's work, it is because she is more free to invent a tradition for herself rather than work within the framework of continuities which provides a grid — however fractured — for different inflections of modernity in the Indian context. One should acknowledge, however, that it is extremely difficult to assess 'modernity' transculturally without a historical base. There is more than one modernity. Chandra, for instance, may seem to be more 'traditional' than Pina Bausch if we are unaware of her deviations from the context she is working within; and conversely, Bausch may seem totally *avant-garde* if we fail to realise that her own work has been much valorised, imitated and assimilated, acquiring in the process an almost 'classical' status in the world of modern dance.

Yantra is, to my mind, a startlingly modernist vision of traditional principles of energy in the body. Drawing on what Chandra describes as a 'vocabulary of inwardness', the production draws us into an elusive journey of the body as it moves through the *adavus* of Bharatanatyam and five breathtaking elaborations of *yantras* (diagrams of the body) into the still point of the *bindu* around which the dancers find their centres in solitude. At one level, the exploration is a deepening and maturation of the quest which was first visible in *Prana,* where the *grahas* (planets) were abstracted through *yantras* — geometric forms shaped through yogic movement. But the significant difference in *Yantra* is the insertion of erotica, inflections of sexual energy animating the intimate spaces within and between bodies.

Inspired by the visionary poetry of *Soundarya Lahari* and the diagrams of the body in Tantra, Chandra has crystallised her choreography around the central image of the *trikona* or triangle — the innermost triangle in the body which in its inverted form embodies the *yoni* on which the *muladhara* rests. The movement in *Yantra* is an attempt to activate this zone of energy through the other *chakras* residing invisibly in the inner trajectories of the spine. What would seem to be esoteric and metaphysical is once again concretised in Chandra's choreography through her immaculate sense of form and realisation of the senses.

Through superimpositions and rotations of the body, caresses of movement and ceaseless flow, the form of the triangle is mesmerisingly dynamised by the dancers in unusual perspectives — vertical and horizontal lines, spirals, even the primordial form of *kurma* or the tortoise. Never is the triangle subject to the banality of illustration. Chandra's *yantras* are processes of movement rather than fixed forms or tableaux. They induce a totally different mode of seeing which necessitates a closer tuning to the 'subtle bodies' enclosed within our physical frames. Without mystifying this process of awakening, Chandra facilitates its experience physically.

Conceptually, the take-off point for *Yantra* would seem to be a re-definition of *soundarya* in the world of dance and beyond. Is it possible to live without *soundarya?* For Chandra, this is not merely the perception of 'beauty' or 'aesthetics' but the capacity to retrieve vital energies coiled within our bodies, which can enable us to 'cope with and confront', in her words, 'the daily assaults on our senses, the unprecedented degradation of our bodies.'

At a more political level, Chandra emphasises the irony that it is the State which understands the body more rigorously than the so-called progressive forces for whom the body continues to remain a neglected (if not forgotten) area of politics. In all the accumulation of theories concerning social and political emancipation, the body is, more often than not, silenced or absent from agendas of change. In the meanwhile, the mechanisms of violence controlled by the State and its agencies have become increasingly sophisticated in legislating discipline, punishment, imprisonment, rape, and birth-control. Invoking the ubiquitous forces of regimentation in our times, Chandra acknowledges: 'They know how to torture and lobotomise our bodies, hit on our nerves. They can kill you from inside without leaving a mark.' Can this situation be countered, physically, spiritually, in and through our bodies?

At this critical level, both Chandra and Bausch are intensely vulnerable as their very search for new possibilities of *soundarya* and love has emerged in direct proportion to the accumulation of violence in our times. In Pina Bausch's envisioning of dance-theatre, the critique of violence is implicated within scenarios of violence, which encompass layers of contradictory emotions ranging from relentless brutality to the most searing tenderness. Her vision alerts us to the paradox of representing violence in the context of a post-modern capitalist society which, nonetheless, has resources (economic, technological, and imaginative) to subvert and transform this violence into art.

In Chandra's work, violence is almost invisible, glimpsed as we have seen earlier in sections of *Sri* depicting women's enslavement in a patriarchal world. However, it would be a profound illusion to imagine that her work exists independently of a consciousness of violence. As I have emphasised earlier, the ethereality of a production like *Prana* is rooted in her awareness of an increasingly polluted universe, where it is becoming almost impossible to breathe. The reclamation of *prana* or life-breath is one of the most potent means of restoring our sense of balance — physically, psychologically, ecologically.

It could be argued, however, that what we see in Chandra's work is the affirmation of life-sustaining forces, whereas in Bausch's dance-theatre, it is the negation of these forces that is most visceral. But neither artist, I would contend, works entirely within this framework of dichotomies and exclusions, even though what they choose to highlight resonates at the expense of what they prefer to suggest or counterpoint in silence: the embers of love within conflagrations of hate (Bausch); the imminence of destruction within seeming timelessness (Chandra).

Beyond *Nelken* and *Yantra*, in whose visions one should not seek a utopian synthesis, one should acknowledge nonetheless that these productions are symptoms, punctuation points in a larger continuum of an emergent world-culture, which can be articulated only if its dimensions are more fully realised and experienced. Instead of searching for transcendental points of reference, it would be more cogent to respect the multiple resources of the body from different contexts, which may still stimulate the re-envisioning and humanisation of our world.

72

73

NOTES

The text of this book has been shaped substantially through conversations, discussions, and interviews with Chandralekha and her associates, including Dashrath Patel, Sadanand Menon, and her company of dancers, over a four year period between 1989-92. While acknowledging all the contributions, I have not attempted to 'footnote' the numerous statements in order to maintain the flow of the text. However, I have provided references for all statements and information relating to published material on Chandralekha and her work, including her own writing.

Chapter One

1. Coomi Kapoor with Sunil Kothari, 'Breaking the Bonds', *India Today*, May 15, 1985, p.134.
2. Ibid., p.136.
3. Harindranath Chattopadhyay, *Diaries* Part II, p.163, Nehru Memorial Museum and Library, New Delhi.
4. Harindranath Chattopadhyay, *Life and Myself*, Bombay: Nalanda Publications, 1948, p.112.
5. Ibid., p.42.
6. Ibid., p.24.
7. Excerpts from *The Curd-Seller Quatrains* first published in a booklet in 1959, later featured in *The Economic Times*, July 21, 1991, in an overview edited by Sadanand Menon.
8. Harindranath Chattopadhyay, *Life and Myself*, op.cit., p.45.
9. Ibid.
10. Ibid., p.61.
11. Harindranath Chattopadhyay, *Freedom Come*, poem written on August 6, 1947, published in booklet form, available at Nehru Memorial Museum and Library, New Delhi.
12. Harindranath Chattopadhyay, *The Curd-Seller Quatrains*, op.cit.
13. Harindranath Chattopadhyay, *Diaries* Part I, op.cit., p.34.
14. Coomi Kapoor with Sunil Kothari, 'Breaking the Bonds', op.cit., p.134.
15. Sunil Kothari, 'Guruparampara', *Bharata Natyam: Indian Classical Dance Art*. Bombay: Marg Publications, 1979, p.131.
16. For more details on the historical background of Bharatanatyam, see Chapter 2.
17. See T. Sankaran's article on 'Kandappa Nattuvanar' for a succinct overview of these 'innovations', published in the special issue on Balasaraswati brought out by *Sangeet Natak*, April-September, 1984, p.56.
18. Ibid., p.55.
19. Chandralekha, 'Contemporary Relevance in Classical Dance', published in the *NCPA Quarterly Journal*, Bombay, June 1984.
20. Ibid.

21. For a feminist perspective on the problem in the Indian context, read Avanthi Meduri's '*Bharatha Natyam* — what are you?', *Asian Theatre Journal*, Volume 5, Number 1, Spring 1988.
22. Chandralekha, 'Rejection of Limits and Confines', unpublished paper presented at workshop entitled 'Limits, Borders, Boundaries' organised by National Centre for the Performing Arts and Max Mueller Bhavan, Bombay, October 2-9, 1990, typewritten manuscript, p.2.
23. Ibid.

Chapter Two

1. Padma Subrahmanyam, 'Sadir', *Bharata's Art: Then and Now*, Bhulabhai Memorial Institute and Nrithyodaya, 1979, p.92.
2. In his authoritative essay on 'Bharata Natya' published in *The Journal of the Music Academy*, Vol. XLV, 1974, p.233, Dr. V. Raghavan specifically states: 'Thus when some time back after a period of disfavour caused by the anti-Nautch crusade, the art was being brought out by enthusiasts and I started calling it in my writings *Bharata Natya*, there was nothing very much new or incorrect'.
3. See Note on `Sadir', p.312-313.
   The problem begins with the word *sadir* itself which is not of Tamil origin. Situating it within the larger category of 'Karnatakam', which was a generic term referring to 'the music and dances of South India', Dr. Arudra asserts that, 'In the Telugu districts, the old *saani*-s (*devadasis*) still call it (*sadir*) as Karnatakam *kutcheri* dances. Since Sadir (*Chaduru*) means a court, the word *kutcheri* crept in'. ('The Format of Bharatanatyam: Historical Background', *Sruti* 73, October 1990) A more speculative hypothesis is offered by Dr. Padma Subrahmanyam in her learned study of *Sadir* in *Bharata's Art: Then and Now* (Bhulabhai Memorial Institute and Nrithyodaya, 1979) when she suggests that *sadir* could have emerged from 'Satara', a possibly eponymous form relating to dances from the Maharashtrian town of Satara itself: 'The *Satara Kacceri* must have gradually become *Satara Kacceri, Satir Kacceri*, and finally *Sadir Kacceri* or *Sadir*'.

   Perhaps, it would be most accurate to see *sadir* as an indigenous, syncretic style of dance that crystallised around the Tanjore court in the eighteenth century rather than as a pure, 'ancient' form of dance descending from the Lasya of the *Natyasastra*. Dr. Subrahmanyam has attempted to identify its multiple sources in the 'folk tradition' of the Tamils, more specifically dances like Kavadi, Karagam, Oyilattam; the contributions of Telugu artists from the erstwhile Vijyanagar Empire, particularly the Vaishnavite celebration of *madhura bhakti*; and solo dance forms like the *nirupanam*, which were performed in the court of the Mahrattas, nurtured through the legendary contributions of the four brothers and residential court musicians and teachers (*nattuvanars*) — Chinayya, Ponnayya, Sivanandam, and Vadivelu who constituted the Tanjore Quartette.

(See 'Sadir', *Bharata's Art: Then and Now*, p.86)

This Quartette is now credited with creating a syllabus for teaching dance and classifying the *adavus* as well as structuring the various components of the *margam* (dance cycle) as it is performed today, including the precise chronology of the *alarippu, jatiswaram, sabdam, varnam, padam, tillana,* and *sloka.*

Today much more work is needed in elaborating on the specific particularities of *sadir* as performed in the court and the temple. The conflation that has taken place in our understanding of *sadir* in different social contexts is further complicated through the larger conflation of *sadir* with Bharatanatyam itself. Instead of assuming a 'continuity' in these forms, it would require a most detailed scholarship to decipher the multiple strands and historical tensions that have contributed to the 'invention' of Bharatanatyam from the fractured legacy of *sadir.* This lies beyond the scope of this note, but it is worth pointing out if only to reaffirm the task involved in 'historicising' Bharatanatyam with sensitivity and depth.

4. See Pupul Jayakar's study of 'Metal Icons of the Mothers' included in her study of *The Earth Mother.* New Delhi: Penguin Books India, 1989, p.170.
5. Sunil Kothari, 'History: Roots, Growth and Revival' included in his edition of *Bharata Natyam: Indian Classical Dance Art.* Bombay, Marg Publications, 1979, p.23.
6. Dr. V. Raghavan, 'Bharata Natya', ibid., p.236.
7. Rukmini Devi, 'Spiritual Background', *Bharata Natyam: Indian Classical Dance Art,* ibid., p.13.
8. Dr. V. Raghavan, 'Bharata Natya', ibid., p.239.
9. Ibid.
10. Rukmini Devi, 'Spiritual Background', *Bharata Natyam: Indian Classical Dance Art,* ibid., p.16.
11. See 'Representing Devadasis: *Dasigal Mosavalai* as a Radical Text' by Anandhi S., *Economic and Political Weekly,* Annual Number 1991, p.746. Other sources of information about the history of the *devadasi* used in this essay are drawn from 'Reform and Revival: The Devadasi and Her Dance' by Amrit Srinivasan published in the *Economic and Political Weekly,* Vol. XX, No.44, November 1984; *Nityasumangali: Devadasi Tradition in South India* by Saskia C. Kersenboom-Story. Delhi: Motilal Banarsidass, 1987; Avanthi Meduri, '*Bharatha Natya* — what are you?', *Asian Theatre Journal,* Spring 1988; 'A Momentous Transition' by Mohan Khokar, *Sangeet Natak,* April-June 1987; 'History: Roots, Growth and Revival' by Sunil Kothari, op.cit.
12. For a succinct account of this 'battle', read Mohan Khokar's 'A Momentous Transition', op.cit., pp.41-47.
13. Amrit Srinivasan, 'Reform and Revival: The Devadasi and Her Dance', op.cit., p.1874.
14. The information and thrust of argument in this paragraph are drawn from 'Representing Devadasis: *Dasigal Mosavalai* as a Radical Text'

by Anandhi S., op.cit., pp.739-741.
15. Ibid., p.740.
16. Ibid.
17. Amrit Srinivasan, 'Reform and Revival: The Devadasi and Her Dance', op.cit., p.1875.
18. By far the most engrossing account of Balasaraswati's thoughts on dance are contained in the article 'T. Balasaraswati: The Whole World in Her Hands' by N. Pattabhi Raman and Anandhi Ramachandran, originally published in *Sruti* and reprinted in *Sangeet Natak*, April-September 1984, pp.15-54. The information in the following two paragraphs of my text is drawn from this article.
19. For a detailed list of the *varnams, padams,* and *javalis,* see 'Balasaraswati's Repertoire', *Sangeet Natak*, April-September 1984, pp.70-74.
20. T. Balasaraswati, 'On Bharatanatyam', *Sangeet Natak*, April-September 1984, p.11.
21. Ibid., pp.8-10.
22. N. Pattabhi Raman and Anandhi Ramachandran, 'T. Balasaraswati: The Whole World in Her Hands', op.cit., p.54.
23. Chandralekha, 'Choreography in the Indian Context', paper presented at Music Academy Annual Conference, Madras, December 27, 1984, later reprinted in *Indian and World Arts and Crafts,* April 1991, p.3.
24. Ibid.
25. Recorded in the valuable video documentation of the lecture demonstration at Kalakshetra. Also quoted in all the publicity folders of Chandralekha's productions.

Chapter Three

1. Coomi Kapoor with Sunil Kothari, 'Breaking the Bonds', *India Today,* May 15, 1985, p.132.
2. All references to *Kamala* in this section are taken from the original copy of the manuscript in Chandralekha's personal archives. Though sections of the prose-poem have been serialised in the *Illustrated Weekly of India,* the original manuscript remains the most reliable text not least because it includes the author's corrections and changes in punctuation.
3. Sergei Eisenstein, *Film Form*. New York: Harcourt, Brace & World, Inc., 1949, p.261.
4. Ibid., p.262.
5. Dr. Chaganty Suryanarayanmurthy, editor and commentator of *Sri Lalita Sahasranamam*. Bombay: Bharatiya Vidya Bhavan, 1989. All references to the text in this paragraph are taken from this edition.
6. Chandralekha, interview with Sai Prashanti, 'Sculpting Space', *Indian Express,* February 16, 1985.
7. Sadanand Menon, 'Chandralekha — Putting the Spine back in Bharatanatyam', unpublished article.

8. For a more detailed examination of Muthuswamy Dikshitar's *navagraha kritis*, read description of Chandralekha's production of *Prana* discussed in Chapter Nine.
9. Chandralekha, 'Synthesising Indian Physical Traditions', unpublished article.

Chapter Four

1. V.S. Naipaul, *India: A Wounded Civilization*, Penguin Books, 1987, p.123.
2. See, for instance, the conceptual background provided by Biswaroop Das in 'Nature, Types and Character of Voluntary Organisations — The Case of West Bengal,' *Man & Development*, Vol. X (3), September 1988. For a broader context on the specific time-frame of Skills' activities, read Franda Marcus, *Voluntary Associations and Local Development in India: The Janata Phase*. New Delhi: Young Asia, 1983. I am grateful to Biswaroop Das for providing me with a cogent background on the subject of 'voluntary associations.'
3. The log-book is a hand-made book in which all the activities of the workshop are documented. It is a telling reminder that workshops on 'education' and 'social transformation' need not deny the aesthetics of their representation. The text of this log contains some of Sadanand's most lucid and eloquent writing from which I quote extensively in the following sections. Hopefully, in time to come, this log-book will be published along with Chandra's writings and graphics.
4. See my 'Letter to the Dead', published in the *Economic and Political Weekly*, April 15, 1989.

Chapter Five

1. Anees Jung, conversation with Susanne Linke, Chandralekha, and Georg Lechner, 'And the feet begin to speak...' *The Times of India*, February 12, 1984.
2. Sunil Kothari, 'History: Roots, Growth and Revival', *Bharata Natyam: Indian Classical Dance Art*. Bombay: Marg Publications, 1979, p.24. See also Uttara Asha Coorlawala 's comprehensive study of 'St. Denis and India's Dance Renaissance,' *Sangeet Natak* No. 104: April-June 1992.
3. Doris Humphrey, *An Artist First*. Middleton: Wesleyan University Press, 1972. See in particular the chapter entitled 'The Orient', pp.44-53, and 'The Breaking Point', pp.62-63.
4. Chandralekha, 'Contemporary Relevance in Traditional Dance — A Personal Note', paper delivered at the first East-West Dance Encounter, later published in the *NCPA Quarterly Journal*, June 1984. All quotations in the following four paragraphs are taken from this paper.

5. Quoted in Anees Jung's 'conversation' entitled 'And the feet begin to speak....,' ibid.
6. Ibid.
7. See Smt. T. Balasaraswati's 'Presidential Address' included in *The Journal of the Music Academy*, Vol.XLV, 1974, p.18; also Dr. V. Raghavan's 'Bharata Natya' published in the same issue, p.249.
8. Quoted in Anees Jung's 'conversation' with Chandralekha and others, 'And the feet begin to speak...', ibid.
9. Chandralekha, interview with Amrita Abraham, 'You cannot translate the ugliness of life directly into dance', *The Sunday Observer*, February 12, 1984.
10. Sadanand Menon, 'Dancers' Dilemma', *Sunday Observer*, April 1984.
11. Chandralekha, 'You cannot translate the ugliness of life directly into dance', ibid.
12. Sadanand Menon, 'Dancers' Dilemma', ibid.
13. Chandralekha, 'You cannot translate the ugliness of life directly into dance', ibid.
14. Pria Devi, 'The Dance, The Dancer and Design for Dance', *The India Magazine*, March 1987, pp.89-91.
15. Ibid.

Chapter Six

1. Dr. Arudra, 'Chandralekha's *Angika*: Striking a Blow for Innovation,' *Sruti*, 1985, p.53.
2. Apart from the visual hieroglyphs of the 'tree' and 'Garuda' held on the outer extremities of the grid, there are a number of familiar *asanas* used in the 'Cosmic Energy' sequence.

    Though there have been changes through the productions, the *karnapidasana* and the *urdhva padmasana* used to be performed at floor level in the middle row. In the former, the body is crouched on the floor with the head placed between the knees which are pressed against the ears ('karna'). The *urdhva padmasana* reveals a 'lotus seen from above.' For more details on these *asanas*, consult Sri B.K. Iyengar's authoritative study *Light on Yoga*. London: Unwin Paperbacks, 1989.

    In the front row, Ashok Kumar used to perform the *chatur-pada asana* in which he would lower his hands on the ground, his forehead touching the knees, so that it would almost seem as if he had 'four feet.' Then, most powerfully, he would stand, stretch his legs, and throw his head back as far as possible with his hands clasped behind in a wrist-hold, the chest thrown out. Complementing this flow of energy, Nagin (also in the first row, on the other side of the grid) would perform the *adho mukha svanasana*, the 'downward looking dog' from which position he would move into the *kurmasana* ('the tortoise').
3. Nandikesvara, *Abhinayadarpanam*, edited and translated by

Dr. Manmohan Ghosh. Calcutta: Manisha Granthalaya Private Limited, 1989, p.36.
4. Describing the space created between the legs of the *aramandi* as a 'rhombus', Dr. V. Raghavan adds that, 'The Sanskrit text *Nrttaratnavali* calls it (the *aramandi*) Kharvata and mentions twelve inches for this lowering of the body; the Tamil text of Aramvalattanar says that if you measure the distance between the two knees bent in Mandala, the two should be equal.' ('Bharata Natya,' *The Journal of the Music Academy*, Vol. XLV, 1974, pp. 252-253.)
5. From V. Raghavan we learn that, 'In an Adavu, we have a particular placement of the hand-foot unit, a particular kind of beating of the floor and a particular further movement of the hand-foot unit, till it reaches a second point at which the hand-foot unit takes on a different pose and a further or different floor-beating occurs. These units are woven into patterns and these patterns into larger sequences.' 'Bharata Natya,' ibid., p. 250.
6. For details of these terms, consult *A Dictionary of Bharata Natya*, compiled by U. S. Krishna Rao. Hyderabad: Orient Longman Limited, 1990.
7. Excerpted from Chandralekha's description of her overall concept of *Angika* which she used to read aloud during the early performances. Typewritten manuscript, unpublished.
8. For the ritualistic context of the *pushpanjali*, read Saskia C. Kersenboom-Story, *Nityasumangali: Devadasi Tradition in South India*. Delhi: Motilal Banarasidass, 1987, pp. 151-64. However, it is significant to note that a 'traditional' scholar like Sri V. Raghavan chooses to secularise the *pushpanjali* in his study of 'Bharata Natya', op. cit. p. 245, by viewing it as 'a later and abridged form of the ancient *purvaranga*.' While acknowledging that it had 'invocatory and benedictory significance,' he nonetheless divests it of any sacred significance by linking it more directly to 'the *melaprapti*, which the *nattuvanar* and the orchestra did, at the end of which the Nati appeared and did the first Nautch-item called *Alarippu*.'
9. I am grateful to Tripura Kashyap and Sadanand Menon for transliterating and translating this passage for me.
10. Translation by Tripura Kashyap and Sadanand Menon.
11. Dr. Arudra, 'Chandralekha's *Angika*: Striking a Blow for Innovation,' ibid., p. 54.

Chapter Seven

Since this chapter relies extensively on reviews, critiques, and press clippings relating to Chandralekha's work in particular (*Angika, Angamandala, Primal Energy*) and Bharatanatyam performance in general, I have included all the relevant sources and dates in the text itself.

Chapter Eight

1. All the 'questions' from the original *Lilavati* text have been translated and adapted by Chandralekha in a predominantly colloquial idiom. They have been included in the folders and publicity material used for the production.
2. U.S. Krishna Rao, *A Dictionary of Bharat's Natya*. Hyderabad: Orient Longman, 1990, p. 13.
3. Chandralekha, 'Production Notes' on *Lilavati,* unpublished article.
4. Chandralekha, interview in *Times of India*, Bombay, February 8, 1989, entitled 'Nature and numbers meet in dance', p. 11.

Chapter Nine

1. B.K.S. Iyengar, *Light on Yoga*. London: Unwin Paperbacks, 1989, p. 21.
2. Ibid., p. 43.
3. Ibid.
4. Sadanand Menon, 'Classical Experiments', *The Sunday Observer*, October 7, 1990.
5. B.K.S. Iyengar, *Light on Yoga*, ibid., p. 408.
6. All information relating to the *navagraha kritis* are taken from Dr. V. Raghavan's definitive study *Muttuswamy Dikshitar*, an NCPA Publication, Bombay, 1975.
7. For a fuller account of *vishranti* read Ranerio Gnoli's insightful introduction to *The Aesthetic Experience according to Abhinavagupta*, Varanasi, 1968.
8. Dr. V. Raghavan, *Muttuswamy Dikshitar*, ibid., p. 5.
9. Ibid., pp. 5-6.
10. Ibid., p. 18.
11. All descriptions of the *asanas* used in the production are derived from Sri B.K.S. Iyengar's authoritative *Light on Yoga*, ibid.

Chapter Ten

1. All statements made by Sumitra Gautam in this section are taken from her written contribution to a feature on 'Chandralekha's *Angika*', *Indian Express*, Madras, November 2, 1985, p. 14. All statements made by the other dancers who are presently members of Chandralekha's company have been drawn from interviews and discussions conducted by me during my research between 1989-91.
2. Sumitra Gautam, statement in 'Chandralekha's *Angika*', ibid.
3. Elaine Scarry, *The Body in Pain: The Making and Unmaking of the World*. Oxford, 1985.
4. Discussion with entire group of dancers conducted at Skills during rehearsals of *Prana* in the summer of 1990.
5. For a particularly perceptive discussion on *aharya* in the larger

context of social attitudes reflected in textiles and dance, see 'Of grace that was', a discussion involving Rukmini Devi and Chandralekha, moderated by Pria Devi. *Indian Express*, July 21, 1984, p. 14.
6. Quoted in conversation with Anees Jung entitled 'And the feet begin to speak', *The Times of India*, February 12, 1984.
7. The information on the workshop is drawn from Sadanand Menon's piece entitled 'Rediscovering the body', *Indian Express*, Nov. 2, 1985.
8. Ibid.
9. My documentation of the Walk Workshop first appeared in the form of an article entitled 'Walking towards Ourselves', published in *The Sunday Observer*, February 4, 1990, p. 10.
10. I have avoided writing about the production in detail because it is a work-in-progress. The first realisation of the production, staged at Kalakshetra, Madras, in April 1993, is likely to go through many changes in the subsequent explorations of the work. What needs to be pointed out, however, is that it is possibly the most 'hybrid' of Chandra's productions to date in its sharp juxtapositions of different dance idioms (Bharatanatyam, Chhau, German expressionist modern dance) and vocal registers (Carnatic music and a minimalist abstraction of 'western opera').

With an entirely female cast, it is not surprising that the production is assertively 'feminine' in its energy and tonalities, perhaps even more so than *Sri*. Certainly, this is the closest that Chandra has ever come to exploring female sexuality in the most distilled and abstracted of forms. In the concluding sequence of the production, in particular, where Ganga and Jamuna meet in a 'confluence of differences', Chandra has created an unprecedented form by almost 'synthesising' the bodies of two dancers trained in Chhau and Bharatanatyam. In the chimera of their combined beings, one enters an almost ceaseless flow of energies that is overpoweringly 'female' in its resonance.

Most of all, one needs to point out that this production is Chandra's response to the fundamentalist categories and absolutes of Hindutva. By invoking the poetic genius of Kalidasa, she has attempted to create in her own language a counter-statement testifying to the intermingling of colours, energies, and sensations that constitute a pluralist vision of 'Indian' culture.

Chapter Eleven

1. I am fully aware that 'feminism' is a 'thick' discourse with multiple idioms. For the purpose of this discussion, I would accept one possible definition of 'feminism' offered by Elaine Marks and Isabelle de Courtivron as 'an awareness of women's oppression-repression that initiates both analyses of the dimension of this oppression-repression, and strategies for liberation.' For a succinct account of the complexities involved in defining 'feminism(s)', read introduction

by Marks and Courtivron in their edition of *New French Feminisms*, New York: Schocken Books, 1981.
2. See '*Request Concert* in Madras' included in my collection of essays entitled *Theatre and the World*. New Delhi: Manohar Publishers, 1990. See also the chapters on the production staged in Calcutta and Bombay for a larger perspective of the entire project.
3. Chandralekha, *One More News*, produced by Skills, screen printed by D.N. Ganguly, 1987. All quotations and descriptions of visuals in this section are drawn from this edition of the book.
4. See, for instance, the description of the dance and theatre workshop held at Skills in November 1983 as part of a larger exploration of Communication and Media. Documented by Kamala Bhasin and participants in *Towards Empowerment*, a publication sponsored by the Food & Agriculture Organisation of the United Nations, April 1985, pp. 145-157.
5. Chandralekha, 'Afterword', *One More News*, op.cit.
6. All references to the narrative of *Fire, Counter Fire* are taken from the original edition of the book, 'made' at Skills/Cultural Centre, and screenprinted by Supaskreen. As in all her books, Chandra avoids pagination.
7. I have already discussed the poster campaign around the subject of parliamentary democracy conducted by Skills in its early years. See Chapter Four for more details. Also read the brief section on poster-making in *Towards Empowerment*, op.cit., pp. 158-168.
8. Quoted in Silvia Bovenschen's illuminating essay 'Is there a Feminine Aesthetics?' included in *Feminist Aesthetics*, edited by Gisela Bocker, Women's Press, p.30.
9. I am grateful to Vibhuti Patel for providing me with this detail.
10. Interview with Vibhuti Patel, Bombay, January 1990.
11. Ibid. Since a cultural history of feminism in India has yet to be written, it is 'oral history' that provides the base for most discussions. I am grateful to Vibhuti Patel for her deep and involved reflections on feminist cultural activities in India, which have enabled me to write this section.
12. Interview with Kamala Ganesh, Bombay, January 1990.
13. Interview with Vibhuti Patel, Bombay, January 1990.
14. The phrase is excerpted from 'Microworld creativity of woman', one of the many texts authored by Chandralekha for *Stree*. All phrases quoted in this paragraph are taken from this article which exists, as yet, in manuscript form. One can only hope that the entire 'text' of *Stree* will be published one day since the exhibition is not likely to be shown in India.
15. Excerpted from Chandralekha's essay 'Matrika — A Perspective', published in *The Economic Times*, March 8, 1992, under the title 'Who are these age-old female figures?'
16. Interview with Kamala Ganesh, Bombay, January 1990. I would like to acknowledge here the critical insight which I received from Kamala

Ganesh that helped me considerably in clarifying my own views on Chandra's attitudes to 'religiosity' and 'traditional iconography'.
17. See the somewhat simplistic critique of male appropriation of female roles in traditional performance offered by Erika Munk in 'The Rites of Women', *Performing Arts Journal*, Vol. X, No. 2.
18. Ananda Coomaraswamy, 'Sahaja', *The Dance of Shiva*. New Delhi: Munshiram Manoharlal Publishers Pvt. Ltd., p. 142.
19. Kamala Ganesh, '*Stree* in Moscow', *The Indian Express Magazine*, May 8, 1988, p. 3.
20. This detail is sensitively highlighted by Kamala Ganesh in '*Stree* in Moscow', ibid.

Chapter Twelve

1. For a contextualisation of *Sri* within the larger spectrum of mother-goddesses, read Kamala Ganesh's 'Mother Who is Not a Mother: In Search of the Great Indian Goddess', *Economic and Political Weekly*, October 20-27, 1990, pp. WS58-64; Pupul Jayakar's study of *The Earth Mother*. New Delhi: Penguin Books India, 1989, p. 170; and David Kinsley's *Hindu Goddesses*. New Delhi: Motilal Banarasidass, 1987.
2. The phrase is excerpted from Chandralekha's 'Who are these age-old female figures?', *The Economic Times*, March 8, 1992.
3. Excerpted from Alice Schwarzer's interview with Simone de Beauvoir in *Marie-Claire*, October 1976, included in *New French Feminisms*, New York: Schocken Books, 1981, p. 153.
4. This is profusely illustrated in Sukumari Bhattacharya's study of 'Motherhood in Ancient India', *Economic and Political Weekly*, October 20-27, 1990, p. WS-53.
5. Ibid.
6. Ibid. pp. WS-55 to 56. All quotations in this paragraph are drawn from these pages.
7. Ibid.
8. Chandralekha, 'Constitution and Family Law: Feminine Perspective: Family and Freedom', typewritten manuscript, originally delivered as a lecture at the Max Mueller Bhavan, March 6-11, 1989. All quotations in the following two paragraphs are taken from this lecture.
9. Ibid.
10. Interview with Vibhuti Patel, Bombay, January 1990.
11. Interview with Neela Bhagwat, Bombay, January 1990.

PHOTO CAPTIONS

Cover Chandralekha performing 'Sakambhari' sequence in 'Sri'
   1 'Namaskar' under the Adyar banyan
   2 Chandralekha, 1991
   3 Chandralekha, 1968
   4 Young Chandra
   5 With 'Baba' Harindranath Chattopadhyay
   6 With Guru Ellappa Pillai
   7 With Mahakavi Vallathol and Bharatanatyam legend Balasaraswati
   8 Chandralekha in 'virahanayika', abhinaya sequence, 1967
   9 With Kamadev in 'Navagraha', 1972
10 A&B 1973 Poster-calendar for Air India based on the Navagraha
  11 In the thick of a women's rally against obscenity, 1977
  12 'Tillana' rehearsal at NCPA, Bombay, for 'East-West Dance Encounter', 1984 — Those sitting include (from left to right) Vidya Shankar, Udupi Lakshminarayan, Kamadev, Bhupen Khakar, Soli Batliwalla, Sadanand Menon, Sunil Kothari, Sonal Mansingh and Chandralekha
  13 Entrance to 'Mandala'
  14 Inside the 'Mandala'
  15 'Navarahana', woman riding man, from 'Angika'
  16 From 'Angika', 1985
  17 Martial sequence, *ashva* (horse) vadivu from 'Angika'
  18 Martial sequence, *kukuta* (cook) vadivu from 'Angika'
  19 Tillana finale of 'Angika'
  20 Tillana finale of 'Angika'
21-24 From 'Angika', performance at Tramway, Glasgow, 1992
  25 'Namaskar' sequence in Kremlin, for Festival of India inaugural, 1987
  26 Chandralekha introducing 'Lilavati' for Doordarshan recording, 1988
27-34 From 'Lilavati'
  35 Chandralekha's interpretation of 'Surya' in 'Prana', 1989
  36 Opening sequence of 'Prana'
37-45 The nine grahas and their positions
46-49 From 'Prana'
  50 Pre-performance ritual — a private moment before going public
  51 Poster by Chandralekha, 1981
52-55 Posters by Chandralekha, 1983-1988
56-57 From 'One More News' by Chandralekha, 1987
58-59 From 'Fire, Counter-fire' by Chandralekha, 1985
60-65 Chandralekha performing 'Sakambhari' sequence in 'Sri', 1992
60-69 From 'Sri'
  70 Dreaming on the swing
  71 From 'Yantra', 1994

72-75 From 'Yantra'
76 'Namaskar' on the beach
Back Jacket Concluding moment of Chandralekha's 'Sakambhari' sequence in 'Sri'

Photo Credits
All photographs by Dashrath Patel except cover, back jacket and nos. 60-65 by Bernd Merzenich, and nos. 2, 11 and 76 by Sadanand Menon.

Index

Abhinayadarpana, 88, 150
Akerman, Chantal, 284
adavu, 100, 155-156, 184, 217, 219-222, 224, 226-227, 246, 338
alarippu, 40, 48, 66
Angamandala, 180-182, 185-188
Angaraka, 229
Angika, 2, 52, 54, 69, 84, 100, 112, 123, 125, 139, 147-180, 182, 189, 195, 207, 227, 241-244, 246, 253, 263-265, 290, 308
aramandi, 58, 155, 246, 252
Aravindan, G., 115, 287, 290, 294, 296, 298
ardha-narishwara, 189, 287, 290, 294-295, 297
Arudra, 168-169
asana, 90, 149, 198, 203, 217-234
ashtavadivu, 153-154, 156
Aurobindo, Sri, 19-20, 121

Balasaraswati, T., 2, 23-24, 37, 46-51, 55-56, 131
Bathtub, The, 256
Batliwalla, Soli, 139
Bausch, Pina, 167, 263-264, 337, 339-340
Bharatanatyam, 4, 22, 24, 38-67, 88, 90-91, 93, 97, 137, 141-142, 154-163, 165-167, 181, 185, 188, 193, 195-199, 208-209, 217, 219, 224, 250, 254, 257-258, 266, 273, 289, 308, 312, 315, 337-338
Bhaskaracharya, 52, 195-197, 208
Bhattacharya, Sukumari, 327-328
Bhinna Pravaha, 266
bhramari, 148, 156, 165, 203
Budha, 229-231

Cage, John, 70
cari, 156, 258, 312, 316

Cartier-Bresson, Henri, 95
Chaitanya, Krishna, 184-185
Chattopadhyay, Aghorenath, 17
Chattopadhyay, Harindranath, 4, 14-23, 26-28, 37, 42, 56, 121, 276-277
Chattopadhyay, Kamaladevi, 298
Chhau, 88, 92, 98, 100, 137, 257, 261-262, 266
Chitrasutra, 60
Citaristi, Ileana, 267
Coomaraswamy, Ananda, 296
Corbusier, Le, 107
Cosmic Energy, 148-150, 167
Cunningham, Merce, 57, 70
Curd-Seller Quatrains, The, 18

Dashabhuja, 316, 319
De Beauvoir, Simone, 325
Devadasi, 2, 4, 26, 38, 52-69, 81, 86, 125, 147, 158, 307
Devarattam, 257
Devi, Mahasweta, 21
Devi, Pria, 135-136
Devi, Rukmini, 2, 39-43, 45, 50, 55-57, 65-67, 125, 128, 246
Dikshitar, Muthuswamy, 90, 222-224, 228
Duncan, Isadora, 51

Eames, Ray and Charles, 107
East-West Dance Encounter, 28, 58, 66, 125-139, 246, 255, 337
Eisenstein, Sergei, 82

Festival of India, 181, 183, 186-188, 190, 195, 291, 298
Fire, Counter-Fire, 280-282
Fuller, Buckminster, 107

Gandhi, Indira, 290-291, 298
Gandhi, Mahatma, 43, 99, 120
Gandhi, Rajiv, 181, 291
Ganesh, Kamala, 290, 293, 299

gati, 156, 183
Gautam, Sumitra, 141, 242-243, 252
Gorbachov, Mikhail, 181
Graham, Martha, 57, 85, 264, 314

Hartmann, Mathias, 259, 262
Hashmi, Safdar, 117
Herder, Chantal, 267
Hoyer, Dore, 255
Humphrey, Doris, 128

Indian People Theatre Association (IPTA), 16, 21, 42, 96
iruthikal, 165
Iyengar, B.K.S., 217-218
Iyer, E. Krishna, 39, 42-43

Jaising, Indira, 71-72
jatiswaram, 48
Jeya Singh, Shobna, 313
Jung, Anees, 126-127
Kalakshetra, 45, 53, 58, 65, 125, 141, 242-243, 246, 248, 250, 253-254, 257-258
Kalarippayattu, 141, 150, 152-153, 250, 257-258
Kali, 96-97, 99, 286, 293
Kamadev, 89-90, 92, 125, 134-138, 221
Kamala, 69, 73-80
Kandappa Nattuvanar, 23-24, 47
Kashyap, Tripura, 162, 246, 250
Kathakali, 40, 257
Kaul, T.N., 287, 298
Kosambi, D.D., 96
Kothari, Sunil, 72, 126, 168, 178
Krishnamurthy, Yamini, 132-133
Kriti Workshop, 288-289
Kumar, Ashok, 138, 141, 164, 180
Kuttishaji, 253-254

Lakhia, Kumudini, 132
Lakshminarayan, Udupi, 16, 121-122, 137, 150, 168, 193, 206, 226, 233, 248

Lasya, 40
Lechner, Georg, 130-131
Lichtblau, Claudia, 257-259, 261-262, 266
Lilavati, 2, 52, 67, 97, 193
lingashtakam, 134, 136, 183
Linke, Susanne, 126, 254-257, 262, 266

Mahapatra, Guru Kelucharan, 296
Mansingh, Sonal, 126, 132
mandala, 58-60, 64-65, 87, 155, 157, 185, 209, 232, 263, 267, 311, 316, 329
Mandala Theatre, 111, 139-142, 230, 261, 333
Mani, G.S., 313
Manushi, 283-284
Manusmriti, 11, 327-328
martial arts, 141-142, 152, 165-166, 177, 191, 308, 337
Max Mueller Bhavan, 125, 127, 130, 331
Maya Darpan, 95-100
Medical, Educational, Rural and General Development (MERG), 113
meippayatt, 165
Menon, Sadanand, 2, 32, 101, 103-123, 125, 132, 137-139, 141, 164, 178, 188, 190, 234, 254, 271, 280, 298, 313
Mukherjee, Hrishikesh, 72
Music Academy, 42-43, 180

Naipaul, V.S., 108
Nair, Guru Kodamalur Karunakaran, 296
Namaskar, 189, 191-193, 232
Namashivayam, Shangitha, 267
Nandakumar, T., 141, 148-149, 162, 221, 224-226, 230, 232-233, 250
Naravahana, 85, 91, 163-165, 290, 293, 319
Narayan, Bhagirathi, 141, 242, 244

Narayan, Jayaprakash, 104
Navagraha, 2, 26, 69, 86-94, 125, 140, 221, 223, 235
National Centre for the Performing Arts (NCPA), 58, 125, 127, 147, 168
National Institute of Design (NID), 70-71, 107-109
Natyasastra, 40, 148, 218
Nehru, Jawaharlal, 37, 291
nerkal, 165
Noh, 81
Non-Government Organisations (NGO's), 106, 112-113, 122

One More News, 276-280, 282

Pandian, V., 141, 151, 242
Panikkar, K.N., 189-190
Paraiattam, 257-258
Patel, Dashrath, 2, 26-28, 94-95, 101, 103, 107-120, 139-141, 148, 187-188, 208, 248, 280
Patel, Vibhuti, 286, 288
Pavlova, Anna, 128
Pillai, Guru Ellappa, 2, 23-29, 51, 53, 56, 88, 92, 100, 121, 123, 158, 198
Plisetskaya, Maya, 181
Poems, '68, 8, 12-13, 246
Pradhan, Sadasiva, 262
prakriti, 138, 182, 292-293, 295, 297, 311, 319
Prana, 2, 81, 87-88, 90, 217-235, 244, 308, 338, 340
Pranayama, 217-218
Premio Gaia, 208, 266
Primal Energy, 84, 88, 125, 134-138, 180, 182-183
pushpanjali, 53, 157-160
Puthli, Asha, 71-72

Raghavan, V., 39-42, 131, 223
Raghuvamsham, 266
Ramalingam, Sujata, 141, 199-201, 206-207, 243-245, 250, 267
Rao, Shanta, 37

Reddy, Dr. Muthulakshmi, 43-45
Request Concert, 3, 31, 193, 272-276,279,312
Roy Chowdhury, Debiprasad, 26

sabadam, 40, 48
sadir, 39, 41, 49
Sahaja, 189, 287, 294
Sahoo, Guru Kedar Nath, 88, 189
Sakambhari, 10, 81, 319-323, 326
Sangeet Natak Akademi, 2, 127, 179
Santiniketan, 26, 332
Sarma Guru Vedantam Satyanarayana, 296
sarukku, 151-152, 207
Satyam, Vempati Chinna, 88
Sathyamurthy,S., 44-45
Sayeeram, Aruna, 267
Shahani, Kumar, 95-100
Shakti, 84-85, 135, 163, 282-283
Shankar, Uday, 23, 37, 128
Shankar Vidya, 57, 92
Shankaracharya, 84, 183
Shawn, Ted, 128-129
Shiva, 135, 137, 150, 198, 218
silambam, 166
Singh, Shanta Serbjeet, 168, 178
Skills, 32, 103, 107, 109-123, 139, 147, 168, 242, 248-249, 255, 257-262
Soma, 227-228
Squire, Robin, 57
Sri, 2, 31, 250, 267, 300, 307-319, 340
Sridhar, S., 250-253
Sri Lalita Sahasranamam, 83-84
St. Denis, Ruth, 128
Stree, 94, 189, 193, 287, 289-294, 298-300
Subbudu, 182-186
Subbulakshmi, M.S., 191
Subrahmanyam, Padma, 132
Subrahmanyam, V.V., 311-312
Surya, 86, 90, 92, 198, 224, 228
Surya Namaskar, 65-66, 90-91, 125, 134, 223, 234

Tagore, Rabindranath, 20
Tanjore Quartette, 24
Tantra, 87, 135, 293, 310, 338
Tanvir, Habib, 189
Theyyam, 297
Thiyam, Ratan, 189-190
Tillana, 38, 53-54, 58-67, 125, 134, 165-167, 246
Tudor, David, 70
utplavana, 156

varnam, 40, 47, 51-52, 159-164

Walk Workshop, The, 257-262
World is My Family, The, 94, 187

Yantra, 337-340
Yoga, 46, 48, 87, 90-91, 93, 134, 141-142, 191, 203, 217-220, 222, 254

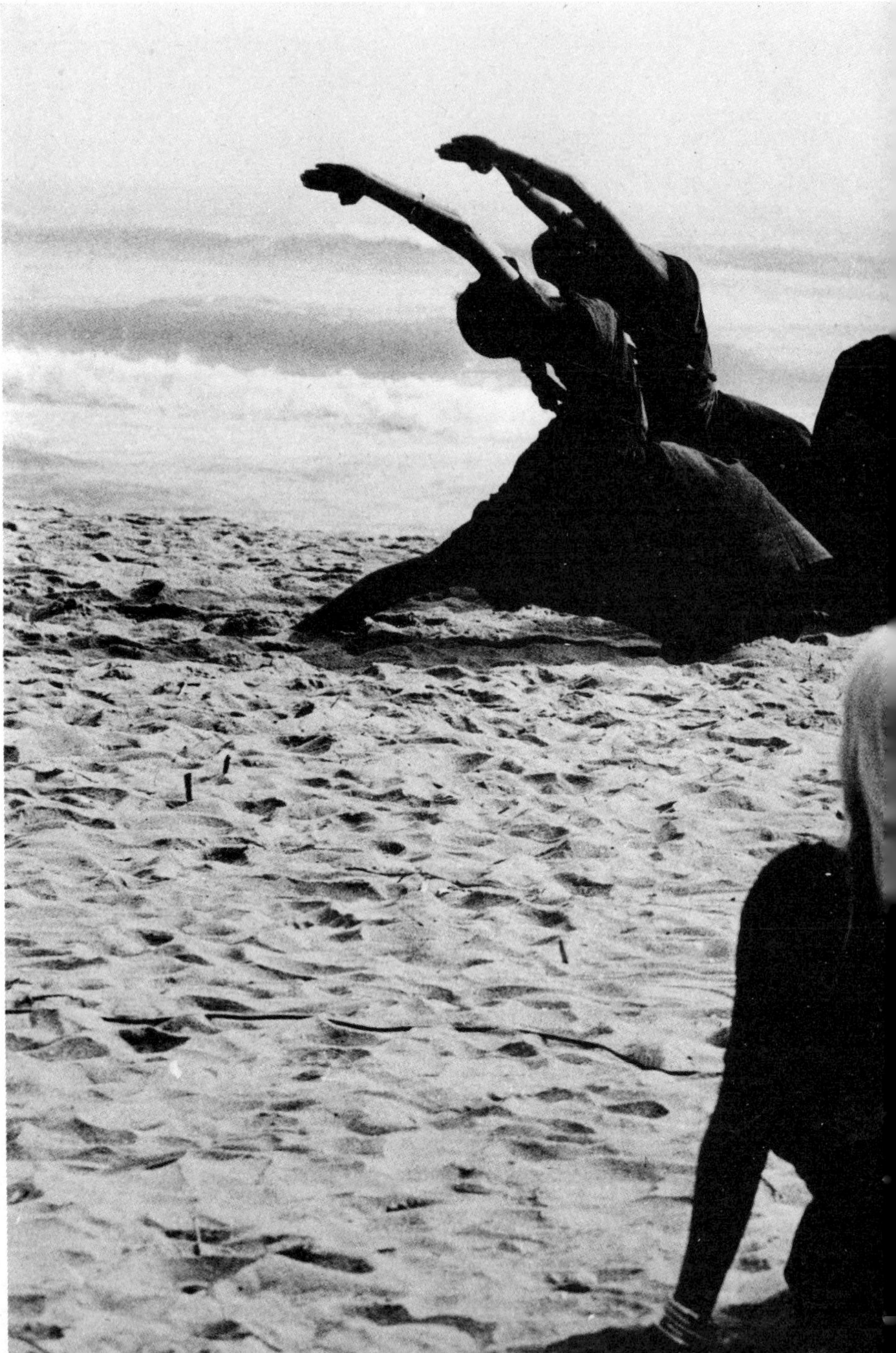

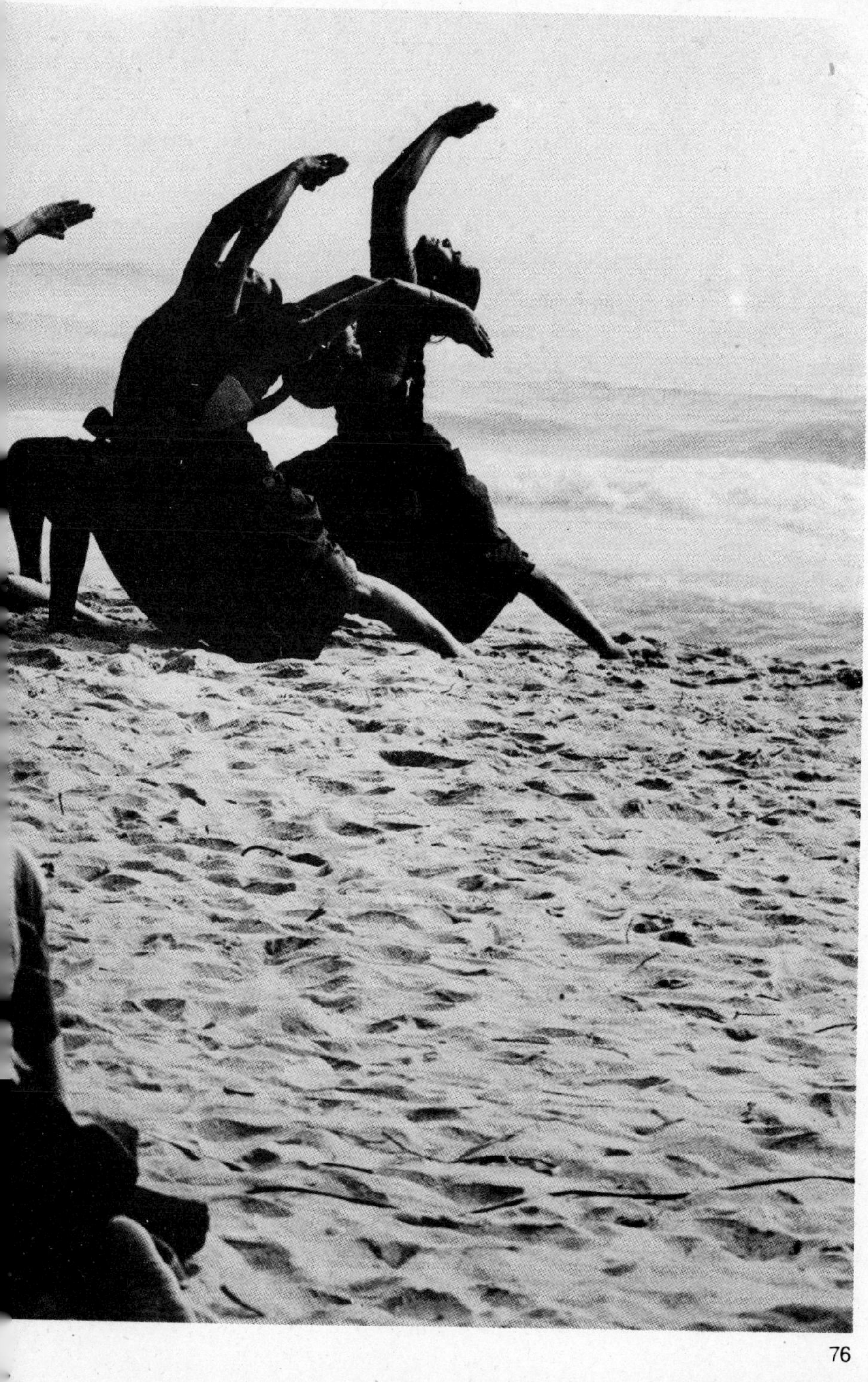